# PERSONAL BEST

## THE JESUS WAY TO FREEDOM

BRIAN SPENCER

HAPPY KID PUBLISHING

Copyright © 2016 Brian Spencer
All rights reserved.
Cover and all interior artwork and design by Trevor & Joanna Stanesby of Blue Pig:
www.bluepigcreative.co.uk
ISBN: 978-0-9956997-0-0

Published by Happy Kid Publishing Ltd

Printed by CreateSpace, an Amazon.com Company

Unless otherwise indicated, all Scripture quotations are taken from the Holy Bible, New Living Translation, copyright © 1996,2004,2007 by Tyndall House Foundation. Used by permission of Tyndall House Publishers, Inc., Carol Stream, Illinois 60188. All rights reserved. Scripture taken from the New King James Version®. Copyright © 1982 by Thomas Nelson. Used by permission. All rights reserved. Holy Bible, New International Version® Anglicized, NIV® Copyright © 1979, 1984, 2011 by Biblical, Inc.® Used by permission. All rights reserved worldwide. Scripture taken from The Message. Copyright © 1993, 1994, 1995, 1996, 2000, 2001, 2002. Used by permission of NavPress Publishing Group.

# DEDICATION

To my wife, Mary Spencer. You have been my best and truest friend on the planet, and you have bravely pressed in not only for your own freedom, but also you have reached out to me and shown me a better way to live. And to our sons, Philip, Adam and James. You have been the observers at close quarters of some of my ups, as well as some of my downs. To the extent that I have played a part in sowing good seed into your lives, may it continue to bear good fruit - you are wonderful young men, and I am immensely proud of each one of you.

PERSONAL BEST

CONTENTS

# ACKNOWLEDGMENTS

First of all, I owe a huge debt of gratitude to my Mum and Dad - Alan & Kath Spencer. They have set a fine example to me of faithfulness, loyalty and provision. Peter & Suzanne Doherty were my pastors for the best part of twenty years and taught me a lot, including how to get over some of my rejection issues. Like countless thousands of people around the world, my life has been impacted in many and profound ways by the outpouring of the Holy Spirit that John & Carol Arnott pastored so brilliantly in Toronto. Steve Long from Toronto generously released his 'Encounter' material to us in the early 2000s and we have used and adapted this over the years. Much of this book represents fruit from seed that was sown by that kind act. Melanie Morgan-Dohner was a force of nature who really challenged me to live a life of freedom - it was such a privilege to be her friend. Dennis and Kristine Dohner, I hope you know how much you mean to me - you play a huge role in keeping me on the good path.

I have been blessed with knowing so many people of goodwill who are helping to shape my life in a way that befits the King and his Kingdom. I will not even try to list all of your names here, but I hope you know who you are!

# INTRODUCTION

This book is about freedom.

In his letter to the church in Galatia, the apostle Paul said this:

*It is for freedom that Christ has set us free.*[1]

Freedom is a fundamentally important part of what being a Christian is really all about. I believe freedom is a key part of the very nature and character of God. Depending on what your experience has been of religion in general and of Christianity in particular, this might seem surprising. Freedom might not have struck you as a major theme of the Christian faith. But, in fact, it really is.

Freedom is about more than getting our problems fixed. It is about moving away from the things that make it hard for us to be more like Jesus. It is about our becoming more and more like the version of ourselves that God always intended - our personal best.

My aim in this book is to provide a comprehensive but hopefully also a concise overview of freedom so that it can be a help to anyone and everyone who is interested. My hope is that, even if you have not consciously ever committed yourself to follow Jesus, you will find something in this book that helps point you to the real Jesus. He loves you, he is worth following, and the life he offers is not dull. Possibly he has been misrepresented to you by people who perhaps ought to know better, and I am sorry for that.

Primarily I have tried to produce a guide that can usefully be put in the hands of anyone but especially including new, or almost new, believers. Why should you have to wait for years before discovering this really important stuff? This book is a distillation of much of what I have learned and experienced over quite a long time. My prayer is that you will find something precious in these pages. May you receive the ability to move quickly into higher heights and deeper depths of freedom.

This book is divided into two parts. Part One, 'Things To Know', deals

---

[1] Galatians 5:1 [niv]

with the 'theory' of becoming free. It lays down a Bible-based foundation for what freedom is. I hope you will find it very illuminating and helpful. I have tried to deliver the truth that has meant a great deal to me personally.

Part Two is much shorter and is called 'Things To Do'. It deals with the practice - the 'how' of becoming free. It attempts to deal with this question: 'well, that all sounds very well, but how can I actually go about enjoying this freedom that Jesus died for?' There are twelve Chapters in Part Two. This is a semi-deliberate acknowledgement of the 'twelve-steps' of Alcoholics Anonymous. Part Two is a kind of twelve-step guide for freedom.

Although Part Two is quite short, it is important. Freedom is a key issue for all of us, whether or not we happen to think that things are going well for us at any given stage in our lives.

Helping Christians find a greater measure of freedom tends to be seen as an exercise of finding a programme, or model, or method, that works. Sometimes we move from one method to another - trying to find something that works for us. By what can look like a process of trial and error, hopefully we eventually see a breakthrough.

I am not by any means going to criticise any of those programmes, models and methods. Some of them are very familiar to me, others less so. Fundamentally, what I want to do is take the mystery out of the whole process of finding the freedom for you that Jesus died for. I want freedom to be easier and quicker for all of us.

I am glad that we have experts and skilled practitioners, especially for people whose need is desperate and whose struggles are complex. But I want to increase the level of understanding about what the underlying principles are that make the various programmes, models and methods work. What makes them work is nothing new.

Could it be that within a healthy worldwide Church, most of the work in moving into greater amounts of freedom can be done just on the basis of individual believers having authentic conversations with Jesus the healer, Jesus the bringer of freedom, Jesus the joy bringer? For those challenging times when, left just to our devices, each of us perhaps lack sufficient objectivity - then, could our friends help? Could it be that major breakthroughs could happen while two friends share an hour or so in a coffee bar?

Could it be that, increasingly, rather than having to wait until we have been Christians for many years before we find some answers, sometimes out of desperation, we can see a culture develop where freedom is much more - well, easy and quick?

I believe that all of this is indeed possible. But for it to happen, we need to see a generation of Jesus followers emerge who are familiar and comfortable with the way to freedom that Jesus invites us to walk along. My prayer is that this book will help you on that journey, that you will have the tools to help others, and that you will be a part of that generation.

May God bless you.

# THINGS TO KNOW

# There's No Way Around It

Shēng | Life

# CHAPTER 1

I must start this book by looking at the Cross. Not just a cross, but the Cross - the one on which Jesus was murdered. Everything and anything useful that I can tell you about freedom depends on what happened there and then. All of the benefits of freedom depend upon what God did on, and through, the Cross. None of us can enjoy here and now all the fulness of the new life that God has for us, unless we face up to what took place at Golgotha in Jerusalem all those years ago. Facing up to not only the way we can benefit from it, but also our own personal responsibility for it. There really is no way around it. Everything swirls around the Cross. All of history, all of the past, present and future. How can this be? How can something that happened so long ago be so relevant and current? This can seem like foolishness - as the Bible itself points out for us:

*The message of the Cross is foolish to those who are headed for destruction! But we who are being saved know it is the very power of God.*[2]

Many Christians wear a cross, or even a crucifix - a cross with Jesus hanging on it - as a sign of their faith in God. In Jesus' time, crosses were well understood as a form of capital punishment. A more modern-day equivalent would be for us to wear something like a model of an electric chair, a guillotine or a hangman's noose. Jewellery like this would certainly look very odd! The horror of what our crosses and crucifixes represent seems to be mostly lost.

Why did this symbol of pain and death become so important for followers of Jesus? If God is love, why is there any need to pay attention to things that seem so dark as sin, pain and death? Even if we can agree that Jesus' death on the Cross was real and necessary, can't we just move on, can't we just look away?

Many do indeed move on, and many do indeed look away. But the path of freedom leads us directly to the Cross. We are going to look at what the Cross does for us, and how we respond.

---

[2] 1 Corinthians 1:18

The Gospels show us that, just before Jesus was arrested, he went through an agony of the soul. He knew what was about to happen, and that his Father God wanted it, but even so, Jesus wanted to find some kind of way out if possible:

*Then Jesus went with them to the olive grove called Gethsemane, and he said, 'Sit here while I go over there to pray.' He took Peter and Zebedee's two sons, James and John, and he became anguished and distressed. He told them, 'My soul is crushed with grief to the point of death. Stay here and keep watch with me.' He went on a little farther and bowed with his face to the ground, praying, 'My Father! If it is possible, let this cup of suffering be taken away from me. Yet I want your will to be done, not mine.*[3]

Jesus was not rebelling against his Father, but he was asking if there was another way. Jesus was then arrested, tortured and then cruelly executed. So, we can tell that from Father God's point of view, there was no other way.

It was a fair question for Jesus to ask - can this cup of suffering be taken away from me? It is also fair for us to be honest about any doubts we might have about the Cross. It is fair to ask why, in Father God's opinion, the Cross was the only way.

Before Jesus was born, God had already delivered to mankind a plan, a blueprint, for how we should live. That plan was all to do with the Jews, with Israel as a nation and with the 'Law' - the Ten Commandments and other rules that God handed down to Moses. God didn't make a mistake, and he didn't change his mind. Once Adam and Eve fell, it was always God's intention to arrive in person and make things right - the first statement of his intent about this is recorded in the first few pages of the Bible.[4]

And yet, God wanted to shape a particular set of people as a good example to all people everywhere. He wanted there to be an actual part of the planet, an actual community where, if you came to visit, you would somehow know that you had come home. God wanted there to be a place where he could be experienced.

---

[3] Matthew 26:36-39

[4] Genesis 3:15

God began this story of the Jews with just one man - Abraham. Starting with Abraham, one of the main themes of God's dealings with his people was the importance of sacrifice and blood. Abraham received amazing promises from God about how he would be the father of a huge nation, and yet in his own lifetime he only had one son from his wife Sarah. This son - Isaac - was a miracle birth, given how very old his parents were. At least Abraham and Sarah had their son, a tangible proof that God was at work in their lives. There was a hope for them that, much further into the future, all of God's amazing words to Abraham would come to fruit.

But God did a curious thing. He told Abraham to kill his son, and to offer him as a burnt sacrifice.[5] In a way, this was not unusual or surprising; in the cultures that surrounded Abraham, there were probably various religions that called for child sacrifices.

Perhaps part of the test for Abraham here was whether the God who had called him really was different from all the other gods of all the other religions. In the story, we learn that Isaac was puzzled about why they were not taking a lamb with them up the mountain to be sacrificed. His father's reply was that God would provide a lamb.[6] I do not know how clear Abraham was about what would happen next. Maybe he was sure that an animal for the sacrifice would be provided. Maybe he sensed that God would bring Isaac back from the dead after Abraham had killed him.

What we are told very clearly is that God is moved by Abraham's obedience and his willingness to even give up his own son, so that the blessings God had already spoken over Abraham are then increased. A ram is provided for the sacrifice - it was trapped by its horns in a nearby bush. As Abraham is about to plunge a knife into Isaac's body, a voice from Heaven interrupts him and tells him the human sacrifice is no longer needed. Now it is clear that Abraham truly fears God.[7]

The apostle Paul tells us in the book of Romans that Abraham was

---

[5] Genesis 22:2

[6] Genesis 22:8

[7] Genesis 22:9-19

declared by God to be righteous because of his faith.[8] This is not just the faith shown by Abraham in this particular test. It was the faith he demonstrated day by day. This particular story is, however, special. It parallels in some way the story of Father God's sacrifice of his son Jesus - but of course, for Jesus there was no ram trapped in a bush nearby who could die in his place.

I believe that part of what moved God to intensify his blessings over Abraham on that mountain was that God saw something in Abraham's heart that reflected, however imperfectly or faintly, a characteristic of God's own heart. Father God was willing to sacrifice his own Son, Jesus. However, we still have a question to answer: why was it necessary for Jesus to die? Why, when Jesus asked if there was any way that this cup of suffering could be removed, was the answer, no?

Hundreds of years after Abraham's time, the Jews were living in Egypt as slaves. Moses was appointed by God to lead them out of slavery and to return to Canaan, the land that God had promised to Abraham. The story of Moses' conflict with Pharaoh is well known. Because of Pharaoh's resistance, the hardships visited upon Egypt intensified until they reached their climax in God killing all the firstborn males in Egypt, boys and animals alike.

The Jews were spared from this disaster by smearing the blood of a sacrificed lamb on the doorposts of their homes. When God saw the blood on their doorposts, he would pass over those homes and not visit death upon them. This event is tied to the Jewish festival of Passover, which God told his people to observe every year in remembrance of that terrible night in Egypt.[9] This festival includes the slaughtering of lambs to provide part of the Passover meal.

As I mentioned earlier, God gave Moses the Law. This happened after the Jews had escaped out of Egypt and were being shaped into a nation. The Law includes many detailed instructions about various sacrifices that

---

[8] Romans 4:3, Genesis 15:6

[9] Exodus 12

should be offered to God. Central to these are a set of instructions[10] about the Day of Atonement. This was the one day in each year when the High Priest entered the 'Most Holy Place' - the most sacred part of the Tabernacle (later, the Temple) - to deal with the Jews' sins. A key role was played by two goats. One of these goats was sacrificed, and the other one had all the Jews' sins laid on to it by the High Priest, and it was then led out into the wilderness. This is where the idea of a 'scapegoat' comes from.

These rituals served a good purpose in reminding the Jews about the importance of taking sin seriously and in pointing to the standards of behaviour that are consistent with godly living. It is difficult, however, to imagine how this mechanism involving two goats could ever, in and of itself, be effective in dealing with a nation's sins. If the Day of Atonement ritual dealt with sin by itself, then surely there would be no need for Jesus to die. Jesus' question in Gethsemane would be all the more telling.

One of the most famous verses in the Bible says this about God's plan for Mankind's salvation:

*For this is how God loved the world: He gave his one and only Son, so that everyone who believes in him will not perish but have eternal life.*[11]

The key to our not perishing is Father God's one and only Son - Jesus. There is no reference in this passage to the two goats on the Day of Atonement. Those rituals that were handed down to Moses by God were a shadow, a prefiguring, of the necessary work that Jesus was going to do at a future date. Several hundred years before Jesus was born, the prophet Isaiah wrote about the coming Messiah as the Suffering Servant:

*All of us, like sheep, have strayed away. We have left God's paths to follow our own. Yet the Lord laid on him the sins of us all.*[12]

Whereas the High Priest each year would in a symbolic act place the Jewish nation's sins on the scapegoat, Father God has placed all of our sins onto Jesus. In the New Testament, the writer of the book of Hebrews

---

[10] Leviticus 16

[11] John 3:16

[12] Isaiah 53:6

compares and contrasts the role of the Jewish High Priest with Jesus as the Great High Priest. Also, the writer speaks of the system that Moses received as being a copy on Earth of something in Heaven that is 'more real' and goes on to say this:

*For Christ did not enter into a holy place made with human hands, which was only a copy of the true one in heaven. He entered into heaven itself to appear now before God on our behalf. And he did not enter heaven to offer himself again and again, like the high priest here on earth who enters the Most Holy Place year after year with the blood of an animal. If that had been necessary, Christ would have had to die again and again, ever since the world began. But now, once for all time, he has appeared at the end of the age to remove sin by his own death as a sacrifice.*[13]

The theme of lambs (or goats) being sacrificed or having sin placed on them, and of this being some kind of picture of a greater reality that is fulfilled in Jesus, is continued right until the end of the Bible. The book of Revelation at various points refers to Jesus Christ as 'the Lamb':

*Then I saw a scroll in the right hand of the one who was sitting on the throne. There was writing on the inside and the outside of the scroll, and it was sealed with seven seals. And I saw a strong angel, who shouted with a loud voice: 'Who is worthy to break the seals on this scroll and open it?' But no one in heaven or on earth or under the earth was able to open the scroll and read it….Then I saw a Lamb that looked as if it had been slaughtered, but it was now standing between the throne and the four living beings and among the twenty-four elders.…..the four living beings and the twenty-four elders fell down before the Lamb. Each one had a harp, and they held gold bowls filled with incense, which are the prayers of God's people. And they sang a new song with these words: 'You are worthy to take the scroll and break its seals and open it. For you were slaughtered, and your blood has ransomed people for God from every tribe and language and people and nation. And you have caused them to become a Kingdom of priests for our God. And they will reign on the earth.'*[14]

Jesus died on the Cross and was later resurrected at a particular point in human history, but the facts of his death and resurrection are fundamentally important for all of Mankind throughout all of history. When Jesus said yes

---

[13] Hebrews 9:24-26

[14] Revelation 5:1-3,6, 8b&9

to his Father's will in Gethsemane, he was saying yes to being the Lamb of God, the supreme sacrifice to whom the Jews' scriptures had been pointing. The book of Revelation shows us that the Lamb of God has the central position in bringing this current age to a final, victorious and glorious end. The Lamb ushers in the complete and permanent rule and reign of God not only in Heaven above, but also on Earth below.

This sort of grasp of God's overall plan in history is important, but it does not necessarily really give us an answer to the question: why did Jesus have to die? We can talk about sin causing a separation between us and God, but does there really have to be blood and death before that separation can be mended?

We all have experience of what it is like to be wounded or damaged by other people. Sometimes it may seem quite easy to forgive those people. At other times, it may seem very hard, if not impossible. Generally speaking, however, we do not insist that someone has to die before we forgive them. Although when the offence is grievous, in our darkest moments we may well wish the perpetrator dead.

Viewed from the other side - when we are the ones who have hurt or offended someone else - we know how we would like to be treated. It can feel very good to be told that we are forgiven, it's OK, there's no problem, it doesn't matter. This attitude of forgiveness, or graciousness, surely in some way reflects Father God's own character. So, when God looks at our sin, why can't he just take the same kind of approach? Why can't he simply tell me I'm forgiven, it's OK, there's no problem, it doesn't matter, without having to go through the process of seeing Jesus Christ crucified?

On this side of eternity, we won't get a complete answer to this question, if only because our capacity to understand is limited. We can, however, get enough of an answer to help us, because God's written words in the Bible and the living inspiration of the Holy Spirit can show us at least some of God's perspective.

One of our problems with the question 'why did Jesus have to die?' is that the question is the wrong question. It is a fair question, but at the same time it is the wrong question. Instead of asking why Jesus had to die, we could ask, how could God possibly bring us to life?

In the book of Romans, Paul spends a lot of time explaining in detail how Christ's death and resurrection play a central role in all of history, and are vital in God's dealings with all of Humanity. This covers not just Jews who lived with the Law in the period between Moses and Jesus, but also everyone else - including people who have lived since Jesus' time who have never had the chance to accept him. Paul makes this very important statement:

*For the wages of sin is death, but the free gift of God is eternal life in Christ Jesus our Lord.*[15]

For all of its flaws - caused by us and all who have gone before us - the world around us is amazing. It is an incredible thing to be alive. The natural world, in all of its complexity and diversity, is wondrous. The universe in which our little planet moves is unimaginably huge and beautiful to behold, insofar as we can comprehend it. The Bible tells us that God made all of this, including you and me. We are his good idea, made in his image, living spirits breathed into existence by God himself and placed in physical bodies in a tangible world. People are amazing! You are amazing!

And yet, without a further act on God's part, we are dead - or at least, as good as dead because we are doomed to die. The free will that God gave us when he made us, and the fact that this free will has been used to live independently of God, means that we must die. In reality, it is impossible to live independently of God. If we can only glimpse a small part of God's view of how the world is, we will see that it is impossible for anyone to continue living forever in some kind of space outside of God's Kingdom.

At the moment, we see evidence around us of a kind of overlap between two kingdoms - God's Kingdom and another, evil kingdom. The evil kingdom will soon come to an end - and would we really want it to last forever, given the pain and suffering that it inflicts on millions of people every day? But when that evil kingdom ends, there will be no place left to hide. Everything and everyone who is part of that evil kingdom must also end, in what the book of Revelation describes as a 'lake of fire'.[16]

One of the problems we have is that we compare sins. While we acknowledge that no-one is perfect, and therefore we ourselves are not perfect, we can so easily look at other people and judge them as being far worse sinners than ourselves. But as Paul says in Romans,

---

[15] Romans 6:23 [nrsv]

[16] Revelation 20:14&15

*For everyone has sinned; we all fall short of God's glorious standard.*[17]

It will always be possible for us to point to a group of people less worthy and more evil than ourselves. We can try to convince ourselves that we are somehow OK in God's sight because we are so much better than 'those people over there' - whoever 'they' are. Many people can claim in all sincerity that they have lead good lives - or at least, they have tried their best to be good.

When we compare ourselves with others in this way, we run the risk of deceiving ourselves. Even if we can think of a group of people who are clearly more evil than us, we don't know everything there is to know about their life circumstances. Perhaps they endured early years of abuse or neglect, for example. And, if we had to live in their shoes, perhaps we would have done even worse things? The biggest problem with the comparison game is that it gets us nowhere. None of us can live life to such a standard that God can allow us to live in his Kingdom, which is the only available place. There is no way we can avoid the wages of sin, which is death, unless God finds some way to intervene.

Without an intervention on God's part, we have all been bound for one simple and awful destination. However much we may feel full of life, in the bigger picture, we are dead. This is why I believe my suggested alternative question is relevant - namely, how could God possibly bring us to life?

You can, if you wish, interpret this question as asking - why did God make us in the first place? If free will is such a problem, and if Adam and Eve's fall led to so much loss, and if so many souls face a horrible future, why bother? In my view, such an interpretation of the question is understandable, but it's also churlish. It comes close to my blaming God for ever thinking of making me. On balance, I am very glad that I exist!

So - given that you and I do, after all, exist; and given that unless God rescues us, we are dead, then what is it God can possibly do that will give us life rather than death?

There are many things that can be said about the Cross, but my main focus here is on the idea or picture of the Cross as a doorway, a gateway, a

---

[17] Romans 3:23

bridge, or an entry point. To life. It was necessary for Jesus to die on the Cross so that the issue of our death could be dealt with. The Cross is our doorway into life, into freedom.

Given our hopeless condition - all of us destined for separation from God because there is no way we can survive long term when nothing exists apart from the Kingdom of God - Jesus came and identified with us. In his death, he took upon himself the punishment that is the result of our independence from God. In his resurrection, Jesus opened the way for us to live a brand new life - one that can thrive in God's Kingdom forever.

One wise Jewish religious leader, namely Nicodemus, came to Jesus under cover of darkness and asked him about the things that Jesus had been teaching. During their conversation, Jesus made this statement:

*I tell you the truth, unless you are born again, you cannot see the Kingdom of God.* [18]

This idea of being born again, or born of the Spirit, or born from above, implies not just a beginning, but an ending as well. Something comes to an end so that something can begin. Something new replaces something old. The Cross makes it possible for God to bring us to life - to move us out from the kingdom of darkness, where we are doomed to die. Through the Cross, God himself enters into our death and takes us out the other side, through Jesus' resurrection.

The issue of sin - both sin in general and my sin in particular - is not something that is solved by working out how we can persuade God to change his mind. Nor can we deal with this issue simply by trying to shift God into a good enough mood that he will decide to be nice to us and dismiss sin as relatively unimportant. On the contrary, the sin issue is an issue of life or its opposite, death. The writer of Hebrews puts it this way:

*Because God's children are human beings - made of flesh and blood - the Son also became flesh and blood. For only as a human being could he die, and only by dying could he break the power of the devil, who had the power of death. Only in this way could he set free all who have lived their lives as slaves to the fear of dying.* [19]

The Cross is nothing to do with changing God's mind or changing

---

[18] John 3:3

[19] Hebrews 2:14&15

God's mood - it is about breaking the power of the devil, and the death that is intertwined with that power. The apostle John said this about the reason why Father God sent Jesus to us:

*The reason the Son of God appeared was to destroy the devil's work.*[20]

Many people see Jesus as a great moral teacher. He certainly is this, but he is also much more. When Jesus was wrestling with his Father's will in the Garden of Gethsemane, He was dealing with the end point of what his mission onEarth had been all along. Not just the delivery of some fascinating moral insights. Nothing less than the destruction of the devil's work - dealing a death blow to death itself.

Here is a passage that uses the image of the way conquered armies were humiliated in ancient Rome by being paraded through its streets:

*When you came to Christ, you were 'circumcised', but not by a physical procedure. Christ performed a spiritual circumcision - the cutting away of your sinful nature...You were dead because of your sins and because your sinful nature was not yet cut away. Then God made you alive with Christ, for he forgave all our sins. He canceled the record of the charges against us and took it away by nailing it to the cross. In this way, he disarmed the spiritual rulers and authorities. He shamed them publicly by his victory over them on the cross.*[21]

The Cross - and Jesus' resurrection, which showed he had broken the power of death - is the means by which we are made alive when we come to Christ. I am not dwelling in this Chapter on the extent and awfulness of the physical pain and emotional torment that Jesus endured as part of his arrest, trial, brutal flogging and crucifixion. This is not because I think these things are unimportant. However, what I do want to stress here is that the Cross is fundamentally about making new life possible for us.

And for this to happen, we need something more than what Jesus endured on this side of the Cross. We need his resurrection. Without the resurrection, all of Jesus' suffering is, of course, a desperately sad story. But it makes no difference to our own sad destiny. The awfulness of the suffering doesn't save us, without something else. Paul makes this very

---

[20] 1 John 3:8 [niv]

[21] Colossians 2:11,13-15

point in his first letter to the Church at Corinth:

*….if Christ has not been raised, then all our preaching is useless, and your faith is useless…And if Christ has not been raised, then your faith is useless and you are still guilty of your sins. In that case, all who have died believing in Christ are lost! And if our hope in Christ is only for this life, we are more to be pitied than anyone in the world. But in fact, Christ has been raised from the dead. He is the first of a great harvest of all who have died.*[22]

The Cross is the means by which we can be moved out of the kingdom of darkness into God's Kingdom, out of death and into life:

*For he has rescued us from the kingdom of darkness and transferred us into the Kingdom of his dear Son, who purchased our freedom and forgave our sins.* [23]

What, then, should our response be? And how does that response fit in with the general aim of this book, which is to help us enter into the fulness of freedom that God has provided for us?

I believe it is vital to focus on the fact that the Cross - Jesus' incredible sacrifice and his victory in the resurrection - is an act of love. I have already quoted this passage, but it is worth quoting again:

*For this is how God loved the world: He gave his one and only Son, so that everyone who believes in him will not perish but have eternal life.* [24]

God was under no obligation to rescue us. Nor did he intervene out of a grudging sense of duty - as if he really had no choice since he is perfect, and he had to save us. Jesus was not sent to the Cross by an angry Heavenly Father. Nor was he sent there out of a cold loyalty to some kind of obligation, as if he had no choice. It was only love that sent Jesus to the Cross. The love of the Father who gave the Son, and the love of the Son who allowed himself to be given.

This love is open to all Mankind, but it is also very specific. It is love for me as an individual, just as it is love for you as an individual. It is not appropriate to settle for responding to the Cross as an act of love for a large

---

[22] 1 Corinthians 15:14,17-20

[23] Colossians 1:13&14

[24] John 3:16

group. It is also an act of love for one person in particular - you. And also, of course, me.

When Jesus told Nicodemus that he had to be 'born again', Jesus was comparing entry into the Kingdom of Heaven with a human child emerging from its mother's birth canal - an intensely personal experience! Jesus didn't just pay a price for everyone; he paid a price for you, and for me. We can't afford to engage with the Cross just at the level of being part of a crowd. Jesus said something along these lines when he said these words about coming into the Kingdom:

*'You can enter God's Kingdom only through the narrow gate. The highway to hell is broad, and its gate is wide for the many who choose that way. But the gateway to life is very narrow and the road is difficult, and only a few ever find it.* [25]

It is one thing to look around at the billions of people in the world, to reflect on the good and bad things they have done, and to wonder at the amazing thing God has done to provide a way for all of us from darkness into his light. It is quite another thing to reflect on the fact that I have personal responsibility. Jesus didn't just die for everyone, he died for me. He died <u>because</u> of me. My sin, and my sin alone, was enough to put Jesus on the Cross.

If we don't face up to this, we miss something that is vital for our freedom. The Cross is my fault - my responsibility, just as it is your responsibility.

As I face up to the enormity of what the Cross represents, and the personal responsibility I carry for it, the appropriate response is to be totally undone. My grievances about the way other people have mistreated me, the injustices I have suffered, my sense of pride and self-justification - all of these things are turned into dust. I might see myself in a number of different ways, for example as a victim, a good person or a master in charge of my own destiny. Whatever I think I see when I look at myself, the more that I gaze accurately at the Cross, the more these ideas and feelings are exposed for what they are. To one degree or another they are mere delusions, fantasies.

---

[25] Matthew 7:13&14

In a sense, I should not move on past this point. Moving on seems to trivialise or minimise what I have just described. It is part of a healthy spiritual life to reflect on a regular basis what it means to be responsible for Jesus' suffering and death. So, please, do not simply move on. Come back to this point. Often.

Shortly before his arrest, Jesus was in a conversation with some religious leaders and he identified himself as a stone that is referred to in the Old Testament as having been rejected by the builders (religious leaders). He said this about himself as that stone:

*And whoever falls on this stone will be broken; but on whomever it falls, it will grind him to powder.*[26]

Everyone has a choice when confronted by Jesus. It is possible to fall onto him, or to let him fall on us. By implication, it is wiser to chose to fall onto Jesus and be broken than it is to have Jesus fall on us. It is more helpful and healthy for us if we perceive accurately who Jesus is, and what he has done for us - each one of us. But this process will break us! Then, once we have allowed ourselves to be broken by Jesus, he can make us whole.

Although it can seem like a contradiction, a proper sense of personal responsibility for the Cross is not meant to leave us feeling like worthless worms. Jesus did not go the Cross to leave you in a state of feeling utterly worthless. God has placed great value on us - including each one of us individually - by the Cross. In God's opinion, you are worth saving, worth suffering for, worth dying for.

We are very used to the idea of things having a value. There are things that we might regard as worthless, and others as priceless. Some things have no value, no-one would pay anything for them. Other things have a value so high that it is almost impossible even to set a price that would enable us to own them. Or, if a price could perhaps be set, only a tiny number of people could ever find the money to pay that price.

Where does a sense of worth, or value, come from? Who or what decides what something, or someone, is worth? A thing is worth whatever

---

[26] Matthew 21:44 [nkjv]

someone else is prepared to pay for it. Market forces of supply and demand come into play. I can have an idea of what my possessions are worth. If I decide to sell them, my idea of their worth is tested in the reality of the marketplace.

I can have an idea of what I am worth. You can have an idea of what you are worth. Where is the marketplace for human souls? God's opinion of your worth matters far more than your own opinion. Your own opinion does not count for very much. Apart from God, the opinions that other people might have about your worth count for even less than not very much. The only opinion that counts is God's opinion. And God has made it clear what value he places upon you. It is very, very, high.

One of the effects of the Cross is, to use a theological term, justification. We are placed in a position where we can stand in God's presence forever and be absolutely OK. The apostle Paul wrote to the Church in Colosse as a group who had accepted Jesus Christ as their Lord[27] and he said this:

*[God] has brought you into his own presence, and you are holy and blameless as you stand before him without a single fault.*[28]

This is all very good news. But…

Following Jesus after we have accepted him as Saviour and Lord cannot amount to just carrying on with life in the same way that we lived before we ever knew him. Sure, we can be confident that we no longer have to worry about what will happen to us after we die because we have gained this justification, this right standing, before God. But we are not given this gift of right standing by God so that we can then abuse it by failing to face up to the realities of life.

If we have truly seen the Cross for what it is, then we have done business with God. Do we really think we can simply carry on with 'business as usual' as we walk away from the Cross?

The responsibility I carry for what Jesus did for me, and the value God has attached to me, place a demand on me to pay attention to how I live. This is not legalism - meaning an attempt to devise a set of rules by which

---

[27] Colossians 2:6

[28] Colossians 1:22

we earn a relationship with God. Nor is this religious performance - meaning a focus on the observation of rituals. This is relationship. In the light of what God has done for me, the love he has shown to me, the value he has placed upon me, he deserves something. It is appropriate that I pay attention to the way that I live.

The Cross provides a gateway for us to a new life, but it really is a life that is new - it is not just a very long (eternal) continuation of our previous life. It calls for a fundamental shift, a change in overall control, an overhaul of our priorities and values.

Jesus said this:

*If you try to hang on to your life, you will lose it. But if you give up your life for my sake, you will save it. And what do you benefit if you gain the whole world but lose your own soul? Is anything worth more than your soul?* [29]

He is calling us to accept 'giving up our lives' as an implication of our being saved. This 'giving up' is more than a momentary surrender when we first accept Jesus into our lives. This is a way of life:

*Then [Jesus] said to the crowd, 'If any of you wants to be my follower, you must turn from your selfish ways, take up your cross daily, and follow me. If you try to hang on to your life, you will lose it. But if you give up your life for my sake, you will save it.* [30]

Jesus is talking about a daily taking up of our cross. This is not <u>the</u> Cross - what Jesus is talking about has nothing to do with somehow perfecting or completing the work of forgiveness and reconciliation that he achieved through his sacrifice. The crowd who were listening to Jesus would have understood him very well. Someone who is carrying a cross is someone who is on their way to die.

What Jesus wants us to do is to make a daily decision to, as the above passage says, turn from our selfish ways. The way to live in God is to put God's priorities first, to put to one side our preferences and inclinations, and to submit everything in our lives to him.

This does not mean we somehow earn the right to be saved by the way we behave. Rather, it means that God, who loves us, wants us to be able

---

[29] Matthew 16:25&26

[30] Luke 9:23&24

really to start living, today, here and now, the forever life that he has provided for us. The truth is, we cannot fully flow in the wonder of our new life unless we participate consciously in the death of our old life. The apostle Paul put it like this:

*My old self has been crucified with Christ. It is no longer I who live, but Christ lives in me. So I live in this earthly body by trusting in the Son of God, who loved me and gave himself for me.*[31]

It is a paradox, an apparent contradiction. The way to life is through death. God has provided an amazing escape for us through the Cross. This is an escape from death, but achieved through death (and resurrection). There is nothing we can do to add to, or complete, the victory that Christ won on the Cross. However, if we want to live lives that are successful in the true sense - lives that are lived in tune with the character of God and the ways of his Kingdom - then we need to adjust our lives so that they fit with that Kingdom.

There is no true freedom outside of God. If we can have a healthy appreciation of the Cross, then we have a good basis to invite the Holy Spirit to show us any areas of our lives where perhaps we are not yet seeing things as they truly are. Jesus always sees things as they truly are, and he wants us to begin to experience that same level of clarity and perception. It is in following Jesus that we will find freedom. I hope this book will help you in that process.

---

[31] Galatians 2:20

# Don't Forget To Forgive

Shù ┃ Forgiveness

# CHAPTER 2

Forgiveness of others plays a vital role in helping us to find freedom for ourselves. It is like a door which opens up a whole realm of possibilities.

As we will see, Jesus' teaching on this subject is very strong and very clear. Although forgiving others is optional in the sense that no one else can make you forgive, in reality forgiving others is not optional for followers of Jesus. He commands us to do it, and he makes our enjoyment of the full benefits of the Cross conditional upon our forgiving other people. It is strange, then, that so many Christians carry on their lives as if they do not need to pay any serious attention to what Jesus is actually telling us to do.

There are some huge obstacles for many people in this area. The pain attached to the awful things that have been done to them can make even thinking about the offences very hard. There can be an understandable desire to see justice done. The offender must be punished, and must also make an appropriate apology first before anything can be forgiven.

No one else has experienced the painful experiences that you have gone through, so no one else has the right to tell you that you should let go. I am not going to pretend that I know what your pain is. I am not going to say that I know how you feel. I will not claim that forgiveness is always easy.

What I will do, however, is take you through what Dr. Jesus' prescription is for unforgiven offences. The fact is, forgiving other people is in many ways a selfish act, rather than a selfless one. When I forgive other people, I am the person who gains most from the process. You forgiving other people is crucial to <u>your</u> freedom, <u>your</u> wholeness, <u>your</u> health, and <u>your</u> fruitfulness.

Some of us will be familiar with a common expression about forgiving and forgetting - 'forgive and forget'. The fact that we cannot forget is sometimes itself used as a justification for not forgiving. In other words, I cannot forget, so how can I forgive? Alternatively, I might say I will forgive as soon as I know I can forget.

In truth, forgiveness really has nothing to do with forgetting. The writer of one of the Psalms asks God not to remember the sins he committed while he was a young man. [32] In another Psalm, there is a beautiful description of our sins having been removed by God 'as far as the east is from the west'.[33] God speaks through one of the Old Testament prophets and promises us that past sins will be 'forgotten',[34] and talks about our sins being blotted out and never being thought of by God ever again.[35] Through another of those prophets, God says he will trample our sins under his feet and throw them into the depths of the ocean.[36]

I find it incredible to think that God could forget in this way. God numbers all of the hairs on all of our heads, and God (in Jesus) holds the whole universe together and stops everything from just falling apart. These Bible verses tell us that God intentionally chooses not to dwell on the sins of those who have been forgiven. They tell us something wonderful about what God's forgiveness is like – how, when he thinks about me for example, his first thought is not about all the many and various ways that I have messed up.

But here's the thing: forgetting is not forgiving, just as forgiving is not forgetting. When God is confronted by the problem of our sin - by the fact that it creates a separation between us and him - the solution to that problem is not simply that he forgets about our sin. He doesn't just say: 'Oh, forget about it, it doesn't matter. All those sins of yours that have got in the way - don't worry, they're not a problem. I have already forgotten about them.'

It is God's forgiveness of our sins that enables him to put a separation between us and those sins, such a separation that is as if those sins were lost

---

[32] Psalm 25:7

[33] Psalm 103:12

[34] Ezekiel 18:22

[35] Isaiah 43:25

[36] Micah 7:19

in the depths of the ocean. That forgiveness comes at a price - Jesus on the Cross. And we only enjoy the benefit of that forgiveness when we accept who Jesus is and put our trust in him. So, this amazing forgetfulness on God's part is not what enables him to have nice warm feelings about us. It is not through some kind of memory failure that God is able to welcome us. God does not forget so that he can then forgive. He forgives, and because he forgives, so he can 'forget'.

I can't see anywhere in the Bible where we are commanded to forget. Such a command would be difficult, if not impossible, to follow. I can catch myself forgetting many things - such as birthdays, names, where I left my keys, and so on. Usually, my forgetfulness is temporary. I cannot, however, choose to forget someone or something as an act of will. The more I try, the harder it becomes.

When I find myself confronted by what the Bible says about my obligations to forgive other people, I am being challenged to make a decision, to forgive as an act of my will. It has nothing to do with whether I feel I am close to the point where I don't really think about the offence any longer. God's word is not calling me to try to get to a place where I am so close to forgetting that I can make the leap of forgiving. The Lord is not saying, 'Get close to forgetting, and once you are there, forgive'. He is saying that forgiveness is a deliberate decision. We are called to forgive before we forget.

We should set our obligations with regard to forgiveness against the background of how Father God himself deals with forgiveness. Here is a fascinating story from the Gospels which might be familiar to you:

*When Jesus returned to Capernaum several days later, the news spread quickly that he was back home. Soon the house where he was staying was so packed with visitors that there was no more room, even outside the door. While he was preaching God's word to them, four men arrived carrying a paralysed man on a mat. They couldn't bring him to Jesus because of the crowd, so they dug a hole through the roof above his head. Then they lowered the man on his mat, right down in front of Jesus. Seeing their faith, Jesus said to the paralysed man, 'My child, your sins are forgiven.'*

*But some of the teachers of religious law who were sitting there thought to themselves, 'What is he saying? This is blasphemy! Only God can forgive sins!' Jesus knew immediately what they were thinking, so he asked them, 'Why do you question this in your hearts? Is it easier to say to the paralysed man 'Your sins are forgiven,' or 'Stand up, pick up your mat, and walk'? So I will prove to you that the Son of Man has the authority on earth to forgive sins.' Then Jesus turned to the paralysed man and said, 'Stand up, pick up your mat, and go home!' And the man jumped up, grabbed his mat, and walked out through the stunned onlookers. They were all amazed and praised God, exclaiming, 'We've never seen anything like this before!'*[37]

The main thing about this story that I want you to consider is this: Jesus seems to have his question to the religious leaders the wrong way round. The issue is, what is it easier to say — that someone's sins are forgiven, or that someone is healed? Common sense indicates that it's easier to say someone's sins are forgiven. Even if you are wrong, who will know? How can your statement be proved or disproved? On the other hand, if you command someone to be healed - in this case, if you tell a paralysed man to get up and walk - and that person isn't healed there and then, everyone can see that something has gone wrong.

Jesus, it appears, had a different perspective. If you study carefully what he says to the religious leaders, it is clear that he believes he has already said the more difficult of the two things to the paralysed man - namely that the man's sins are forgiven - but that as a proof of this, Jesus will say the easier of the two things, so that everyone can draw their own conclusions when the man walks.

From Jesus' point of view, why would it be harder to say that the man's sins had been forgiven? One answer is that, quite rightly, the religious leaders were sensitive to the fact that Jesus seemed to be taking on the role of God. Since sin separates us from God, it is up to God to say when and if that separation has been dealt with.

Another answer - and one that I believe is equally true -is that Jesus as God can only pronounce any of us as being forgiven at an enormous price. That price is what Jesus endured when he was tortured and then crucified. This is why it is harder for Jesus to tell the paralysed man that he is forgiven than it is to tell him to get up and walk. Jesus knows he can only say this on the basis that he is going to be the fulfilment of Old Testament prophesies about the innocent Messiah who will suffer in our place.

We need to understand that it is not an easy thing for God to tell us we

---

[37] Mark 2:1-12

are forgiven. He can only say this on the basis of his having dealt with the sin issue. The cost to God of being able to say to each of us that we are forgiven was huge. May we continue to grasp this hugeness more and more. May we also continue to grasp that God does not have to pay this cost again. His payment was once, once for all, and once and for all. The writer of Hebrews expresses this very clearly:

*Under the old covenant, the priest stands and ministers before the altar day after day, offering the same sacrifices again and again, which can never take away sins. But our High Priest offered himself to God as a single sacrifice for sins, good for all time. Then he sat down in the place of honour at God's right hand…For by that one offering he forever made perfect those who are being made holy.*[38]

In our individual dealings with God, each one of us must reckon with Jesus and the Cross. I must face up to the fact that Jesus went to the Cross for me. You must face up to the fact that Jesus went to the Cross for you. That said, Jesus doesn't have to carry on dying. He did it once, and that was enough.

Part of the Gospel account of Jesus' crucifixion tells us something amazing about Jesus' willingness to forgive. As he is hanging there, in the process of dying an agonising, humiliating death, he looks around at the people who have crucified him and he says this:

*'Father, forgive them, for they don't know what they are doing.'*[39]

In one sense, those responsible indeed didn't know what they were doing. As part of his address one day to a crowd who were outside the Temple in Jerusalem, Peter acknowledged that the crowd and their religious leaders had acted in ignorance when they killed Jesus.[40] Perhaps it's true that for most of the time when we sin, we don't really appreciate the full implications and consequences of what it is that we are doing. Be that as it may, Jesus is clearly being remarkably kind. It's as if he is pleading their case before Father God. This shows us something amazing about God's heart of forgiveness.

---

[38] Hebrews 10:11&12,14

[39] Luke 23:34

[40] Acts 3:17

The idea I want to submit to you is that God is forgiving. Really, really, really forgiving. I like the way the Amplified Bible puts it:

*If we [freely] admit that we have sinned and confess our sins, He is faithful and just (true to His own nature and promises) and will forgive our sins [dismiss our lawlessness] and [continuously] cleanse us from all unrighteousness [everything not in conformity to His will in purpose, thought, and action].*[41]

If we repent, we connect with God and find that he deals with us in a way that is 'true to his own nature and promises' – in other words, we connect with a God who forgives. He is not carrying on a debate with himself about whether or not you deserve to be forgiven. On his side, he has already done everything he can do. He has already decided to forgive you - and me. Whether you and I enjoy the benefits of that forgiveness is up to us!

God decided to forgive me long, long before I ever thought of repenting of my sins. When I eventually came to him, God was not waiting to be persuaded. Now that I belong to him, I don't have to worry about what will happen to me if I die without having repented of some particular sin, or even sins. On the other hand, now that I belong to him, it is appropriate that on an ongoing basis I learn to recognise and acknowledge any actions or attitudes of mine that are out of line with God's own character - in other words, sin.

God forgiving my sin - and your sin - has very little to do with you and me. God decided to forgive us before we were even born. Yes, repentance is essential if we are to enjoy, to receive, that forgiveness. But on God's part, this forgiveness has already been given to us. God forgiving us is a done deal. The gift has been given. Whether or not we receive it, that is up to us to decide.

If we reject God, then that is our problem, and not his. We are then left with the consequences of our sin - death and eternal separation from God. This is not because God has failed to forgive us; it is because we have failed to accept the gift of forgiveness that we have already been given by God.

We are now going to move on to Jesus' major teaching on the subject of

---

[41] 1 John 1:9

forgiveness. But I want to do this against the background of what is a simple, but vitally important idea, one that I feel is very often overlooked. It is vitally important we forgive because being forgiven is a key facet of God's own character. God wants us to forgive because he wants us to be like him, to carry the family likeness. Our heavenly Father is the supreme example of forgiveness. He wants us to be like him.

There must have been something that Jesus said, or more likely a whole number of things that he said, that prompted Peter to ask him a question about forgiveness. It's quite possible that Peter was not just acting on his own, but was in fact reflecting the questions that many, if not all, the disciples had about forgiveness. For whatever reason, Peter was left wondering just what limits Jesus was placing on this forgiveness thing. Peter's question triggered this answer from Jesus:

*Then Peter came to him and asked, 'Lord, how often should I forgive someone who sins against me? Seven times?' 'No, not seven times,' Jesus replied, 'but seventy times seven! Therefore, the Kingdom of Heaven can be compared to a king who decided to bring his accounts up to date with servants who had borrowed money from him. In the process, one of his debtors was brought in who owed him millions of dollars. He couldn't pay, so his master ordered that he be sold - along with his wife, his children, and everything he owned - to pay the debt. But the man fell down before his master and begged him, 'Please, be patient with me, and I will pay it all.' Then his master was filled with pity for him, and he released him and forgave his debt.*

*But when the man left the king, he went to a fellow servant who owed him a few thousand dollars. He grabbed him by the throat and demanded instant payment. His fellow servant fell down before him and begged for a little more time. 'Be patient with me, and I will pay it,' he pleaded. But his creditor wouldn't wait. He had the man arrested and put in prison until the debt could be paid in full. When some of the other servants saw this, they were very upset. They went to the king and told him everything that had happened. Then the king called in the man he had forgiven and said, 'You evil servant! I forgave you that tremendous debt because you pleaded with me. Shouldn't you have mercy on your fellow servant, just as I had mercy on you?' Then the angry king sent the man to prison to be tortured until he had paid his entire debt. That's what my heavenly Father will do to you if you refuse to forgive your brothers and sisters from your heart.* [42]

---

[42] Matthew 18:21-35

In this parable, Jesus uses the metaphor of financial debt for the offences we endure. This is interesting, if only because we often think or feel about offences in the sense of having suffered a loss, or of the offender 'owing' us something.

The first of the two servants in the story couldn't possibly pay off the debt he owed - it was hopelessly large. The master didn't simply give him generous terms for payment. The master completely wrote off, cancelled, the debt. This was a remarkably generous and gracious act. The second servant receives much less kind treatment - at the hands of the first servant. The unfairness of what has happened is so objectionable to some of the other servants that a report of the affair gets back to the master, who pronounces a serious sentence: prison and torture until the first servant can repay the debt, which means a life sentence.

The linking of our receiving forgiveness, and our forgiving others, finds an echo in part of the Lord's Prayer:

*'…and forgive us our sins,*

*as we have forgiven those who sin against us…* [43]

Forgiveness from God is a gift, but this gift cannot be received without repentance. Similarly, if I choose not to forgive others, I am changing my position so that I am no longer in the place where the gift of forgiveness can be received. I am borrowing from John and Carol Arnott's teaching on this subject[44] when I say that when we receive God's forgiveness, we move from the level of legal rights and wrongs - the justice level - to the level of grace. If we refuse to forgive others, we are keeping hold of our rights, our sense of being entitled to some kind of revenge and/or punishment and/or restitution. If we decide to keep hold of our rights, this means we are also letting other people keep hold of their rights against us. We are choosing to move down to the justice level, rather than living on the higher and better grace level.

These Bible passage I have just quoted contains a sober warning that we must be careful not to disqualify ourselves from experiencing forgiveness

---

[43] Matthew 6:12

[44] 'Grace & Forgiveness'

by holding on to our own rights.

There is something else in Jesus' story here that I want to focus on. In response to Peter's question, Jesus is presenting Peter with a paradigm shift - he is fundamentally challenging Peter's idea of how you work out whether you are under an obligation to forgive someone. At the heart of Jesus' challenge is this idea: for someone like Peter to even ask this question shows that he has no true grasp of how much he himself has been forgiven.

So often, the reason why Christians struggle with Jesus' command to forgive is that basically it seems so unfair. It is very significant that Jesus' story here is really all about fairness. However, it is fairness with a difference. We are invited to take a look at what true fairness is like - not fairness as seen through the blinkers of our limited understanding and our prejudices, but fairness as seen through God's eyes.

It is the unfairness of the unforgiving servant's treatment of the second servant that gets him into trouble. Other servants are observers of this, and their sense of fairness is offended, and so a report goes back to the master, who takes action.

Let me try to summarise what Jesus is saying here. For each and every one of us, the gift of forgiveness that we have received from God is huge. It cost God a very high price, and it is equivalent to our being released from a debt that we could never, ever, repay. Any offences that we suffer at the hands of other people - however horrible - are, in comparison, insignificant. Having received from God the gift that we have received, it is hypocritical and ridiculous to hold other people to the debts they owe us. If we insist on following this course of action where we want to pursue our rights, then we are choosing to act as if God's grace means nothing. God's level of grace is a higher level of living than the level of justice, or law. On the grace level, we can enjoy all the benefits that forgiveness brings. We can truly experience what this book is all about - freedom. On the justice level, we give our enemy the opportunity to harass and accuse us.

It is as if Jesus is showing us a set of weighing scales. If we could accurately weigh in those scales the debt we owe him, in comparison with the weight of the debt that others owe to us, there is simply no comparison. Jesus' forgiveness of us always trumps our forgiveness of others.

This can be very difficult to accept, for example in the case of someone who has led a good life but suffers something heinous such as a rape or some other kind of serious abuse. The trouble is, as human beings, we are very limited in how much we can take in of the bigger picture. Hurts that are suffered by us personally, or by people we love, are of course felt very keenly. We are probably less sensitised about the pain that we inflict on other people beyond our close circle of family and friends. Most important of all, we can be somewhat blind when it comes to the effect that our own sins have had on God.

For many of us, although we accept that we were sinners who needed Jesus to bridge the gap between us and the Father, we see ourselves as people who have led, or at least now are leading, lives that are basically decent. We accept, of course, that all sin is sin. And yet, when we consider our own sins and compare them with the sins of others (especially those others who have sinned against us) we seem to be, in relative terms, the innocent party.

We accept that when John 3:16 speaks about Father God loving all the world so much that he sent his only Son, we are part of that 'world', and that our own sin was part of the problem. But perhaps in our hearts we find it hard truly to grasp that our individual sin - your own sin and, equally, mine - prompted Jesus to visit this planet on his mercy mission and put himself on the Cross.

Even it it happens subconsciously, we can so easily compile a kind of league table of sin, and of sinners. Very often, there will in such a league table be a large number of people who are in our view very much worse sinners than we were (or are).

There is a rather subtle deception at work in this type of thinking. It is as if yes, Jesus did die for me as well as everyone else. But in the overall scheme of things my own individual sins don't really amount to very much. Really where this takes us is to a place where we deny the central importance of the Cross, because we ignore our personal responsibility for Jesus' sacrifice. This brings us back to the thrust of Jesus' answer to Peter's question about forgiveness. If we truly know how much we have been forgiven, we will embrace the relatively small matter of forgiving others. If we can't forgive others, perhaps we have forgotten, or have not ever properly grasped, just how much forgiveness we have ourselves received.

There is an opposite problem, that of the person who is gripped by guilt about the horror of the sins they have committed and can't easily embrace the gift of forgiveness that God offers. We can have a problem really accepting God's forgiveness because we feel our sins are so bad. Although at the conscious level we might rarely, if ever, own up to this, we can feel that yes, God forgives us, but he does so more reluctantly than he forgives other people, because our sins are worse. Or, we may live with a sense of continuing to blame ourselves so that yes, God forgives us, but we don't forgive ourselves.

We could even have some kind of complaint against God himself — perhaps we blame him for the bad circumstances of our life. God has never sinned and does not need our forgiveness, but from our human point of view we might need to forgive God. If we can't resolve that big problem, then surely we will find it very hard to forgive anybody else.

Although I am focusing mainly on forgiving others around us, please bear in mind that there are these three directions, or dimensions of forgiveness. The first is forgiveness of others around us. The second is being prepared to forgive ourselves. The third is, if we find we are blaming God, forgiveness of God himself. Even so, clearly, God has not committed any sin.

The big mistake that the unforgiving servant made in Jesus' story was that he had lost any sense of the true nature of things. He dealt with a relatively small thing - the debt that was owed to him - as if the very, very, very big thing - his being let off an impossibly huge debt - had never happened. As a result, he traded something very precious, namely freedom, for something inferior: living in the realm where everyone gets what they deserve.

I want to zero in on the question of whether we really grasp the enormity of what it is that Jesus has done for us: for each one of us, regardless of how terrible we think our own sins have been.

Here is a fascinating story of a meal that Jesus shared with a religious leader called Simon:

*One of the Pharisees asked Jesus to have dinner with him, so Jesus went to his home and sat down to eat. When a certain immoral woman from that city heard he was eating there, she brought a beautiful alabaster jar filled with expensive perfume. Then she knelt behind him at his feet, weeping. Her tears fell on his feet, and she wiped them off with her hair. Then she kept kissing his feet and putting perfume on them. When the Pharisee who had invited him saw this, he said to himself, 'If this man were a prophet, he would know what kind of woman is touching him. She's a sinner!' Then Jesus answered his thoughts. 'Simon,' he said to the Pharisee, 'I have something to say to you.' 'Go ahead, Teacher,' Simon replied.*

*Then Jesus told him this story: 'A man loaned money to two people - 500 pieces of silver to one and 50 pieces to the other. But neither of them could repay him, so he kindly forgave them both, canceling their debts. Who do you suppose loved him more after that?' Simon answered, 'I suppose the one for whom he canceled the larger debt.' 'That's right,' Jesus said. Then he turned to the woman and said to Simon, 'Look at this woman kneeling here. When I entered your home, you didn't offer me water to wash the dust from my feet, but she has washed them with her tears and wiped them with her hair. You didn't greet me with a kiss, but from the time I first came in, she has not stopped kissing my feet. You neglected the courtesy of olive oil to anoint my head, but she has anointed my feet with rare perfume.'*

*'I tell you, her sins - and they are many - have been forgiven, so she has shown me much love. But a person who is forgiven little shows only little love.' Then Jesus said to the woman, 'Your sins are forgiven.' The men at the table said among themselves, 'Who is this man, that he goes around forgiving sins?' And Jesus said to the woman, 'Your faith has saved you; go in peace.* [45]

There is, at least potentially, a terrible irony in this story that might not be immediately obvious to you. It is quite possible that Simon drew a particular conclusion from Jesus' teaching here, and it is a conclusion that we might also reach.

You can read this story as a very simple lesson: the level of devotion we can give to Jesus, the intensity of our feelings of gratitude and worship, are connected with and are in proportion to the amount of wickedness that we have committed. If this were true, then we would all be stuck - within some kind of range of responses. None of us would be able to get to a level of worship, gratitude, call it what you will, that is 'above' the corresponding level of the seriousness of our sin.

Possibly Simon felt Jesus was accepting that he, Simon, as a righteous man, would not be able to relate to Jesus in the same way that the woman had done. After all, there was such a huge gap between them in terms of moral conduct. Did Simon feel regret that he would not be able to enter into the same world of worship that the woman was moving in? I do not know. Alternatively, did Simon feel relieved that he did not have to worry

---

[45] Luke 7:36-50

about trying to go to the same extremes as the woman? My own guess is that this is more likely. What did Simon make of Jesus' rebuke of his own behaviour, about the absence of what were some common courtesies within the culture of those times? Again, I don't know.

Here is the irony. It is possible that Simon, and it is possible that we ourselves, can completely miss the real point that Jesus is making. Simon compared himself to the woman and saw himself as morally superior. To paraphrase this possible interpretation, it's as if Simon heard Jesus say something like this: 'It's like this, Simon. This woman is clearly a very bad sinner, whereas you are a morally upright, respectable member of society. She has a big burden of awful sins that need to be forgiven, whereas in comparison your sins are of course very minor blemishes. You need to understand and excuse her over-the-top behaviour against the background of the terrible things that she has done.'

My suggestion is this. Jesus' perspective is completely different. I don't know whether he weighed or compared the two sets of sins, the woman's sins and Simon's sins. Even if he did, I am sure that Simon would have been shocked and surprised if he could see things from Jesus' point of view. Jesus is not letting Simon off the hook because Simon hasn't sinned very much. On the contrary, he is inviting Simon to discover that he really has no idea just how much he has himself been forgiven, and how in the overall scheme of things there really isn't much difference between Simon and the woman. To God, we are all big sinners. Each one of us has sinned enough to put Jesus on the Cross.

Applying this idea to ourselves, if we put ourselves into this story, do we identify more with the woman, or with Simon? Is it possible that somewhere along our journey of life, we have lost contact with the reality of just how much we have been forgiven?

Going back to the parable of the unforgiving servant, and Jesus' central teaching about forgiving others, we all have something in common with the unforgiving servant. We all owed a debt that we could not ever repay. What Jesus is calling us to obey is the logic of what we said yes to when we accepted him in the first place. For each of us, we have been given an unimaginably huge free gift. The debts that others owe us - in the sense of the wrong things they have done to us - are, in comparison, insignificant. We need to trust God to deal with those offenders as he sees fit. As for ourselves, each one of us needs to focus on living in the good of what God has done for a particular offender, namely me and you.

I am an offender, someone who has committed enough sins to put me in serious trouble, and enough sins to prompt Jesus to go to the Cross. May I deal with others in a consistent way: may I not deny the reality of what my Jesus has done for me. And may this also be true for you. If we hold on to unforgiveness, then we create prison cells, or bondages, for ourselves. May each one of us learn how to let go of unforgiveness, and experience the freedom that comes when we operate in the realm of grace. As we move within that realm of grace, may we discover more and more of our personal best.

# 'Hearing' God

Zì ǀ Word

# CHAPTER 3

Romans 10 tells us that the key to salvation is confessing with our mouths that Jesus is Lord and believing in our hearts that God raised him from the dead. Paul goes on in that Chapter to explain that this believing cannot happen unless the message of the good news has been heard, and therefore it is essential that messengers of the good news are sent out into the world. Communication is essential. God is the first and greatest communicator. He spoke the universe into existence, and if we are willing to hear its message, the very universe itself speaks of who God is and what he is like:

*"The heavens proclaim the glory of God. The skies display his craftmanship. Day after day they continue to speak; night after night they make him known. They speak without a sound or word; their voice is never heard. Yet their message has gone throughout the earth, and their words to all the world.* [46]

We also have the Bible itself. Paul says this about the Bible in his second letter to Timothy:

*'All Scripture is inspired by God and is useful to teach us what is true and to make us realise what is wrong in our lives. It straightens us out and teaches us to do what is right.* [47]

It is possible, of course, for someone to read the Bible without it making any sense at all. Unless the Holy Spirit brings understanding, then at best the Bible is going to be an interesting piece of literature, a collection of stories, or a useful historical document.

The Bible is often referred to as the word of God, and rightly so. But the Bible itself speaks of another word - <u>the</u> Word, God's ultimate work of communication with his creation. This Word is Jesus, and is described by John at the start of his Gospel:

*In the beginning the Word already existed. The Word was with God, and the Word was God. He existed in the beginning with God. God created everything through him, and nothing was created except through him. The Word gave life to everything that was*

---

[46] Psalm 19:1-4

[47] 2 Timothy 3:16

*created, and his life brought light to everyone. The light shines in the darkness, and the darkness can never extinguish it...So the Word became human and made his home among us. He was full of unfailing love and faithfulness. And we have seen his glory, the glory of the Father's one and only Son...No one has ever seen God. But the unique One, who is himself God, is near to the Father's heart. He has revealed God to us.* [48]

What incredible communication from God to us. If you want to know what God is like, look at Jesus. If you want to know what God thinks about something, find out what Jesus says about it. If you wonder how God would deal with people like you and the people in your world, look at Jesus' behaviour and you will have your answer.

Encountering Jesus is fundamentally important for freedom. Jesus told his followers that they were truly his disciples if they kept obeying his teachings. Jesus' promise to such disciples is that they will know the truth, and the truth will set them free; and if Jesus sets you free, you are free indeed.[49] The twelve disciples knew what it was to have daily encounters with the giver of freedom. When many people stopped following Jesus because his teaching had offended them, Jesus asked the 'Twelve' if they also wanted to leave him. This was Peter's reply:

*'Lord, to whom would we go? You have the words that give eternal life.* [50]

Clearly, the most significant encounter that we have with Jesus is when we say our first yes to him and begin our journey of discipleship with him. But the process of finding freedom is an ongoing one. Jesus himself said,

*'My sheep hear my voice; and I know them, and they follow me.* [51]

and,

*'..the Spirit of truth.....will guide you into all truth; for he will not speak on his own authority, but whatever he hears he will speak; and he will tell you things to come. He will glorify me, for he will take of what is mine and declare it to you.* [52]

---

[48] John 1:1-5,11&18

[49] John 8:31&32,36

[50] John 6:68

[51] John 10:27

[52] John 16:13&34

We have to be clear that these promises are as true for us today as they were for the first disciples two thousand years ago. It's wonderful and important, of course, that we have the Bible. But what Jesus said the Spirit would do was not just a reference to the Holy Spirit inspiring the writing of the New Testament, which for us is now a matter of history.

Today, the Holy Spirit is helping us when we read the Bible. He is also helping us hear the new things that Jesus wants us to hear today. When Jesus spoke about his sheep hearing his voice, he didn't mean that once the first generation of disciples had died, no-one would hear from him first hand ever again.

As a believer, it is part of your birthright to be able to hear the voice of your shepherd, to hear his words of life. When we know we are hearing from Jesus direct, the power that flows from this is amazing.

So, we have seen that God the great communicator is still in the business today of talking to his children. How are you enjoying that conversation at the moment? Some Christians don't believe that this conversation is possible. If you have such a belief, it will certainly get in the way. Some Christians feel they have difficulty hearing what God is saying to them. I have often heard comments such as, 'I don't hear from God anymore', or 'God doesn't talk to me - what's wrong with me?'.

My intention in this Chapter is to make two big points. So far, we have been considering the first of those, namely that God is still speaking today, and he wants to have an ongoing conversation with each of his kids. The second point is this: if we believe we have problems hearing God, those problems might be rooted in false expectations about what 'hearing' God is really like.

The word 'hearing' in the title of this Chapter is in quote marks for a special reason. Hearing from God so clearly that it feels as if an audible voice is traveling through the air into your ears is relatively rare. Much, much more common is a sense of picking up what God is communicating in a way which is perhaps something like physical hearing, but which really is quite a different thing.

The way we 'hear' from God can usefully be divided into three broad types of communication: dialogue; seeing; and sensing. I am using the word 'dialogue' to describe one of the three communication types simply in an attempt to avoid confusion. It is almost embedded in our language that any kind of communication with God must be 'hearing' God. So, in talking about three different kinds of communication, I want to avoid labelling one of these three as 'hearing'.

If your primary way of communicating with God is by sensing or seeing rather than dialogue, please do not be put off or discouraged when I or anyone else talks about 'hearing' God, or having a dialogue with God. All three communication types are equally valid and important. While we can all experience and use all of these, probably there will be one communication style in particular that works best and most easily between you and the Great Shepherd.

The dialogue communication type is easy to explain. This type includes not only hearing God speak as if his voice is actually moving through the air around you, but also the sort of conversation that goes on, so to speak, inside your head. It can range from snatches of conversation, perhaps a few words, to complete sentences, even to a conversation which is as clear as any other conversation you might have with someone face to face.

There are examples in the Bible of God speaking with an audible voice. 1 Samuel 3 tells the story of the prophet Samuel when he was a boy who was working as an assistant to the priest, Levi. It was uncommon, the story tells us, in those days for people to receive messages from God. The boy Samuel heard God so clearly that it woke him up, and he assumed it must have been Eli who was calling him!

However, I very much doubt that every single time the Bible refers to someone 'hearing' God, it is always a reference to this kind of audible voice experience. If you have never heard God's voice in that audible way, do not be discouraged. This could, of course, happen for you soon (who knows?!) but in any event, the conversations you have with God that seem to go on just inside you are, nevertheless, conversations with God. So do not despise them.

What about the 'seeing' type of communication? In the Old Testament era, prophets were often called 'seers', which shows us that it was well understood that God often spoke through pictures and visions. On the Day of Pentecost Peter preached to the crowd who were amazed by what they had seen and heard when the Holy Spirit was poured out on the disciples. Peter quoted the promise from Joel:

*'In the last days, God said, I will pour out my Spirit upon all people. Your sons and daughters will prophesy, your young men will see visions, and your old men will dream dreams.* [53]

God is very, very, smart. He completely understands the power that images have to convey information clearly and quickly. We can see something of the power of visual communication in the amount of money companies spend on creating, and sometimes re-creating, their logos and brands. Depending upon how you best process information, when you are in a learning or studying environment you might find yourself drawing some kind of picture or diagram to help you understand or remember something.

Even if you are primarily a seer, there is again, within this type of communication, a wide range. Some people seem able very easily to see scenes in great detail, sometimes moving pictures as if they are watching a film, sometimes open visions so that it is like being inside the scene. Others might get a picture of an object, either in detail or it might be the impression of an object, perhaps just in outline. All of this counts.

Here are a couple of examples of seeing from the Bible:

*Then as I looked, I saw a door standing open in heaven, and the same voice I had heard before spoke to me like a trumpet blast. The voice said, 'Come up here, and I will show you what must happen after this.' And instantly I was in the Spirit, and I saw a throne in heaven and someone sitting on it.* [54]

Interestingly, this shows two stages of seeing: first a door, and then a view through that door.

*That night Paul had a vision: A man from Macedonia in northern Greece was standing there, pleading with him, 'Come over to Macedonia and help us!' So we decided to leave for Macedonia at once, having concluded that God was calling us to preach the Good News there.* [55]

Both of these passages point to a combination of seeing and hearing.

---

[53] Acts 2:17

[54] Revelation 4:1&2

[55] Acts 16:9&10

There is certainly no reason why someone who primarily dialogues should not also be able to see, and likewise someone who primarily sees can also have a dialogue. The three communication types are available to all of us, but the fact remains that for each of us there is likely to be a primary way of communicating with God.

The third communication type is what I am calling sensing. Sensing is perhaps the hardest to explain, partly because it operates at a level where there are no words or pictures. A person who communicates with God primarily by sensing might use this kind of language. 'I don't quite know how to explain this, but...', or 'I just have this feeling that...', or 'It seems to me that what the Lord is saying is...' Someone whose primary style is sensing often 'hears' from God in the depths of his or her being. Depending upon your culture, you might talk about 'gut feelings', or 'having a feeling in your waters (or your bones)', 'in my heart of hearts', or something similar.

My belief is that many people who think they have a major problem 'hearing' God are in fact primarily sensers who are comparing themselves against others who seem to have either a dialogue with God or who seem to see amazing pictures. They then decide that, since they are not communicating as other Christians do, something must be wrong with their own receiving equipment. If you are primarily a senser, please be released into who and what the Lord has made you to be!

My suggestion that there are three primary types when it comes to hearing God is not something that I can prove by quoting a simple proof text from the Bible. I will, however, venture that there seem to be hints of this in Scripture.

*All the believers were united in heart and mind. And they felt that what they owned was not their own, so they shared everything they had.*[56]

We are not told how the first Church in Jerusalem came to the point of feeling as they did about their possessions. I do find it interesting that the word 'felt' is used here. Perhaps we are looking here at a powerful example of a corporate sensing? Here is a possible example of Paul 'sensing':

---

[56] Acts 4:32

*Afterward Paul felt compelled by the Spirit to go over to Macedonia and Achaia before going to Jerusalem. 'And after that,' he said, 'I must go on to Rome!'*[57]

Here is another hint, in the book of Isaiah:

*And he said, 'Yes, go, and say to this people, Listen carefully, but do not understand. Watch closely, but learn nothing. Harden the hearts of these people. Plug their ears and shut their eyes. That way, they will not see with their eyes, nor hear with their ears, nor understand with their hearts and turn to me for healing.*[58]

This passage is part of the account of what happens to the prophet Isaiah when he receives his amazing vision of God on his throne. There is a strong suggestion here of a threefold communication - twice we have reference to this. First there is the hardening of the heart, the plugging of the ears and the shutting of the eyes. Second there is not seeing (with the eyes), not hearing (with the ears) and not understanding (with the heart).

Did Jesus also refer to this threefold communication?

*'Keep on asking, and you will receive what you ask for. Keep on seeking, and you will find. Keep on knocking, and the door will be opened to you. For everyone who asks, receives. Everyone who seeks, finds. And to everyone who knocks, the door will be opened.*[59]

This is part of a teaching which Jesus gave about prayer. The thrust of this teaching is that we shouldn't give up or be discouraged if we feel our prayers aren't being answered. God is a good father. He knows what we need. If we ask him for something good, we can be confident that we will receive something good, but we must be prepared to persist.

As part of that teaching, Jesus makes reference (again, twice) to three kinds of making requests in prayer: asking; seeking; and knocking. Asking is to do with talking and hearing. Seeking is to do with looking and seeing. And knocking is to do with an action - what you would feel - like sensing, and certainly something different from dialogue or seeing.

I am not going to try here to give any practical advice about how to tune

---

[57] Acts 19:21

[58] Isaiah 6:9&10

[59] Matthew 7:7&8

into God. That is for later, in Part Two of this book. For now, please be encouraged that 'hearing' God is possible, indeed you may already have been 'hearing' God very well, but failed to credit yourself with the ability to do so.

If you are primarily someone who does dialogue but the snatches of conversation you have with the Lord seem to be nothing compared with the hugely detailed conversations your friends seem to have with the Almighty on a daily basis - be encouraged!

If you are primarily someone who sees but your grainy, black and white snapshots pale into insignificance when you hear stories of Hollywood-style 3D extravaganzas that are enjoyed by others in your Church - be encouraged!

And last, but by no means least, if you are primarily someone who senses, but you feel embarrassed by, or you hardly know how to explain, the sometimes vague feelings that are churning within the depths of your being - be encouraged! If everyone else around you appears to be full of sound and/or vision, may you, especially, know that you are indeed in intimate contact with the God who loves you so very, very dearly.

God has never stopped communicating with you, and he never will stop. Are you ready for what he will say next?

# Really Knowing

Xīn | Heart

# CHAPTER 4

What is the secret, the key, to making real progress as a follower of Jesus? If there is one thing that you need to do, or to believe, what is it?

If we spend any time pondering this question, most of us will probably think that the key (if indeed there is any single key) is maybe knowing more about what the Bible. Or praying more. Or witnessing more. Or working harder. Or something else that we have to do, some action we have to take.

Possibly we are waiting for a change in our life circumstances. Such as, to finish our education, to move to a better job, or to find a better Church. We might be pinning our hopes on meeting a special someone who will make everything better for us. Whether we admit it or not, many of us will tend to think in terms of needing more power from God to do a better job for God.

The fact is, there is a significant key that is in plain view when we read our Bibles. This key is radically different from the sort of thing I have just mentioned. It is in many of Paul's letters to the Early Church. What Paul spends time praying for those Churches tells us a lot about what was important so far as he was concerned. The limitations of our language make it difficult to say in one or two words what this key is, but a rough summary would be this: you need to really, really know in the depths of your being that God loves you, and that he is your biggest fan.

Let's look at some of the prayers that the apostle Paul said he was praying for various Churches. He was asking God to connect Christians - people who had already said yes to Jesus, people who were already committed to him - with the reality of God's love. So one of the lessons we can learn is that this deeper connection is not automatic and complete on the day a person first becomes a Christian. Another lesson is that this deeper connection is very important.

*Ever since I first heard of your strong faith in the Lord Jesus and your love for God's people everywhere, I have not stopped thanking God for you. I pray for you constantly, asking God, the glorious Father of our Lord Jesus Christ, to give you spiritual wisdom and insight so that you might grow in your knowledge of God. I pray that your hearts will be flooded with light so that you can understand the confident hope he has given to those he called - his holy people who are his rich and glorious inheritance. I also pray that you will understand the incredible greatness of God's power for us who believe him.*[60]

It is good to take a little time here to unpack some of the original Greek language which Paul was using when he wrote these words. This is because English, at least, is a language where the concept of 'knowing' has become somewhat devalued. This devaluing is similar to what has happened to other words, such as 'love'. We can use the word 'love' to describe Jesus' sacrificial love for us, but at the same time I can talk about 'loving' a certain movie, or 'loving' chocolate ice cream. Taking another devalued word as another example, when trying to say something about God's nature and character, we can say that God is 'awesome'. But a pizza can also be 'awesome'!

The way we talk about what we 'know' is similar. We can say that we know something merely on the basis of having read something in a magazine, or on the internet, or because we've heard a few sentences on the tv or the radio. One way of expressing the different levels of knowledge is to contrast 'head knowledge' with 'heart knowledge'. I can, at an intellectual or rational level, say that I know something. This is 'head knowledge'. On the other hand, there is stuff that I am utterly convinced about in my heart - in the very depths of my soul. This is 'heart knowledge'. There can even be a conflict, sometimes a hidden conflict, between these two levels of knowledge. We look at that conflict in the next Chapter.

So, let's go back to the passage from Ephesians 1. Paul is asking that these Christians receive 'spiritual wisdom and insight'. The Greek word here is *epignosis*, which means full discernment. This is more than just intellectual box-ticking. It goes beyond our saying we believe or understand something while in reality in our hearts we believe something quite different.

This passage goes on to link the state of our hearts with what we truly understand. The prayer here is about our hearts - *kardia*. This Greek word is where words such as cardiography come from. Paul wants our *kardia* to be

---

[60] Ephesians 1:15-19

'flooded with light'. Another word used here is *eido*, which means to see. As some other translations put it, Paul's prayer is that the eyes of our hearts are opened. So, our hearts have eyes! Paul is talking about us shifting from head knowledge to heart knowledge.

Here is another one of Paul's prayers:

*Then Christ will make his home in your hearts as you trust in him. Your roots will grow down into God's love and keep you strong. And may you have the power to understand, as all God's people should, how wide, how long, how high, and how deep his love is.*[61]

I find it interesting that this is a prayer about our having power. Not about the power to perform amazing signs and wonders, but rather, to understand how great God's love is. The Greek word here is *katalambo*, which means to take eager hold of something. This is much more than merely agreeing on an intellectual level that God's love is big. This word *katalambo* is about the truth, the reality of God's love, travelling down from our heads into our hearts. It is about our grabbing hold of this truth.

Here is another of Paul's prayers:

*I pray that your love will overflow more and more, and that you will keep on growing in knowledge and understanding. For I want you to understand what really matters, so that you may live pure and blameless lives until the day of Christ's return.*[62]

Again, the Greek word in this passage about understanding is *epignosis* - full discernment. Notice the link in this prayer of Paul between what we understand and how we live. My conduct, my behaviour, flows from what I believe inside. The key to living right is believing right. But again, believing right is not a question of giving mental assent to a list of beliefs which someone else puts in front of you. It is a question of what do you really, in your heart of hearts, know to be true.

A huge part of our spiritual journey as followers of Jesus is breaking away from the ways of thinking that we have learned from the world around us. As Paul puts it,

*Don't copy the behaviour and customs of this world, but let God transform you into a*

---

[61] Ephesians 3:17&18

[62] Philippians 1:9&10

*new person by changing the way you think. Then you will learn to know God's will for you, which is good and pleasing and perfect.*[63]

There is a link between the type of people we are, and the way we think. This idea is expressed rather beautifully in J.B. Phillips' version of Paul's words:

*Don't let the world around you squeeze you into its own mould, but let God re-mould your minds from within...*[64]

Quite possibly, we did not know that when we became Christians, we volunteered to join a process that involves the remoulding of our minds! However, we are probably more familiar with the concept of repentance. John the Baptist preached a message that was about the need to repent. On the Day of Pentecost, when the Holy Spirit was poured out on many people in Jerusalem and the crowd asked Peter what they needed to do to be saved, Peter's reply was that they needed to repent, and to be baptised.[65]

But what exactly is repentance? It is easy to think repentance is just another word for saying sorry, or feeling sorry. Speaking personally, sometimes in my own journey what I thought was my own repentance might not have been much more than feeling sorry that I had somehow been found out!

This is another example of important ideas being hidden by the use of an English word that robs the idea of much of its true meaning. It is an example of a devaluing of an idea. The word in the Bible that is time and again translated as repentance is the Greek word *metanoia*. This means much more than feeling sorry, or saying sorry. It is about going through a change in frame of mind and feeling, or making a change of principle and practice.

What all of this points to is that becoming a Christian, and living as a Christian, means that we need to allow the ways we think and feel to be challenged by God. It means we need to co-operate with God in the process of re-shaping some of the basic ways we believe the world around

---

[63] Romans 12:2

[64] 'New Testament In Modern English' by J.B. Phillips

[65] Acts 2:38

us works, and what life is all about.

Here is a final look at one of Paul's prayers on the subject of knowing - the key to success:

*So we have not stopped praying for you since we first heard about you. We ask God to give you complete knowledge of his will and to give you spiritual wisdom and understanding.*[66]

*Epignosis*, full discernment, is again the word here for understanding. The fact is, in Paul's prayers for the Church there is this constant theme of the need to enter into a deep understanding. We would all do well to pay serious attention to this theme, this key.

It is easy for us to fall into the trap of thinking that what we desperately need is for some kind of external change to happen. Even if what we hope for is for example a mighty, fresh encounter with the Lord (which would always be wonderful) we are missing something about how God's world works. Circumstances change. Sometimes they are good, sometimes they are bad. We encounter helpful people as well as unhelpful people. There are times when we can feel God is very close, and times when it feels as if he is a million miles away.

The key, the secret to success, is not just about the quality of our knowing. Moving from 'head knowledge' to 'heart knowledge' in and of itself is not the key. It is also about the object of our knowing. What is it that we want to know more about? Who is it that we want to know more about?

What really matters, what is really important, is what we know in or hearts about God. Paul's prayers that we have glanced at are all about us connecting with the reality of what God is like, how much he loves us, and how significant we are as a result. This is the stuff that matters, far above anything else.

I will agree with Paul by praying that you will find the truth of God's goodness, of his kindness and affection for you. May this truth percolate more and more down from your head into your heart, and may your heart be able to connect more and more with the reality of the God who is love. I

---

[66] Colossians 1:9

pray this so that you will be best equipped to lead a life of victorious freedom, over and above whatever the circumstances of life may be. May you be propelled towards your personal best.

# Truth Is Relational, Not Informational

Rén | Person

# CHAPTER 5

We must have the truth, we must know the truth, if we are going to be free. This will not necessarily be obvious to you. You might think that freedom is all about, for example, escaping from a bad relationship, moving out of a bad employment situation, gaining some new education or qualification, getting more money, moving to a different country, and so on.

God most definitely wants to bless you; he wants to guide you through the circumstances of life. He wants you to make good decisions, he wants to connect you with your destiny and to give you a life of fulfilment and adventure. But if we want to align ourselves with God's good (very good) will for our lives, we need to work with God, we need to tune in to how God's world actually works. We need to grasp the huge importance of truth.

The reason why I say that having the truth, or knowing the truth, is necessary for freedom, is because the Bible tells me so. More precisely, Jesus says so. Here are some of his words on the connection between truth and freedom:

*'You are truly my disciples if you keep obeying my teachings. And you will know the truth, and the truth will set you free.* [67]

This is taken from an account of a conversation Jesus was having with a crowd of people. Jesus was making a very interesting connection between sonship (and this includes daughters) and freedom from sin, which we look at elsewhere in this book. Later in that conversation, Jesus adds:

*'...if the Son sets you free, you will indeed be free.* [68]

I like to paraphrase it like this: if Jesus sets you free, you will be good and free - really and truly free - free beyond any shadow of doubt.

So, this is the deal: if we want to be free, we have to accept the importance of knowing the truth. We have to make it our priority to know the truth. Greater freedom is not secured by a change in our circumstances,

---

[67] John 8:31&32

[68] John 8:36

but by a better connection with whatever the truth is about us and our circumstances.

Given the importance of the truth, what then is the truth? One answer might be that the Bible is the truth. The Bible is certainly God's word. Interestingly, different people can all claim to believe the Bible and yet those same people can hold some contrasting views on a variety of subjects. This may be partly because some of those subjects are complex and we all assess what the Bible is saying through the filters of our own life experiences, our ideas - dare I say, even our prejudices.

Another answer might be that Science is the truth. I am a fan of scientific discovery, even though in some quarters Science is hijacked by those with a defiantly anti-God agenda. Scientific discovery reveals new facts about our amazing universe. Even though Science is concerned with facts, there is a human, subjective element in the process. Theories are developed and advanced, sometimes amid controversy within the scientific community. Experiments are devised to prove, or disprove, certain theories - and perhaps the results of those experiments are interpreted through some subjective filters. Some theories become so well established and accepted that they are regarded as fact. Sometimes, at a later date, those very 'facts' come under challenge from a new theory - and so on.

There may be other types of truth which occur to you. In a western culture that is described by some as 'postmodern', the idea of there being any kind of single, absolute truth may seem impossible to grasp.

Great as the Bible is, good as scientific discovery is, as good as any other other type of truth might be, where do we find the truth of which Jesus speaks - the truth that sets us free?

There is a clue in the title of this Chapter. Pontius Pilate, when he had Jesus in front of him after Jesus had been arrested, came agonisingly close to the answer, and yet he missed it.

*Pilate said, 'So you are a king?' Jesus responded, 'You say I am a king. Actually, I was born and came into the world to testify to the truth. All who love the truth recognise that what I say is true.' 'What is truth?' Pilate asked.*[69]

---

[69] John 18:37&38

Pilate was perhaps cynical about whether truth could be found anywhere at all. Given that he was enmeshed in the system of Roman government and administration, perhaps all he could see was a world ruled by the exercise of military power and political wheeling and dealing. But Pilate, like so many people in our world today who might wonder about truth, asked the wrong question. Rather than ask, 'what is truth?', if he had asked, 'who is the truth?', I wonder what Jesus would have told him.

There is an irony in this story. Pilate was wondering where truth might be found, and yet standing in front of his very eyes was truth - not truth itself, but truth himself. Truth is not a set of facts. Truth is a person. Truth is relational, not informational.

Perhaps this sounds odd. I have taken some liberties with English grammar and/or language in the title of this Chapter. But please bear in mind that I am agreeing with what Jesus says about himself:

*'I am the way, the truth, and the life. No one can come to the Father except through me.*[70]

Jesus is, in his own words, the Truth. The Bible is God's word and it is true, however all truth is not completely contained even within that good book. That book is certainly full of truth. Some truth can even be found in some other books. And yet, the Truth is not fully expressed in a book, because the Truth is in fact a person. There is a clue to this at the very beginning of the good book, the Bible, itself:

*In the beginning God created the heavens and the earth.*[71]

The universe in which we live was all made by God, a person. All of its principles, all of its workings, are his idea, his creation. He doesn't need any books to find anything out. The internet has added nothing to the sum total of his knowledge. Every law of nature is his design. He doesn't worry about whether his idea of the truth is just his own personal subjective take on reality. Without him, outside of him, there is no reality. God is the truth. Truth is a person, and we know who he is.

When I first became a Christian, I had what was my most significant

---

[70] John 14:6

[71] Genesis 1:1

encounter with this person who is the truth. I love the way every person's story of how they became a Christian is different, it is uniquely their own story, their own personal encounter with the God of all truth.

In some senses, I didn't know what I was doing. When Nicodemus came to see Jesus under cover of darkness, my guess is he was surprised to hear that he had to be 'born from above'. Romans 8:15 tells us we have become God's very own children, adopted into his family. 2 Corinthians 5:17 says that Christians are 'new persons', and that a new life has begun.

Could it be that, when we become Christians, we don't have much real understanding what what is happening to us? We may well have responded to God out of some level of desperation or a sense of emptiness. We may have been concerned most of all about not going to hell. I am very glad that God in his infinite wisdom has set the bar very low for us in terms of what we have to do, and what we have to understand, before we become new creations, before we get adopted into God's family.

Whatever your level of understanding was (or is), the fact remains that your conversion was the start of something personal, something relational. A new life began, like a baby being born. A new life, one that will never end, was ushered into the universe. The remainder of your life in this present age is meant to be spent exploring the wonderful reality of this new reality.

So: when do we get to know <u>all</u> of the truth? When does a Christian finally know all that he or she needs to know? If you have already understood that truth is relational, not informational, if you have already grasped that the truth is not an 'it', but that the Truth is a person, then the answer should be clear. Knowing the Truth is an ongoing, developing process. This is precisely because it is about a relationship, not learning a set of facts or principles.

The disciples who were closest to Jesus didn't know everything, even though they had been in close proximity to Jesus throughout his public ministry. As part of his goodbye message to his disciples before he was arrested, Jesus said this:

*'Oh, there is so much more I want to tell you, but you can't bear it now. When the*

*Spirit of truth comes, he will guide you into all truth.*[72]

This process of being guided into all truth never ends. As a disciple of Jesus, there will never come a point where I can tell the Holy Spirit that there is nothing more I need to know. How absurd that would be! It would be the height of arrogance (and ignorance) for me to say to the God who is the Truth that there is no more truth for me to know.

Being a disciple, being a follower of Jesus, is primarily the story of a relationship. You might feel there are certain expectations about how, as a Christian, you are supposed to behave. There may be things that other people tell you, or that you yourself believe, that you should do, or not do, to help you grow in your walk as a Christian.

Many of these things, possibly even all of them, may well have some value. However, I want to dig a little deeper here. I want as it were to look under the surface of things and invite you to consider what your life's journey as a Christian is really all about, and how it really works.

This is part of what Jesus prayed during his final address to his disciples after the Last Supper, the night he was arrested:

*'I have given them the glory you gave me, so they may be one as we are one. I am in them and you are in me. May they experience such perfect unity that the world will know that you sent me and that you love them as much as you love me.*[73]

This prayer is sometimes used as a focus for unity between various Church congregations. I am in favour of unity (although I am sceptical about the value of a unity based just on some kind of organisational/institutional alignment). The emphasis about unity in Jesus' prayer is on the unity we find first of all in God. That is the basis of real unity. Christian brothers and sisters begin to flow in a unity together as a result of being immersed, soaked, baptised in the unity they find as individual children of God when they go deeper into the reality of who God is and what God is like.

This unity matters to Jesus, since it is a key to evangelism. The world, people who don't yet know Jesus, will detect this kind of unity and it will

---

[72] John 16:12&13

[73] John 7:22&23

actually help them know that Jesus really was sent by the Father. The devil fakes whatever he can, he tries to fob us off with highly dubious counterfeit merchandise, however this God-inspired unity cannot be faked. It has the distinctive aroma of the Kingdom of Heaven around it.

There is something else about this unity. It will cause people who don't yet know Jesus to conclude that, looking at Christians - ordinary believers such as you and me - God loves us just as much as God loves Jesus. That is quite a statement for Jesus to make.

It suggests a strategy for evangelism, a key for evangelism, which is not often mentioned. It raises this question: how will the world get to know that God loves Christians as much as God loves Jesus? This must, surely, mean that Christians must know for themselves that God loves them as much as God loves Jesus. Here is a key to effective evangelism. Here is something for you to aim at in your journey of Christian discipleship. Make it a priority to be utterly, completely convinced that, when God the Father looks at you, he has the same feelings about you as when he looks at Jesus. It is important for you to know that if God has a wallet, your photo is in his wallet; that if God has a fridge, there is a picture of you on that fridge.

This knowledge is not just important for you. It is important for everyone else. God's plan is that people around the world will be confronted by the reality of God's love for them as they encounter Christians who know they are loved by God in the same way that God the Father loves God the Son.

When people think about what truth is, often truth can be seen as a set of black-and-white propositions; rather hard-edged or hard-nosed. In contrast, we have been looking at truth as a matter of a relationship with a person. The journey into more truth is not an exercise in ticking boxes on a list of statements. Fundamentally, it is journey into a heart of love. It is because of the impact of the reality of this journey into love that Paul could write,

*Prophecy and speaking in unknown languages and special knowledge will become useless. But love will last forever!*[74]

---

[74] 1 Corinthians 13:8

and,

*I am convinced that nothing can ever separate us from God's love. Neither death nor life, neither angels nor demons, neither our fears for today nor our worries about tomorrow - not even the powers of hell can separate us from God's love.*[75]

And John wrote this in one of his letters:

*God is love, and all who live in love live in God, and God lives in them. And as we live in God, our love grows more perfect. So we will not be afraid on the day of judgment, but we can face him with confidence because we live like Jesus here in this world. Such love has no fear, because perfect love expels all fear. If we are afraid, it is for fear of punishment, and this shows that we have not fully experienced his perfect love. We love each other because he loved us first.*[76]

The suggestion here is that is possible, for at least some of the Christians who received John's letter, that they had not yet 'fully experienced [God's] perfect love'. John is clearly encouraging people to make progress towards an ever more complete experience of God's love. Just as it was true for the very first readers of John's letter, it is true for us. Possibly our everyday experience of life is some way short of being intimately connected with the reality of God's perfect love. Even if we have been Christians for a long time.

Since the story of life as a Christian is the story of a relationship, the way it will develop should not be presented as some sort of pre-packaged, one-size-fits-all product. In the remainder of this Chapter I will share two stories about my own experience, in the hope that these will help to illustrate what it is like to have an ongoing relationship with the person who is the Truth.

What I want to try to illustrate is that Jesus, who is the Truth, is in the business of delivering truth to each of us in a way that is perfectly designed to fit our particular characters, our particular personal histories and our particular needs. My stories, because they are personal, might not register or resonate with you at all. But I hope that come what may they will encourage you to pursue you own special conversations with the Truth - with Jesus. Because, after all, truth is relational, not informational.

---

[75] Romans 8:38

[76] 1 John 4:16-19

My two personal stories are examples of two important aspects of having a living, ongoing relationship with the Truth. The first aspect is, letting Jesus take my baggage. The second aspect is, letting Jesus deal with my ungodly beliefs.

'Baggage' is the clutter of the unhealed hurts, ungodly character traits, and ungodly parts of my personality that we bring with us when we become Christians. Jesus dealt with all this stuff on the Cross, however the process of our letting him take all the baggage from us takes time. It is a process.

Those friends who know me well would probably express it better, but let's say I have a strong sense of what is right and what is wrong. This can tip over into me not only my having clear ideas about how I should be living, but also sharing advice (whether or not it is wanted) with others about how they should be living.

What was highlighted for me, through some trusted friends, was that a further part of this character trait was that I tended to react unhealthily and unhelpfully in a certain way in certain situations. It was as if it wasn't enough for me to know that I was the one who was right, even if everyone else was wrong; I needed the other people involved to recognise and acknowledge that I was right and they were wrong. I'm not proud about this - but baggage is baggage!

So, with some help from those friends, I had a conversation with Jesus about this sense of my needing to feel vindicated. Here's a brief summary of what happened during that encounter.

I was shown a scene which I took to be the Day of Judgement, when every knee will bow, and every tongue will confess that Jesus Christ is Lord. I realised that something vital in this scene was all the people who were having to acknowledge Jesus, even though they had denied him during their lives, perhaps they had even despised him or ridiculed him. These people were being shown to be wrong, and Jesus was being shown to be right. He was being vindicated.

Jesus told me that he was happy that this day had arrived - he didn't have any reservations about it. He was totally secure in who and what he was and is and will be, and it was good that he was being acknowledged as Lord. However, Jesus said something else to me that utterly undid me. Looking at all these people who were having to acknowledge him, effectively against their will, he said the fact that they were all wrong and that they had to admit he was right, gave him no pleasure at all. He had never wanted them to be in this position, he had so much wanted them to be at this event of their own free will, happily meeting with their Lord as not just Lord but also saviour and big brother.

And there was a final thing that Jesus told me. Although he knew it was not possible, he said that if there had ever been anything else he could ever have done that meant these people could be in the right rather than in the wrong, he would have done it in a heartbeat. Even if that would have meant that he needed to be wrong so that they could be right.

Now this might strike you as bad theology and/or trite and/or meaningless. On a theological level, I think this attitude of Jesus, as I perceived it in this kind of vision, is completely consistent with the Cross. He has in fact done everything that he can, and it included him taking on a planet-load of shame and accusation.

What I so much want to convey to you is that what I received that day was my Jesus talking to me. Someone else could use more or less the same words that Jesus used when he spoke to me, but the real point was that I knew it was Jesus who was talking to me. Perhaps he might not use quite the same words with anyone else, I really do not know. But, for me, the words that he spoke, to me - well, as the disciple Peter said, they were truly words of life.

I will not pretend that I am now 100% clear of the un-Christlike traits which lead some dear friends to propel me into that encounter in the first place. Yet, I know that something fundamentally changed that day. I am sure that I still have some work to do in that area in the future. I should not be complacent about my ability to fall back into some old and unhelpful patterns of behaviour. That said, if I were to tell you that there was no significant breakthrough for me that day, that would be a lie.

As a reminder, this little testimony is about Jesus dealing with my baggage. To my mind, it's as if Jesus on occasions comes into our lives as something like a hospital porter, or someone very helpful at a railway station or an airport. He sees that we are burdened with our baggage, he gently comes alongside us and asks, 'Can I help you with that?' This is the same Lord of all who once said,

*Come to me, all of you who are weary and carry heavy burdens, and I will give you*

*rest. Take my yoke upon you. Let me teach you, because I am humble and gentle at heart, and you will find rest for your souls.*[77]

If Jesus - who is the Truth - comes to you and suggests he help you with your baggage, I urge you to take him up on his offer!

My second personal story is about Jesus dealing with an ungodly belief. An ungodly belief is a belief which has its roots in the heart of a person, and which runs contrary to God's truth. It is possible to have an ungodly belief and not realise it, even to believe God's truth in your head, but to believe something very different in your heart.

My wife Mary and I were attending a ministry training course in Toronto in January 2008. I had more than once been on the receiving end of ministry for my various ungodly beliefs, and I had also taught on this subject, and ministered on it, a number of times. When our group came to look at the whole subject of ungodly beliefs, therefore, I felt I was on relatively 'safe' ground. In due course we were all invited to ask the Holy Spirit to shed light on any ungodly beliefs which we might have.

Purely as an aid, we had sheets to look at which listed a large number of fairly common types of wrong belief, grouped under various headings. Without producing a list here, these beliefs can include junk such as: 'I'm too old/young/fat/thin', 'I must be careful not to disclose what I really feel', 'I cannot afford to trust a man/woman', and so on.

I looked through each heading and list of common ungodly beliefs in turn, and I was asking the Holy Spirit to reveal anything to me that needed to be dealt with. I believe I was totally genuine in that prayer, but at the same time I might have been a little casual about the whole process - after all, I had been through this sort of thing several times already.

I won't bore you with all the details of how it emerged, but what is important is that I found myself having a conversation with God about an ungodly belief that I didn't know I had. It had been well hidden on two levels. The first was that I was not conscious of believing this thing. The second was that I felt this belief was actually true.

In summary, this was my ungodly belief. I was holding back from

---

[77] Matthew 11:28&29

trusting God fully. I believed it actually is dangerous to let go completely and follow God. This was because I thought God was unreasonable. I even had a Bible verse to back up my unbelief:

*Since he [God] did not spare even his own Son but gave him up for us all...*[78]

Of course, there's a context for that scripture which is all about God's love, not his unreasonableness. The point is, in my twisted-out-of-shape belief system, Jesus' sacrifice had been given a distorted meaning. In my head, I knew that already. But the problem wasn't in my head. It was in my heart.

It is hard for me to convey the shock and surprise I felt that day, not only at discovering that I had been living with this ungodly belief, but also that I could not simply shake it off. On an intellectual, rational, Bible-based level, I knew I could demolish this belief very easily. What surprised me was that this didn't work. I could not make this belief go away simply by an exercise of head knowledge. My heart also needed to be engaged.

It took around 24 hours for the healing process to be completed. I discussed, I prayed, I read the Bible, I paced the room, I laughed, and I cried a bit as well.

I will share what the end of this process was for me, however I must add a qualification to this. If what I have just shared makes you suspect you perhaps have the same, or a similar, wrong belief, it is very unlikely that God's answer for me will be exactly the same as his answer will be for you. His answer (for me) works (for me). It needs to, because the direction of the rest of my life will be hugely affected by whether or not I truly know that God is to be trusted with my welfare.

Truth is relational, not informational. It is about me hearing from him, and about you hearing from him. To some degree, we can help each other along the way, with words that we hear from God that are messages to be passed on for the benefit of someone else. But, above all, we need to hear Jesus for ourselves, about ourselves. Jesus has the words of life for you that will change your life. Jesus' words are tailored and special.

Dealing effectively with ungodly beliefs must include a process of

---

[78] Romans 8:32

finding a new belief, a replacement belief that can take the place of the ungodly belief that is being demolished. So, the following day, this is the replacement belief which emerged for me. Jesus did not go to the Cross because of an unreasonable God making him do it; it was Jesus' own love that drove him to the Cross. Whatever circumstances I may encounter, Jesus and the Father will always be with me. God has given me the heart of a lion that is strong enough to stare suffering in the face.

Now, I'd like you to notice something that is not in this replacement belief. There is no promise that everything in life will be easy, or that I won't come to any harm. For me, this is very important. Don't get me wrong, in no sense do I want to go looking for suffering. All I know is that, for me, I need a truth that can help me through a difficult day. I need something that helps me know, if it feels like a fire is raging all around me, by God's grace I will be able to walk through that fire - rather than run away from it.

So there you have it, a couple of personal stories, as an illustration. The truth that has been revealed to me fits perfectly with who I am, what my life experiences have been and what I need. The reason it fits me perfectly is because Jesus is most excellent at delivering truth. He is the best person to take our baggage away, to lighten our loads. When all is said and done, Jesus is the Truth.

What things will Jesus say to you? Well, that is for you to discover as you explore your relationship with Jesus who is the Truth...

# Laws And Grace

Fǎ ｜ Law

# CHAPTER 6

This is a book about freedom, and yet we spend some time looking at the importance of respecting certain rules or principles. For example, there is the vital principle of forgiveness. How can there be a valid connection between freedom - which is surely about not being bound by rules - and the need to be aware of principles? Even more seriously, how can a book which claims to be consistent with the gospel of Jesus Christ place an emphasis on following principles? Isn't this a denial of what happened on the Cross? Am I in danger of forgetting about grace?

Whether or not this objection is alive and bubbling within you at the moment, it is something that needs to be addressed head on. In this Chapter I aim to show that a follower of Jesus who is seeking to live a life of freedom must take account of various rules or principles. We can even dare to call these 'laws'. I aim to show that this approach takes nothing away from Jesus' sacrifice and God's grace.

Jesus' arrival on planet Earth marked a new covenant between God and Mankind, the story of which is told in the New Testament. Jesus spoke about this new covenant at the Last Supper, the same night he was arrested. He spoke about his body being given for us and his blood being shed. When Jesus finally died on the Cross, the huge curtain which hung in the Temple in Jerusalem in front of the Most Holy Place was torn from top to bottom, signifying the end of the old covenant - the process of our trying to make ourselves acceptable to God by observing Jewish religious laws.

Being saved is a matter of faith in Jesus and grace, not observing such laws. As the story of the Early Church unfolded, it became clear that gentiles (people who were not Jews) who found faith in Jesus did not have to become Jewish to make their salvation complete. Any idea of it being necessary to observe Jewish religious laws as part of Christian discipleship is an unbiblical distortion of the gospel. As it says in the Bible, I am not under law, I am under grace:

*For sin shall no longer be your master, because you are not under the law, but under grace.*[79]

It is clear, then, that healthy Christian discipleship is all about embracing the reality of grace. But we will do well if we can also grab hold of what grace really is, and whether grace means we are somehow immune from the forces at work in God's universe.

We need to understand the context of the verse I have just quoted. It is worthwhile spending some time on Chapters 6, 7 and 8 of Romans in detail. Paul is talking about how we become acceptable to God: if you like, how we get saved. He compares the effectiveness of what Jesus achieved on the Cross with the 'law'. The law here is not the law of the land, but the law which Jews knew they were supposed to follow as part and parcel of their identity as God's chosen people. This law is the Ten Commandments revealed to Moses by God, together with all the other requirements which are detailed in the books of Exodus, Leviticus, Numbers and Deuteronomy.

Paul is very clear that the law is good, and yet the law is not able to save anyone. The law shows us the correct way to live, but none of us can live up to the high and holy standard that it sets. Paul explains that our being acceptable to God was never, even after the law was given, just a matter of trying to do as good a job as possible of obeying the law; it was always about faith.

The story of the Jewish people as told in the Old Testament did not begin with Moses and the Ten Commandments, but with Abraham, the father of the nation, some 400 years previously. Paul makes this connection between Abraham, faith, and the fact that faith is the only way to God:

*There is only one God, and he makes people right with himself only by faith, whether they are Jews or Gentiles. Well then, if we emphasise faith, does this mean that we can forget about the law? Of course not! In fact, only when we have faith do we truly fulfil the law. Abraham was, humanly speaking, the founder of our Jewish nation. What did he discover about being made right with God? If his good deeds had made him acceptable to God, he would have had something to boast about. But that was not God's way. For the Scriptures tell us, 'Abraham believed God, and God counted him as righteous because of his faith.' When people work, their wages are not a gift, but something they have earned.*

---

[79] Romans 6:14 [niv]

*But people are counted as righteous, not because of their work, but because of their faith in God who forgives sinners.*[80]

And there is a beautifully clear statement of the gospel earlier in chapter 3 of Romans:

*But now God has shown us a different way of being right in his sight - not by obeying the law but by the way promised in the Scriptures long ago. We are made right in God's sight when we trust in Jesus Christ to take away our sins. And we all can be saved in this same way, no matter who we are or what we have done...For God sent Jesus to take the punishment for our sins and to satisfy God's anger against us. We are made right with God when we believe that Jesus shed his blood, sacrificing his life for us.*[81]

Some of the strongest language in the Bible can be found in Paul's letter to the Churches in the region of Galatia. Paul is addressing the claims from 'Judaizers' - those who claimed that non-Jews, gentiles, who had become Christians needed somehow to perfect their faith by embracing the law, including the need for circumcision.

Paul's attack on this trend includes: wishing a curse upon anyone who preaches a message other than the real gospel;[82] detailing how he corrected Peter in public for his hypocrisy;[83] and wishing that the Judaizers would mutilate themselves.[84] Eugene Peterson puts it quite graphically in the Message:

*Why don't these agitators, obsessive as they are about circumcision, go all the way and castrate themselves!*[85]

This issue - what does the gospel mean in terms of religious observance, and do non-Jewish Christians also have to take on the law of Moses - is one of the main threads in the story of the Early Church as it is recorded in the

---

[80] Romans 3:30 -4:5

[81] Romans 3:21&22,25

[82] Galatians 1:8&9

[83] Galatians 2:11-16

[84] Galatians 5:11&12

[85] 'The Message' by Eugene Peterson

book of Acts.

Peter is challenged about the 'unclean' gentiles and he sees the Holy Spirit poured out in the home of Cornelius, a Roman soldier/officer.[86] Paul, previously Saul, a hyper-devout Jew and an enthusiastic persecutor of Christians, is not only dramatically converted but also receives a commission from the risen Jesus to take the good news to the gentiles and to kings, as well as to the Jews.[87]

The pressure from Judaizers, especially around the question of circumcision, builds up to the point where Paul, with Barnabas, travels from Antioch - which has become a main centre of gentile Christianity - to Jerusalem, the centre of the first Church, the Church of Jewish converts. A conference is called, which addresses the controversy of whether gentile Christians should be called upon to be circumcised. In conclusion, the wording of a letter is agreed that tells gentile Christians to abstain from eating meat sacrificed to idols, from sexual immorality, and from eating the blood or meat of strangled animals.[88]

So, the argument over circumcision, which so exercises Paul in Galatians, was won in favour of his position. As a matter of Church discipline, it was settled that gentile Christians did not have to suffer circumcision.

Did that conference at Jerusalem get it right? Did the leaders of the Jewish church in Jerusalem give too much away, or were they perhaps too conservative and cautious? Sometimes the Bible makes clear what is right or wrong - but sometimes the Bible simply records what actually happened, leaving it to us to discern the rights and wrongs of it. Perhaps the decision which came out of Jerusalem was exactly what the Holy Spirit wanted; perhaps there was an element of compromise. I am certain that, if the Church in Jerusalem had tried to insist on circumcision, that would have been a serious error.

---

[86] Acts 10

[87] Acts 9:1-19

[88] Acts 15:1-31

Here is the conclusion I draw from this. The whole thrust of teaching in the New Testament on this subject, mainly but not exclusively from Paul, is that the law of Moses does not bind followers of Jesus. However - and this is important - there may be moral principles underneath that law that apply to us, even though we are 'under grace'. For example, one of the Ten Commandments tells us not to commit murder. Murder remains a sin issue, even in the age of grace.

I am 100% with Paul in his severe warning in Galatians about not adding to the true gospel. Even so, we need to be awake to whatever fundamental moral issues still apply to us. I don't have to act like a good Jew to make my salvation valid. But the fact remains I am alive in a moral universe - a world where my actions have consequences. I seem to be agreeing with Jesus, which is always a very good idea. As part of his Sermon on the Mount, Jesus said this about the law:

*Don't misunderstand why I have come. I did not come to abolish the law of Moses or the writings of the prophets. No, I came to accomplish their purpose. I tell you the truth, until heaven and earth disappear, not even the smallest detail of God's law will disappear until its purpose is achieved. So if you ignore the least commandment and teach others to do the same, you will be called the least in the Kingdom of Heaven. But anyone who obeys God's laws and teaches them will be called great in the Kingdom of Heaven. But I warn you - unless your righteousness is better than the righteousness of the teachers of religious law and the Pharisees, you will never enter the Kingdom of Heaven!*[89]

Bearing in mind what Paul says in Romans about our inability to satisfy the requirements of the law of Moses, Jesus' teaching in the Sermon is all the more amazing. Time and again he takes one of the laws - which are hard enough for us to follow - and he adds whole new dimensions to it, examining the very condition of our hearts, opening our eyes to our attitudes and intentions.

So, for example, the apparently straightforward commandment about not murdering anyone becomes a springboard for Jesus to talk about anger and the need to pursue reconciliation.[90]

---

[89] Matthew 5:17-20

[90] Matthew 5:21-26

What is going on here? Paul makes it clear that the law is good.[91] Do not be mistaken by thinking that the Bible says something about the law having been nailed to the Cross. Such an idea is possibly based on a misunderstanding of this passage from Colossians:

*You were dead because of your sins and because your sinful nature was not yet cut away. Then God made you alive with Christ, for he forgave all our sins. He canceled the record of the charges against us and took it away by nailing it to the cross. In this way, he disarmed the spiritual rulers and authorities. He shamed them publicly by his victory over them on the cross.[92]*

What has been nailed to the Cross is not the law - after all, the law is good - but the record of charges against us, in other words the sins we have committed. Evil spirits - the spiritual rulers and authorities - have not been disarmed by the law having been done away with; they have been disarmed because Jesus has dealt with the issue of sin.

One of the things the law does is it shows us the gap between how we are supposed to live and what our lives are actually like. As Paul puts it in Romans:

*God's law was given so that all people could see how sinful they were.[93]*

Personally, I think of the law as something like a scaffold - a structure that was given by God to help people understand how to build their lives in a godly way. Or to put it another way, the law is some kind of road sign or direction pointer, drawing our attention to something quite far off in the distance - the place where there is no sin, and where God is pleased with everything that happens.

In contrast, what is going on in the Sermon on the Mount is radically different. Jesus is not adding fresh burdens on our backs, making tough law even tougher. Whereas the law is pointing us to a place where really by our own efforts we cannot go, Jesus has come from that very place. He has arrived from Heaven, from the Kingdom of God, and he is announcing the

---

[91] Romans 6:7-13

[92] Colossians 2:13-15

[93] Romans 5:20

arrival of that same Kingdom here on Earth.

Everything that Jesus discloses in the Sermon is a disclosure of what Jesus' own world is like. It's as if Jesus is saying to us, this is what I am like, this is how I live, this is the godly environment I carry around with me wherever I go. Would you like to come and join me? As we track through with Jesus his teachings in the Sermon and elsewhere in the Gospels, we will find that we are uncovering clues, principles, about what a Jesus lifestyle is like, how to live like Jesus.

This is what I was referring to earlier when I said there are moral principles underneath, or within, the law of Moses. This is why the title of this Chapter speaks not of 'the law' but of 'laws' - the principles of a moral universe that we would be wise to observe. Jesus mentions many of them in the Sermon on the Mount itself. We will look briefly at some of those laws at the end of this Chapter, but before we do that, I want to look at the amazing subject of grace.

Grace and mercy are often spoken of together. You can say that mercy is not getting what I deserve: being let off, if you like. In contrast, grace is getting what I don't deserve: receiving a free gift. A fairly traditional and well-established definition of grace is receiving 'unmerited favour' from God. A definition from Strong's[94] which I feel is especially helpful is, 'a gift or blessing brought to Man by Jesus Christ'.

The word grace that appears in English language Bibles is a translation of the Greek word *charis*. It is one of those words packed with significance and sometimes it's worth trying to come up with a new translation so that we can see something new about the truth within the concept. For example, in one of my Bibles *charis* is often translated not as 'grace' but as 'wonderful kindness'.

I suspect that often when we talk about grace, really we are talking about mercy, or we are talking about that part of grace which reflects the 'niceness' of God. Please don't misunderstand me - I am extremely glad that God is indeed 'nice' and this characteristic of his is certainly part of what *charis* is all about. But probably, all of us could do with a bigger and

---

[94] 'Strong's Concordance' by James Strong

better grasp of all that grace really is.

One reason why it's important to have a good understanding of grace is because grace is how we get saved. Faith certainly plays a vital part, but it isn't faith that actually does the saving - it is grace:

*For it is by grace you have been saved, through faith - and this is not from yourselves, it is the gift of God - not by works, so that no one can boast.*[95]

Great light is shed on the question of what grace is by this very famous scripture which explains the gospel:

*For God loved the world so much that he gave his one and only Son, so that everyone who believes in him will not perish but have eternal life.*[96]

Grace originates from God's love. It is expressed through, in, with, and by Jesus, who is given by the Father as a gift. Grace is not just a description of the kindness of God, it includes the acts of God, it is an expression of the person of God. Christians become Christians by accepting Jesus, putting their trust in Jesus, believing that Jesus is God and that he died for us. Without my response of faith, I could not become a Christian. But almost all of the work has already been done. By Jesus, sent by the Father. I didn't deserve it, and I didn't earn it. God did it. God graced it.

Compared to his work, what I have had to do - muster a little faith and make my response - is very little, albeit vital. Basically, God did it all. Because of his great love and kindness, and his having paid a huge price personally to make it possible, he took my little response as a yes, and he saved me. Amazing grace!

If you are already a Christian, and if this is indeed grace, if this is how you actually get saved, what about the rest of your life? If this is grace at the beginning of your new life, what about grace day to day?

Paul said a great deal about grace. Sometimes he is known as 'the apostle of grace'. I am not going to try to summarise all of that teaching here. However, I do very much want to establish some clear view of what it is to be 'under grace'. With that objective in mind, this is a key passage:

*...just as sin reigned in death, so also grace might reign through righteousness to bring*

---

[95] Ephesians 2:8&9 [niv]

[96] John 3:16

*eternal life through Jesus Christ our Lord.*[97]

Here, Paul is comparing and contrasting grace with sin. Sin is a powerful force, which has exerted a terrible influence. Grace is also at least in some sense a force, and is capable of having a tremendous impact on our lives.

In one of his letters, Paul discusses the 'thorn in the flesh' which has been troubling him. Some people interpret this thorn as a physical ailment of some kind. I do not know what it was, however the word which Paul uses to describe it - *kolaphidzae* - is only used one other time in the New Testament, and that was to describe the abuse which Jesus endured at the hands of the Temple Guards. My view is that this thorn was some difficult situation or person, as opposed to a sickness. In any event, it clearly troubled Paul and he asked God three times to take it away:

*Three times I pleaded with the Lord to take it away from me. But he said to me, 'My grace is sufficient for you, for my power is made perfect in weakness.' Therefore I will boast all the more gladly about my weaknesses, so that Christ's power may rest on me. That is why, for Christ's sake, I delight in weaknesses, in insults, in hardships, in persecutions, in difficulties. For when I am weak, then I am strong.*[98]

Paul was discovering that Jesus' grace was sufficient in challenging circumstances. We get a glimpse here of a very different way of living - where we reach an end of ourselves, our own strength and our own abilities; where we rely on God's strength and on God's power.

This reveals at least something of the very heart of what grace really is. It is not our performance, our work, our strength. It is God's performance, God's work, and God's strength. It is not my inability, but God's ability. Given the vastness of the subject, I almost hesitate to offer any kind of definition of grace, however based upon all that I have read and reflected on, here is my attempt. Grace is God's exercise of his favour, presence and power in our human lives in and through the person of Jesus Christ in all his fulness.

For me, there is an ever-growing realisation that there is a vital connection between truly understanding grace and also truly understanding

---

[97] Romans 5:21 [niv]

[98] 2 Corinthians 12:8-10 [niv]

that I am 'in Christ'. We can have some quite peculiar ideas about what our relationship with Jesus is really like.

If being a Christian seems mostly about making sure I have a reservation in Heaven, maybe Jesus is not much more than a bystander, observing my life from a distance. When the time comes for me to die and I'm waiting to get in through Heaven's gates, Jesus is there and he indicates to angelic gatekeepers that yes, I can come in, I'm with Jesus. I would label this kind of idea as 'Jesus the VIP nightclub buddy'. When I really need his help to get me in, he will get me in. Perhaps it is only I, the writer of this book, who has ever lived on this low level of understanding. That said, I am very glad that Jesus will indeed get me in!

Moving to a higher level of understanding, there is the very important concept of Jesus in me, Christ in me. Jesus spoke to his disciples about Jesus and the Father coming to them and making a home in their hearts.[99] Paul prays in his letter to the Ephesians that Christ will dwell in the hearts of the believers.[100] It is a wonderful thing to experience something of the reality of Jesus in me. But if we stop at this point in the journey, we still miss something very important - for there most certainly is more to discover.

The 'problem' with the idea of Christ in me is that, because I am very small, maybe in my thinking and attitudes, the Christ who is in me will be smaller still. But if I go on from this and understand that not only is Christ in me, but also I am in Christ - well, on that basis, Christ is certainly not small!

Let's consider some of the things Paul wrote on this subject. He makes it a priority to gain Christ and 'to be found in him'.[101] We have been created in Christ Jesus to do good works.[102] Everyone who has been baptised into

---

[99] John 14:23

[100] Ephesians 3:17

[101] Philippians 3:9

[102] Ephesians 2:10

Christ has clothed themselves with Christ.[103] If someone is <u>in</u> Christ, a new creation has come into being.[104] We are all parts of the body, and Christ is the head. We are one <u>in</u> Christ, so that worldly distinctions such as age, gender and race mean nothing.[105]

We will return to this passage from Colossians, however here for me is a clear statement about what lies at the very heart of being under grace:

*...your life is now hidden with Christ in God*[106]

The more that I consider Paul's writings, the more I am struck by how he seemed to be almost lost - but in a very, very, good way. He was so lost in the wonder and reality of Jesus being in him, and him being in Christ, that it seemed impossible for Paul to think in terms of his life being his own. It was as if Paul's own sense of identity was melting away into the vastness of God. For example, he says that he no longer lives - it is Christ who lives in him,[107] and that for him, to live is Christ, and to die is gain[108] - or, as it is put in The Message:

*Alive, I'm Christ's messenger; dead, I'm his bounty. Life versus even more life! I can't lose.*

Let me try to convey some sort of image of what I believe it is to be under grace. The moment I said yes to Jesus, my new life began - not the promise of some new life in the future, but an actual new life, starting immediately. I was rescued by Jesus from all of the consequences of my sin and he took me into himself.

When this age ends, even if that will involve the destruction of every single atom which exists in the universe, I will be OK, because I am in Jesus. In all of the circumstances of life, no matter what troubles or attacks

---

[103] Galatians 3:27

[104] 2 Corinthians 5:17

[105] Galatians 3:28

[106] Colossians 3:3

[107] Galatians 2:20

[108] Philippians 1:21

are thrown at me, no matter what demonic forces might try to attack me, first of all they have to get past Jesus, which is impossible. I may feel some pain, some hurt. But nothing can change this fact: I am in the safest place in the universe.

Being under grace means that Jesus has, as it were, folded you into himself. You still exist as a real person, you still experience the world around you, but in fact Jesus is between you and every circumstance of life. No wind, no flood, no storm, no earthquake, no attack, no sickness can stop you being in Jesus - who is alive and will never die, who will never forget you.

Again from The Message, Paul's revelation of this profound truth is why he could say:

*I'm absolutely convinced that nothing - nothing living or dead, angelic or demonic, today or tomorrow, high or low, thinkable or unthinkable - absolutely nothing can get between us and God's love because of the way Jesus our Master has embraced us.*[109]

That is a very fine picture of being under grace - the embrace of Jesus our Master; an embrace that never releases us, an embrace that wraps us up into him so that, in effect, we cannot be seen - because God is in between us and everything and everyone.

If this is true, there is a question to be answered, namely: how then should I live? What does the daily life of someone who is in Christ look like? If we have a low level concept of grace - that it is merely about being 'let off', as it were - then perhaps this will not seem like an important question. But if we have a high concept of grace - what then?

This very question is addressed by Paul:

*Well then, since God's grace has set us free from the law, does that mean we can go on sinning? Of course not!*[110]

Given the enormity of what God has done for me, how can I possibly carry on living in the same old way, as if it doesn't matter how I live? I have a responsibility to aim to live a life which is worthy of, and which is consistent with, the life of the one who saved me by his grace. To return to

---

[109] Romans 8:38&39 [The Message]

[110] Romans 6:15

the book of Colossians:

*Since, then, you have been raised with Christ, set your hearts on things above, where Christ is, seated at the right hand of God. Set your minds on things above, not on earthly things. For you died, and your life is now hidden with Christ in God. When Christ, who is your life, appears, then you also will appear with him in glory.*[111]

I have a choice - to focus either on earthly things, or on heavenly things.

I am not under law. I don't have to fret about trying to please God by acting like a good Jew. I am under grace.

Although I am not under law - the law of Moses - there are even so various natural laws which bind me. Unless God chooses miraculously to suspend his own natural laws, if I hold my car keys out and then let go of them, they will drop to the floor. I experience the working of the law of gravity, and mostly I am very grateful for it.

As well as the laws of the natural world, there are various man-made laws to which I am still subject. Certainly, I am free to disobey them if I choose, yet I am not free of the consequences of any such disobedience. If I try to defend myself in a court of law against a motoring offence on the basis that I am under grace, I will fail.

Much, much more importantly, there are moral, or spiritual, laws. Many of these can be discerned behind, or under, the law of Moses. Many of them are touched upon in the Sermon on the Mount. These laws reflect something of the very character of God. This is why Jesus spoke of fulfilling the law of Moses, rather than abolishing that law. It is foolishness under the banner of grace to try to live as a Christian as if none of our actions - whether good or bad - have any consequences.

My salvation by grace has not shifted me into some kind of alternate, consequences-free world. Within the Sermon on the Mount itself, Jesus makes it clear that a refusal to forgive others blocks our own ability to receive forgiveness.[112] If we judge others, Jesus tells us that we will also be judged.[113] Having received his wonderful grace, Jesus is encouraging us all

---

[111] Colossians 3:1-4

[112] Matthew 5:14&15

[113] Matthew 7:1&2

to carry on with the process of growing up, to demonstrate more and more the character traits of our Father in Heaven.

I will stress here one particular moral, or spiritual, law that applies to us all. This is the law of sowing and reaping. Jesus often used in his parables the picture of a farmer sowing seed. His audience would have understood very well ideas connected to the life of a farmer. There is a lot that can be discovered about parallels between the way God's Kingdom works and the way that plants and trees grow.

But the main point I want to make here is that there is a vital spiritual connection between how we spend our time and energy: between how we act (this is what we sow) and what we experience or receive (this is what we reap). As Paul puts it in his letter to the Church in Galatia,

*Do not be deceived, God is not mocked; for whatever a man sows, that he will also reap.*[114]

There is connection between what we do, and what happens to us. There is a connection between what we give and what we receive. Jesus himself said:

*Take heed what you hear. With the same measure you use, it will be measured to you; and to you who hear, more will be given. For whoever has, to him more will be given; but whoever does not have, even what he has will be taken away from him.*[115]

And, speaking about the need to not judge, he said something again about the connection between our actions and what happens to us:

*The standard you use in judging is the standard by which you will be judged.*[116]

It is true that grace folds us into Jesus. It is not true, however, that grace wraps us up in some kind of fuzzy, sentimental super-spiritual cotton wool that means we have no need to pay any care or attention to the way we live our lives. Jesus has set us his example. His call on our lives is to grow more and more into the everyday reality of living on planet Earth in just the same way that Jesus would live, if he walked in our shoes.

---

[114] Galatians 6:7 [nkjv]

[115] Mark 4:24&25 [nkjv]

[116] Matthew 7:2

If grace really is about the embrace of Jesus our Master, then surely we must more and more be caught up in the wonder of who this Master is. What kind of person is he, how can we please him, and how can we become more and more like him? This is the call of true Christian discipleship - to follow Jesus, to be changed from one degree of glory to another.[117]

I do not have to do any of this to earn my salvation - that is impossible and it is contrary to the gospel of Jesus Christ. However, given the reality of what my Jesus has done for me, I feel compelled by his love, his character, his example, to live a life which, however imperfectly, in some way reflects the wonderful reality of his love for me. I cannot, dare not, will not, remain unmoved by such love.

Apart from anything else that such a journey will involve, my willingness to be moved will mean that I will take seriously what God says about a number of things. These include: the consequences of not forgiving; the consequences of judging; the power of the words that I choose to use; the reality of the occult; the significance of my sexual choices; and so on.

May we all be delivered from any false concept of 'cheap' grace, from such a low level concept of grace that we remain detached from the realities of how this world - God's world - actually works. May we all be released into a glorious freedom to become more and more like the wonderful Father God who loves us and who sent his son Jesus to save us, now and forever.

---

[117] 2 Corinthians 3:18

# Freedom From Sin

Ài | Love

# CHAPTER 7

This Chapter is not primarily about you and me being forgiven by God for our sins. To use a theological term, that forgiveness brings about our 'justification', our being put in a right relationship with God. This can only be achieved by what Jesus did on the Cross. And of course, we started this book with a reflection on the Cross.

Rather than justification, in this Chapter we are going to look into 'sanctification', another theological concept. Sanctification is about saying goodbye to our previous sin-filled lifestyle; it is to do with living a life that becomes more and more like the kind of life that Jesus himself lived.

The idea of your life changing so that it becomes like Jesus' own life might be provoking some interesting reactions within you right now. Perhaps you feel daunted by the apparent impossibility of it all. You might be very aware of bad habits that you have been unable to break and of which you feel ashamed. You might groan at the prospect of having to pursue a path of what looks like hypocrisy. This is because looking ahead, you can see that you will end up hiding the wrong things that you do, so that you can fool other people into accepting you as a nice, well-behaved Christian.

Facing up to reactions such as these is part of what it is all about to be a disciple, a follower, an apprentice, of Jesus. Jesus is God and God is all-powerful; and yet, one of the things Jesus either will not, or perhaps more accurately cannot do, is deny his own character. Even though it may well make me uncomfortable, Jesus will not pretend that he is happy about my current sins. He will not settle for me feeling that it's OK with him if I carry on sining. He does not want any of us to be deceived into believing that our daily failures here on planet Earth don't matter.

After all, we might tell ourselves, God does forgive us. After all, one day we will all be in Heaven together and there will be no more sin. Come on - Jesus died for more than this. Eternal life is supposed to start in earnest now, not later on. Later in this Chapter, we will again dip into John's letters, but for starters here is a challenge from him:

*Those who say they live in God should live their lives as Jesus did.*[118]

The issue of how we deal with our current sins is fundamentally about how good a grasp we have of what our identity truly is as sons and daughters of God. It's about whether we are content to carry on living like slaves, or whether we will press in for a greater measure of the freedom that Christ has won for us.

It's about what happens within us when we read Chapters 7 and 8 of Romans. Fundamentally, we can identify ourselves as people who on an ongoing basis live life as a struggle against sin. That is Romans 7. Alternatively, we can see ourselves as people who are living the life of the Spirit, full of freedom and without condemnation. That is Romans 8.

Although it might seem perverse to do it, I want to consider the attractiveness of sin. It is important that we have some kind of understanding about what draws us to sin so that we are better equipped to resist evil.

The Bible tells us that Jesus was tempted, just as we are tempted.[119] It is not sin to be tempted. Jesus remained without sin, even though he was tempted to sin.

We know that, until Jesus comes back to bring this current age to an end, we live in a kind of overlap of two kingdoms. Jesus has already ushered in God's Kingdom, and he has given us a mandate to extend it throughout the whole earth. At the same time, there is still a world system that is manipulated by the devil. With this in mind, John gives us a piercing analysis of how sin works:

*Do not love the world or the things in the world. If anyone loves the world, the love of the Father is not in him. For all that is in the world - the lust of the flesh, the lust of the eyes, and the pride of life - is not of the Father but is of the world. And the world is passing away, and the lust of it; but he who does the will of God abides forever.*[120]

John is saying that this evil world system operates on the basis of three

---

[118] 1 John 2:6

[119] Hebrews 4:15

[120] 1 John 2:15-17 [nkjv]

drives – two lusts, and one pride. The lust of the flesh, the lust of the eyes, and the pride of life. There is a very clear correlation between this analysis and the account in Genesis of the fall of man – the story of how sin came into the human family at the start of our history:

*So when the woman saw that the tree was good for food, that it was pleasant to the eyes, and a tree desirable to make one wise, she took of its fruit and ate. She also gave to her husband with her, and he ate.*[121]

The serpent's temptation of Eve operated on these three levels. There were all sorts of things that Eve could eat, but she entertained the idea that she was hungry and that this particular fruit would be a good way of satisfying that hunger. There were many beautiful things to look at, but she entertained the idea that this particular fruit looked good. She had access to the creator of the whole universe, but she entertained the idea that it would be good to find a source of wisdom that operated independently of the creator. She was attacked on the levels of physical appetite, the external appearance of things and her desire to be significant.

As I have already said, temptation is not sin. Giving in to temptation does, however, result in sin. I have heard temptation explained using the analogy of a tree and some birds. Using the picture of my life as a tree, a bird comes and lands in my branches. The bird represents, for these purposes, temptation. I can't stop birds from time to time landing in my branches, but I don't have to build a nest for them so that they feel welcome to stay. That would be a kind of picture of what sin is.

As with many pictures, this isn't completely consistent or logical – for example, you might struggle with the idea of a tree building a nest! Anyway, I believe this picture is helpful because it does convey something important about what we do with temptation after it has arrived.

The threefold attack on Eve is a stunningly accurate description of how we ourselves can experience temptation. The appetites or desires that are targeted in this story are not in and of themselves sinful. It is not, for example, a sin to have a desire to eat. The true issue is this: to what extent will I lay out a welcome mat for the enemy as and when he comes to call?

---

[121] Genesis 3:6 [nkjv]

To what extent will I entertain unhelpful thoughts and ideas?

When Jesus teaches about prayer, in response to his disciples' request that he would show them how to pray, he gives them what is commonly called the 'Lord's Prayer'. Included within that model for prayer is this statement about temptation:

*And don't let us yield to temptation, but rescue us from the evil one.*[122]

You might be familiar with a slightly different translation, along the lines of 'lead us not into temptation'. That well-known language almost seems to suggest that it is God who sets us up in situations where we are tested by temptation. This cannot be what Jesus is really saying, since elsewhere in the Bible we are told clearly that God doesn't tempt anyone.[123]

Here is the heart of what Jesus is saying in the Lord's Prayer about temptation. We should be ready to dismiss temptation quickly as and when it comes calling at our door. The normal, daily attitude of our hearts should be that we don't even want to find ourselves in a situation where we experience temptation.

This is not because we are afraid of temptation, or because we feel that there is a serious risk that we will give in to it.

Quite the opposite – we have determined, in advance, that as and when temptation comes, we will make it go away. We will not be inviting it in for a cup of something nice to drink so that we can have a discussion. Since we have already decided in advance that we will not be giving temptation even the time of day, it is as if we know that any encounter we might have with temptation will be a waste of our precious time. Therefore, our preference is that, looking at the day we are living today, we don't want to have our time wasted by a caller at our door who will only be sent away with, so to speak, its tail between its legs.

Sad to say, this has not always been a description of my attitude towards temptation. Based on my own personal experience, and talking to other people, I would say that we often have two other relationships with temptation, and these are utterly contrary to what Jesus sets out for us in

---

[122] Matthew 6:13

[123] James 1:13

the Lord's Prayer.

Those two other relationships are to do with (1) fear and (2) flirtation. We can say this part of the Lord's Prayer and believe we are agreeing with Jesus when in fact we are afraid of what will happen when temptation arrives, because we feel like we are bound to give in to it, and we know it will be destructive. Also, we might be praying that prayer, but at some deep, or hidden, level we might be relishing the prospect of maybe, perhaps, possibly, giving into that temptation as and when it arrives.

I hope that, if you are at some level struggling with sin, or if you know that you have an unhealthy heart attitude towards that door-to-door visitor called temptation, this Chapter will help you. May you come to a place of victory so that you can increasingly live each day with the genuine, realistic hope that you will reach the end of that day without having given in to sin. This is part of God's will for you and me. Taking each day at a time, we can explore the glorious possibility that we can actually live that particular day in exactly the same way that Jesus would live our day.

To summarise the story so far, we have looked at the threefold pull of the current world system – the lust of the flesh, the lust of the eyes, and the pride of life – and we have looked at what our attitude is supposed to be towards temptation. With that in mind, let's move on to see a point in the Bible story where this threefold attack is demonstrated, and where we see how Jesus himself deals with temptation. Here it is, a story which comes just after Jesus has been baptised by John the Baptist and he goes on a journey into the wilderness where he fasts for 40 days:

*Then Jesus was led by the Spirit into the wilderness to be tempted there by the devil. For forty days and forty nights he fasted and became very hungry. During that time the devil came and said to him, 'If you are the Son of God, tell these stones to become loaves of bread.'…Then the devil took him to the holy city, Jerusalem, to the highest point of the Temple, and said, 'If you are the Son of God, jump off! For the Scriptures say, 'He will order his angels to protect you. And they will hold you up with their hands so you won't even hurt your foot on a stone.'…..Next the devil took him to the peak of a very high mountain and showed him all the kingdoms of the world and their glory. I will give it all to you,' he said, 'if you will kneel down and worship me.*[124]

---

[124] Matthew 4:1-3,5-9

Can you see it? The lust of the flesh is within the first temptation, 'tell these stones…'. Jesus was hungry, and the Devil targets that hunger. The lust of the eyes is within the second temptation, 'jump off!'. Being rescued by angels at the Temple would look really good. The pride of life is within the third temptation, 'I will give it all to you'. Jesus was being offered the chance to dominate all of humanity.

The other account of this episode in Jesus' life is in Luke Chapter 4, where it is made clear that this was not the one and only time that Jesus was tempted. We are told that the Devil then left Jesus, and waited for his next opportunity.[125] This detailed account of this attack on Jesus from the enemy at the beginning of his public ministry is given to us in Scripture for good reason. There is a lot that can be, and has been, said about this passage but for our purposes here, I will set out the following key ideas, most of which we have already covered:

Temptation is not sin.

Temptation does not last forever - it is seasonal.

Temptation operates on three broad levels - the lust of the flesh, the lust of the eyes and the pride of life.

Jesus succeeded, always, in resisting temptation.

Meditating on God's word is a vital weapon in resisting temptation.

Temptation is an attempt to undermine our confidence in our identity.

Before we move on from looking at the story of Jesus being tempted, I need to explain something about the last two points in this list of ideas, namely knowing God's word and having confidence in our identity.

Jesus uses the Bible as part of his defence against the Devil's attack, in contrast to the way the Devil actually misuses the Bible as part of his strategy. The three different Scriptures quoted by Jesus all come from the same part of the same book in the Old Testament, the book of Deuteronomy.

Jesus knew the Bible very well and he could have quoted a great number of different passages if he chose to do so. His example is an excellent one; if we want to keep on growing as Christians, it will serve us well to apply

---

[125] Luke 4:13

ourselves to absorbing more of what the Bible actually says. But more is going on in this story than Jesus just selecting from his memory bank some particularly relevant proof texts. I suggest that Jesus had recently been meditating upon - in other words, he was spending time considering, reflecting upon, thinking about, imagining - the book of Deuteronomy.

When you look at the point in his life where Jesus was at the time, Deuteronomy is an interesting book to ponder. Moses is at the end of his life, and he is reviewing with God's people what he has been doing with them during the 40 years that they have been travelling through the desert – a wilderness. Moses is about to die and God's people are about to start something new, a major change is about to take place in their history - their entry into the land that God had promised to them. And here is Jesus: he stands at the crossing over point between the Old and the New Testaments. He has been living in obscurity and now he is going to start the public ministry that in a relatively short time of around three years will lead to his death and resurrection. Physically, at the exact point in time of this temptation, he is in a wilderness where he is fasting for 40 days.

I believe that Jesus was meditating on this part of the Bible around the time that the Devil showed up. Presumably the Devil, given that he has only limited resources, times his approaches carefully, choosing times when we are at our most vulnerable. Even at this vulnerable point, Jesus was thinking about God's word. This gives us an important clue about how to do a better job in resisting the Devil. We will have more success in saying no to the Devil if we are thinking more about God stuff.

Fundamentally this is about an attitude of the heart where we choose to make time to consider the things of God, because we place a high value on the things of God. This attitude will put us in a state of readiness, or alertness, so that when we are tempted it is less difficult for us to tune into the reality of God's love us, and what his plans and destiny for us are.

The final point I want to draw from this story is that there is something going on that is even deeper than the threefold attack of temptation: the playing upon the lust of the flesh, the lust of the eyes and the pride of life. When we look at this story of Jesus being tempted in the wilderness, it is fundamentally an attack on his identity.

What happens in Jesus' life just before this wilderness experience is his baptism. As he comes out of the waters of baptism, he hears the Father tell him,

*'This is my dearly loved Son, who brings me great joy.'*[126]

In other words, Jesus receives a tremendous affirmation of his identity, a confirmation of who he is. The Devil begins the first two of the three temptations with a statement that challenges this affirmation. He says, 'if you are the Son of God...' This is as if part of what the Devil is testing is, does Jesus really know who he is? Or is he so unsure or insecure about it that he will feel the need to prove it to me? And then the third and final temptation challenges how important Jesus' identity is to him. Would he be prepared to trade it for some immediate status and prestige?

The Devil was launching an attack to see how good a grasp Jesus had of his identity as the Father's loved Son, Could it be that for us, too, there is some kind of connection between being secure in our identity as sons and daughters of the Father and our being able to resist temptation? We will come back to this idea.

Bearing in mind that Jesus always succeeded in resisting temptation, how well am I doing in comparison, and how well are you doing? The inescapable conclusion is that it is possible for us to resist, even if our actual experience has been that we seem to fail miserably. The whole thrust of the Gospel message is that Jesus really does set an example that he believes we can follow. This is part of what he said to his closest circle of followers on the evening before he was arrested and then killed:

*'I tell you the truth, anyone who believes in me will do the same works I have done, and even greater works, because I am going to be with the Father. You can ask for anything in my name, and I will do it, so that the Son can bring glory to the Father.'*[127]

If some of those 'greater works' include things like praying for other people to be healed physically, or to be released from demonic bondage, surely they must also include, for ourselves, being able to resist the Devil.

The book of James contains this promise:

*Resist the devil, and he will flee from you.*[128]

---

[126] Matthew 3:17

[127] John 14:12&13

[128] James 4:7

Don't misunderstand me, I am not trying to prove that 'real' Christians never sin, or that we somehow can earn our salvation by behaving well. There is, however, a connection between the reality of having a new life in Jesus and the ability of that new life to begin to change how we live. Many sayings of Jesus make it clear that he knows we will sin. But he also talks about how vital it is that we repent: to turn our backs on, change our thinking about, our sins. More than once, he seems to set a very high standard for people he has interacted with.

The man who had been lame for 38 years who was healed by Jesus at the pool of Bethesda was hunted down by Jesus at the Temple and Jesus told him to stop sinning.[129] The woman who was caught in adultery and who was brought to Jesus to test him was at risk of being stoned to death. Jesus rescued her by challenging the religious leaders only to cast the first stone if they themselves were without sin. Jesus himself refused to condemn her, but he also told her to 'sin no more'.[130]

What we find in these words of Jesus is both a challenge and an encouragement. The challenge is that we are being called to live a different kind of life and to make a break with our old ways. The encouragement is that this change is actually possible. When Jesus told the previously lame man and the adulterous woman to stop sinning, he was opening up for them the possibility that life could actually be different. He was setting them free from the expectation that life was going to just carry on as usual.

If all of this is true, then how do we reconcile this with the reality of our walk with the Lord, if that reality seems to be filled with failure, compromise, and repeated defeats when faced with the attack of temptation?

This is a valid and important question. It lies at the heart of what I want to address in this Chapter. In an attempt to do this effectively, let's now look at this issue from a slightly different angle, namely how we see ourselves when we read Romans 7 and 8, and how 'normal' or otherwise we think it is to have struggles with sin.

---

[129] John 5:14

[130] John 8:11

Here is a key section from Romans 7:

*…..The trouble is with me, for I am all too human, a slave to sin. I don't really understand myself, for I want to do what is right, but I don't do it. Instead, I do what I hate. But if I know that what I am doing is wrong, this shows that I agree that the law is good. So I am not the one doing wrong; it is sin living in me that does it. And I know that nothing good lives in me, that is, in my sinful nature. I want to do what is right, but I can't.*

*I want to do what is good, but I don't. I don't want to do what is wrong, but I do it anyway. But if I do what I don't want to do, I am not really the one doing wrong; it is sin living in me that does it. I have discovered this principle of life - that when I want to do what is right, I inevitably do what is wrong. I love God's law with all my heart. But there is another power within me that is at war with my mind. This power makes me a slave to the sin that is still within me. Oh, what a miserable person I am! Who will free me from this life that is dominated by sin and death? Thank God! The answer is in Jesus Christ our Lord. So you see how it is: In my mind I really want to obey God's law, but because of my sinful nature I am a slave to sin.*[131]

This passage describes a struggle with sin that I imagine is very familiar to us. Possibly it either describes some current battle we find ourselves in, or it brings back memories of a past battle.

Of course, I have no idea precisely what sort of reaction or response you feel when you read these words of Paul. For myself, I feel a strong identification with it. The struggle that Paul speaks of seems so clearly to describe what I have felt for so much of the time. It seems to sum up very accurately many of my weaknesses and failings.

But here is the problem: we can fall into the trap of thinking that this part of Romans 7 provides us with some kind of excuse for sin. We can think of this passage as a kind of 'human nature defence'. If we find ourselves suddenly feeling uncomfortable about the sins we keep doing, or if someone else challenges us about them and tells us that we need to change, we might at some level believe that our behaviour is, after all, only human nature.

Paul himself describes this very struggle, so aren't we simply living in the

---

[131] Romans 7:14-25

reality of what he teaches? OK, we might grudgingly admit, the passage does talk about Jesus being the answer, but the freedom that he brings is something that we will only truly experience when we get to Heaven. That, we might argue, is when this 'life that is dominated by sin and death' is replaced by a new life in the age to come.

If we think along these lines, then we have a belief system that fits with what we see around us. The reality of our own struggles with sin, and the struggles that are at work within other people around us, all seem to confirm that such struggles are normal, that there is no escape from them this side of Heaven. Such beliefs get us off the hook, so to speak. They give us an excuse to stay pretty much as we are, to continue to struggle, to carry on feeling like a failure.

However, if we are going to enjoy freedom, we must embrace the truth, and it is not true that this passage from Romans 7 sets out a description of normal christian life. I use the word 'normal' in the sense of what is proper and possible, rather than in the sense of what is commonly experienced, or generally popular. This struggle with sin is not 'normal'. As followers of Jesus, we do not have to settle for a life that is thoroughly compromised by failure and disappointment, leaving us looking back on our lives with regret, but excusing ourselves by saying that we were the victims of our human nature.

There is a clue to this fact within the passage itself. In verse 25, Paul says, 'Thank God! The answer is in Jesus Christ our Lord': so, we see that there is, after all, an answer to this problem.

This passage does look, at least at first glance, like a current description by Paul of some struggle that he lives with on an ongoing, daily basis. The language is all about what is happening now - the trouble is with me, oh what a miserable person I am, and so on. Once I heard a famous historian being interviewed on the radio about the British royal family. He referred to King Henry VIII, who of course lived and died hundreds of years ago. This historian was so engaged with the historical events he was describing that he used the very same kind of language to talk about events in the life of this long-dead King. So for example, the historian didn't say that in year whatever Henry married whoever. Instead he said, Henry 'marries'…as if he were commenting on a live, current event.

I believe something similar is going on with Paul's use of language in this passage. We can see that something else must be going on if we take the time to see this passage in its context, and if we also look at it in parallel with what other parts of the Bible have to say on the same subject. It is worthwhile doing this, because what we truly believe about this passage will have a great bearing on how serious and persistent we are prepared to be about seeing victory in our own personal struggles with sin. If we really are serious about this, we will win – and not only in the age to come.

This particular passage is part of a teaching by Paul about what the 'law' – in other words, the Ten Commandments and the other instructions that Moses received direct from God - could do, and what it could not do. The law points to the need for some other solution to a particular problem. That problem is this: we human beings fail to follow God, even when he shows us the way. The solution to this problem is: Jesus.

Here is part of what Paul says earlier in Romans 7, which we must take account of if we are to engage accurately with what he says about the struggle with sin:

*Now, dear brothers and sisters - you who are familiar with the law - don't you know that the law applies only while a person is living?....this is the point: You died to the power of the law when you died with Christ. And now you are united with the one who was raised from the dead. As a result, we can produce a harvest of good deeds for God. When we were controlled by our old nature, sinful desires were at work within us, and the law aroused these evil desires that produced a harvest of sinful deeds, resulting in death. But now we have been released from the law, for we died to it and are no longer captive to its power. Now we can serve God, not in the old way of obeying the letter of the law, but in the new way of living in the Spirit.*[132]

If you read this carefully, you will not find in it the testimony of someone who is ruined by failure in an ongoing fight against sin. Paul talks about having been united with the resurrected Christ. He is able to produce: good food; good fruit; a harvest; a plentiful supply of good deeds; and right behaviour, as opposed to wrong behaviour. He is no longer captive, imprisoned, by the power of sinful desires. He is able - in the here and now, not waiting for the hereafter - to live in the Spirit, and he is able to serve God.

---

[132] Romans 7:1,4-6

So when Paul moves on later in Romans 7 to describe the struggle with sin, he is not painting a picture for us of a typical day in the life of Paul. Instead, having stepped back to look at the big picture of God's redemptive plan – how in his love he gave the law to his people, and how again in his love he gave his Son to the world – Paul as it were steps into the picture, and in a sense re-enacts part of it, to emphasise or highlight what it is that we needed to be delivered from.

Let's carry on looking at the context in which Paul speaks of the struggle. Bear in mind that the book Romans was a letter, written without any chapter or verse numberings, and that there is a flow in it, a progression in the ideas that are presented. Moving on from the struggle, a very different scene is before us in what we know as Romans 8:

*So now there is no condemnation for those who belong to Christ Jesus. And because you belong to him, the power of the life-giving Spirit has freed you from the power of sin that leads to death. The law of Moses was unable to save us because of the weakness of our sinful nature. So God did what the law could not do. He sent his own Son in a body like the bodies we sinners have. And in that body God declared an end to sin's control over us by giving his Son as a sacrifice for our sins. He did this so that the just requirement of the law would be fully satisfied for us, who no longer follow our sinful nature but instead follow the Spirit.*

*Those who are dominated by the sinful nature think about sinful things, but those who are controlled by the Holy Spirit think about things that please the Spirit. So letting your sinful nature control your mind leads to death. But letting the Spirit control your mind leads to life and peace....But you are not controlled by your sinful nature. You are controlled by the Spirit if you have the Spirit of God living in you. (And remember that those who do not have the Spirit of Christ living in them do not belong to him at all.)....Therefore, dear brothers and sisters, you have no obligation to do what your sinful nature urges you to do. For if you live by its dictates, you will die. But if through the power of the Spirit you put to death the deeds of your sinful nature, you will live. For all who are led by the Spirit of God are children of God. So you have not received a spirit that makes you fearful slaves. Instead, you received God's Spirit when he adopted you as his own children. Now we call him, 'Abba, Father'. For his Spirit joins with our spirit to affirm that we are God's children.*[133]

---

[133] Romans 8:1-6,9,12-16

Great volumes can be written about this passage, but all I am going to do is highlight some of the ideas that are crucial for us in having a healthy approach to the problem of sin in our lives.

A Christian is someone who belongs to Jesus. If you belong to Jesus, then through Jesus' sacrifice, Father God has declared an end to sin's control over your life. We still have a sinful nature that wants to draw us away from pleasing God. So, we have a choice. We can refuse to obey that sinful nature, and instead we have the ability to let the Holy Spirit, who is living inside us, guide us into a meaningful and fruitful life.

Although this is a choice, really we have an obligation to choose for the Holy Spirit. To do otherwise means we would be deliberately opting for a life full of negative, fruitless consequences: something more like death than life. To make such a bad choice means we would be denying the reality of what Jesus did for us when he died on the Cross and rose again. It means we would be shutting our spiritual eyes so we don't see the pain he suffered - for you, and for me. It means that we would be denying who we really are - sons and daughters of God.

Doing a better job of removing sin from our daily lives is not about trying desperately to placate an unplacatable god, out of a sense of duty or of fear. Deciding to let ourselves be 'controlled' by the Holy Spirit rather than our sinful, selfish desires is not evidence of weakness or of fear; it is fundamentally an act of love.

In my own life, I have found it to be true that love is a much more powerful motivating force than fear. If my understanding of my relationship to God is that he is some kind of cold, distant, possibly unreasonable disciplinarian, I will tend to focus on my performance. I will try hard to act correctly so that I am not punished, and I will hope that my good performance will earn me some treats or privileges in due course.

By contrast, if I understand that I am a dearly loved and accepted member of Father God's family, that he dotes over me, and that he has paid an enormous price to make all of this possible, then I will learn how to live in a way that is consistent with his own character. Because I love him, I will celebrate the family likeness that there is between us: the family likeness that was sealed when the Holy Spirit came into my life and took up residence.

Fundamentally, experiencing a greater measure of freedom from sin is not about the exercise of great willpower as if it is a huge struggle against all the odds. Perhaps we feel the chances of failure outweighing the chances of success. No: true freedom is about being prepared to make decisions and choices that are more consistent with who and what we are. It is about living in the reality of who and what we are.

To check this interpretation of what Paul is really saying in Romans 7 and 8, it's worthwhile taking a sideways look at what is said elsewhere in the New Testament about the process of sanctification and whether we are supposed to live in victory over sin. So, here goes:

*For the Lord is the Spirit, and wherever the Spirit of the Lord is, there is freedom. So all of us who have had that veil removed can see and reflect the glory of the Lord. And the Lord - who is the Spirit - makes us more and more like him as we are changed into his glorious image.*[134]

Our expectation of what is normal in our development as followers of Jesus is that we continue to go through a process of change: that we see more and more freedom in our lives and we become more and more like him. In the following passage from Galatians, we see Paul once again addresses head on the question of how we should deal with our sinful nature:

*So I say, let the Holy Spirit guide your lives. Then you won't be doing what your sinful nature craves. The sinful nature wants to do evil, which is just the opposite of what the Spirit wants. And the Spirit gives us desires that are the opposite of what the sinful nature desires. These two forces are constantly fighting each other, so you are not free to carry out your good intentions.*

*But when you are directed by the Spirit, you are not under obligation to the law of Moses. When you follow the desires of your sinful nature, the results are very clear: sexual immorality, impurity, lustful pleasures, idolatry, sorcery, hostility, quarrelling, jealousy, outbursts of anger, selfish ambition, dissension, division, envy, drunkenness, wild parties, and other sins like these. Let me tell you again, as I have before, that anyone living that sort of life will not inherit the Kingdom of God.*

*But the Holy Spirit produces this kind of fruit in our lives: love, joy, peace, patience, kindness, goodness, faithfulness, gentleness, and self-control. There is no law against these things! Those who belong to Christ Jesus have nailed the passions and desires of their*

---

[134] 2 Corinthians 3:17&18

*sinful nature to his cross and crucified them there. Since we are living by the Spirit, let us follow the Spirit's leading in every part of our lives.*[135]

John, sometimes known as 'the disciple whom Jesus loved', was perhaps best placed of all the apostles to reflect upon what it was like to live life with Jesus, to deal with the challenge that Jesus must have posed. In one place, he says this:

*….God is light, and there is no darkness in him at all. So we are lying if we say we have fellowship with God but go on living in spiritual darkness; we are not practicing the truth. But if we are living in the light, as God is in the light, then we have fellowship with each other, and the blood of Jesus, his Son, cleanses us from all sin. If we claim we have no sin, we are only fooling ourselves and not living in the truth. But if we confess our sins to him, he is faithful and just to forgive us our sins and to cleanse us from all wickedness. If we claim we have not sinned, we are calling God a liar and showing that his word has no place in our hearts.*[136]

The call on our lives is to 'live in the light', to let God's love and holiness reveal our sins for what they are. In the light is where our sins can be forgiven, and where we can move on. This is good news. From time to time this living in the light might feel uncomfortable, but it is good news.

Part of what living in the light will mean is not only being honest with God about where we are failing, but also being honest with ourselves and some other people, even if it is just one trusted friend. It will mean living with the tension of not wanting to carry on with sin as we have before, but being real enough to admit our mistakes. It will mean being serious enough to begin to do something to change things, however long this process might take.

There is a sobering challenge in this. Would it not be more convenient, and more realistic, to accept that at least for some people we just seem to be destined to stay stuck with addictions, or bad habits, or destructive cycles of behaviour, or whatever? Isn't it, after all, biblically true that we will always struggle with sin? Isn't this the selfsame unwinnable struggle that Paul so vividly describes in Romans 7?

---

[135] Galatians 5:16-25

[136] 1 John 5:5-10

Such an interpretation of Romans 7 is irreconcilable with what John goes on to say:

*Anyone who continues to live in him will not sin. But anyone who keeps on sinning does not know him or understand who he is. Dear children, don't let anyone deceive you about this: When people do what is right, it shows that they are righteous, even as Christ is righteous.*

*But when people keep on sinning, it shows that they belong to the devil, who has been sinning since the beginning. But the Son of God came to destroy the works of the devil. Those who have been born into God's family do not make a practice of sinning, because God's life is in them. So they can't keep on sinning, because they are children of God. So now we can tell who are children of God and who are children of the devil. Anyone who does not live righteously and does not love other believers does not belong to God.*[137]

Do not think this teaching from John should simply be ignored because it is too tough, or because it is unrealistic. This passage is about the basic direction of your life. What kind of person are you turning into? Do you know who you are? Do you realise how much Jesus paid to bring you into his family? As a child of God, are you going to face up to the long-term consequences of who and what you are, or will you mess around with sin, using your 'human nature' as an excuse?

Jesus himself made a very clear connection between sin and not living like a member of God's family:

*'You are truly my disciples if you remain faithful to my teachings. And you will know the truth, and the truth will set you free.' 'But we are descendants of Abraham,' they said. 'We have never been slaves to anyone. What do you mean, 'You will be set free'?' Jesus replied, 'I tell you the truth, everyone who sins is a slave of sin. A slave is not a permanent member of the family, but a son is part of the family forever. So if the Son sets you free, you are truly free.'*[138]

The problem with sin is that it traps us, it enslaves us, it takes away our freedom. When Jesus was tempted by the Devil in the wilderness, there was something else in the temptations that was even deeper that the Devil seeking to play upon the lust of the flesh, the lust of the eyes, and the pride

---

[137] 1 John 3:6-10

[138] John 8:31-36

of life. The Devil asked a deeper question: did Jesus really know he was the Son of God?. Just a few days before, Jesus had heard his Father speak approving words to him on the day of his baptism. The Devil was testing Jesus to see whether Jesus really knew who he was.

The fact that Jesus was securely grounded in his identity was vital in his ability to resist evil. The Devil also understood the importance to Jesus of knowing who and what he was. If the Devil could weaken that confidence, the Devil would have landed a terrible blow on Jesus.

Is it possible that, when we feel we have failed God because we have fallen back into sinful behaviour, we end up focusing on the wrong issue? Do we condemn ourselves, do we waste our time and energy beating ourselves up, when our efforts would be far better spent getting back to a place of intimacy with our Father in heaven? I believe the answer is: yes!

There may well be practical steps we can usefully take as part and parcel of 'putting to death the deeds of our sinful nature'. I make some suggestions about these in Part Two of this book. And yet, there is a foundational issue, lying much deeper, that we need to be clear about.

If we get this, anything is possible. We are sons and daughters of God. We already carry the Lord's family likeness. We could never have earned this privilege, but it is God's indescribably precious gift to us, written as it were into our spiritual DNA.

If you feel you are struggling with sin, my prayer is that you will more and more clearly see this struggle from God's perspective. You win. You are family. Your destiny is to grow up into him. Enjoy the ride!

# The Family Tree

Fù | Father

# CHAPTER 8

Genealogy - research into who our ancestors were, and how they lived - is a subject of huge interest for many people. The U.K. television programme called 'Who Do You Think You Are?' says something important about this subject in its very title. There is implied in this title the idea that, for each of us, our very identity is at least in part shaped by our parents, their own parents, and other members of our particular family tree.

What does the family tree have to do with freedom, with moving into our personal best? The better we understand the family influences that helped to shape us, the better understanding we will have of ourselves. Families are one of God's great ideas, and his intention always was that they would be a means, a vehicle, for being a blessing - nurture, encouragement, education and so on. This remains true today.

Sadly, what is also true is that our families can to a greater or lesser degree have been places of brokenness, of dysfunction, of pain and neglect. Sometimes our personal journey into greater freedom will involve facing up to the reality of this.

You may be familiar with expressions such as, 'like father, like son', 'he/she is a chip off the old block', or something similar. The gist of these kinds of sayings is that not only do we inherit physical characteristics from our parents – the colour of our hair, our height, the shape of our nose and so on – but also something of the way we behave, our very personality, is handed down to us.

Because of advances in science we now know a lot more than previously about the mechanics of how our physical characteristics are shaped. The discovery of DNA and the decoding of the human genome have been amazing breakthroughs. We should be honest with ourselves about the challenges that modern discoveries and knowledge present to us as we try to settle on an understanding of our own identities as children of a God who is there, and who loves us. God's word is very clear that you are not an accident. You are not merely the product of some random shuffling and re-shuffling of genetic code:

*You made all the delicate, inner parts of my body and knit me together in my mother's womb. Thank you for making me so wonderfully complex! Your workmanship is marvellous - and how well I know it. You watched me as I was being formed in utter seclusion, as I was woven together in the dark of the womb. You saw me before I was born. Every day of my life was recorded in your book. Every moment was laid out before a single day had passed.*[139]

There is a potential controversy about 'nature versus nurture'. Is your personality shaped primarily by your DNA, by what you have biologically inherited from your mother and father? This is 'nature'. Or should we focus on your upbringing and your experiences within the environment in which you were raised? This is 'nurture'. If the truth lies in a combination of the two, what are the proportions?

Is there anything about your personality that is truly a reflection of the choices which you have made, an expression of your genuine individuality? Or is everything about you determined by circumstances beyond your control? Are you not very much more than a product of what other people (your parents) have given you in terms of your genetic makeup working in combination with what other people (the world around you) have done to you?

The Bible leads us to conclude that each one of us is much, much more than just our DNA, and much, much more than just an automatic, determined response to the conditions that we find around us. This is regardless of the hand I have been dealt when I think about my biological inheritance and my life circumstances - which country I was born in, where I went to school, whatever.

I, like you, am a unique creation, made in God's image, and fully responsible for my actions and also for the choices I make as I travel along the road of life. Each one of us is fundamentally a spiritual being, living inside a physical body. Because of the Fall, our current bodies have all sorts of problems and weaknesses. These issues, following on from the Fall, are only a temporary problem for us. But, as Paul pointed out to the Church in Corinth, the fact that we are spirits living in bodies is not temporary, it is part of our eternal destiny:

*We grow weary in our present bodies, and we long for the day when we will put on our heavenly bodies like new clothing...Our dying bodies make us groan and sigh, but*

---

[139] Psalm 139:13-16

*it's not that we want to die and have no bodies at all. We want to slip into our new bodies so that these dying bodies will be swallowed up by everlasting life.*[140]

Identical twins - twins who have the same genetic coding - are sometimes studied by sociologists, for obvious reasons. From time to time news stories surface about identical twins who for whatever reason were separated at a relatively young age, only to be reunited many years later, often finding that their separate lives still have some remarkable things in common.

For me, such stories are fascinating, however I have no idea what is the true nature of any invisible connection that there may be between twins. My reason for mentioning identical twins is simply this. Some twins may well say something they feel like just one half of one whole person. But the reality is that these people, although they start life with exactly the same DNA, are most definitely separate, distinct, unique persons.

You are not defined primarily by your DNA; you are a spiritual being, and if you have given your life to Jesus, you have been born again, born of the Spirit, born from above.[141] You are a new creation. Any earthly labels which might be attached to you, such as male/female, black/white, rich/poor, are, relatively speaking, insignificant.[142]

This truth can fairly lead us on to wonder whether our actual family tree is of any relevance to us at all. Perhaps we can build a justification that looks and sounds very spiritual for paying no attention to where we came from and who raised us. For some of us, whether or not we are conscious of doing it, we might try hard to avoid looking at our family issues because they are simply too painful.

The Bible has a lot to say about generations, but it is perhaps not very easy to discern precisely how all of this applies to followers of Jesus, to those who have agreed to be part of his new covenant. Perhaps it is easy to accept the idea of good things (blessings) coming down to us through the

---

[140] 2 Corinthians 5:2-4

[141] John 3:3

[142] Galatians 3:28

generations. But perhaps it is less easy to accept the idea of bad things coming down to us in the same way.

A lot of the Bible material on this subject is in the Old Testament. I am going to use the term 'generational sin' to describe the process of the sins of parents being visited upon later generations. We will have to take some kind of view about whether generational sin is a complete non-issue given that we no longer live in the age of the Old Testament writings on this subject. We will also need to keep some balance between the negative and positive aspects of the family tree. We should never lose sight of the fact that God's plan for you is always that your family tree is a means for you to be blessed.

God visiting generational sin - the sins of parents - onto their children, and even to later generations, seems to be almost a part of God's character, as it is revealed in the Old Testament. This is part of what God tells Moses when he gives Moses the Ten Commandments:

*'Do not worship any other gods besides me…You must never worship or bow down to them, for I, the LORD your God, am a jealous God who will not share your affection with any other god! I do not leave unpunished the sins of those who hate me, but I punish the children for the sins of their parents to the third and fourth generations. But I lavish my love on those who love me and obey my commands, even for a thousand generations.'* [143]

In God's original plan, families were always supposed to be a means by which blessing was transferred, even increased. The experience of humankind upon this planet was supposed to be one of ever-widening, ever-deepening knowledge of God, his ways, and the wonders of his creation. Rather as Sir Isaac Newton, the great scientist, once said of his forerunners in the scientific community, we were all supposed to be standing on the shoulders of giants.

It is no coincidence that one of the other Ten Commandments is this one:

*'Honour your father and mother. Then you will live a long, full life in the land the*

---

[143] Exodus 20:3,5&6

*LORD your God will give you.*[144]

We will come back to this Commandment later in this Chapter. For the time being, please notice that God places a high value on honour between the generations, and that there is a curse implied in the blessing that is promised here. Failure to give this honour to parents may well result in the opposite of a long, full life.

Clearly, the relationship between parents and children matters to God. I wouldn't pretend to know all the reasons for this. However, I'm sure that one very important reason is that being a parent reflects part of the very nature of God. There are numerous references in the Old Testament to God as Father, and with Jesus' public ministry this was spelled out and emphasised. Another reason is that honour is part of the mysterious complexity and beauty in the inter-relationships between the three different parts of the Godhead: God the Father, God the Son and God the Holy Spirit. Since God himself operates on the basis of honour, he wants us to do likewise.

As if in a direct challenge to what God said in the Ten Commandments about his being a jealous God, and about not worshipping idols, the multitude who were with Moses in the wilderness blew it very quickly. They slipped into worshipping an idol, a golden calf, while they were waiting for Moses to come back down from the mountain. In his anger, Moses smashed the stone tablets on which the Ten Commandments had been written. At a later time, when the Commandments were given again by God to Moses, God restated something about parents' sins having an impact upon their children, as if to make it clear that this is really important:

*He passed in front of Moses and said, 'I am the LORD, I am the LORD, the merciful and gracious God. I am slow to anger and rich in unfailing love and faithfulness. I show this unfailing love to many thousands by forgiving every kind of sin and rebellion. Even so I do not leave sin unpunished, but I punish the children for the sins of their parents to the third and fourth generations.*[145]

Here, God's visiting the sins of the parents upon the children is

---

[144] Exodus 20:12

[145] Exodus 34:6&7

expressed, even more clearly than before, as a reflection of part of God's very character, since it follows on from God's declaration to Moses of God's name. Punishing children for generational sins is, it seems, not just something that God does: it is a reflection of who he is, and of what he is like.

We need to address the fact that there is an apparent contradiction between what these passages tell us about God's forgiving, gracious and merciful nature and what they tell us about God punishing children for what their parents did wrong. Put simply, this does not seem fair, even by our lowly and corrupted human standards.

As I have already said, God's intention for families from the outset was that they would be a vehicle for blessing. God is good, and he wants to bless us. Part of the way in which he clearly does lavish his love on us, even for a thousand generations, is by sending Jesus to us. This over-arching act of mercy and grace trumps all of our sins. God did not become nice only when the New Testament period started. The God of the Old Testament is the same as the God of the New Testament! The actual arrival of Jesus as a human baby at a specific point of time in our human history is foreshadowed and predicted throughout the Old Testament and it colours all of God's prior dealings with mankind.

I suggest that sins being visited upon children for three or four generations is, in and of itself, another sign of God's 'niceness'. The consequences of evil of are being reined in as it were, they are being held in check. We can stumble over what looks like the injustice of innocent children suffering for what guilty parents have got wrong, when in fact God is placing a limit upon the effects of sin.

What God will not do is place us in a fairytale-type world where we can never feel the real effects of sin. The effects of sin are reverberating all around us. My own sin, your sin, the sins of our forbears, the present and past sins of our nations and cultures, the structural sins of our governments, our institutions, our schools, our businesses – they are all real sins and they have real effects.

There is a particular story in the Old Testament which illustrates very well two apparently contradictory things happening at the same time, namely the flow of God's love and forgiveness on the one hand, and on the other hand God permitting us (and the people with whom we are connected) to experience at least some of the real consequences of sinful actions. This story concerns King David, who was described by God as a man after God's own heart[146] – an amazing compliment.

David was having a relaxing time in his palace when he should, apparently, have been out fighting and smiting – it being the season when kings customarily went out to war. From a roof terrace he saw a beautiful married woman, Bathsheba, taking a bath and he allowed one impulse to follow after another. He committed adultery, and Bathsheba became pregnant. Her husband Uriah was away at the war that David was supposed to be fighting.

Desperate to cover up his sin, David summoned Uriah back from the war and tried, unsuccessfully, to engineer a situation whereby Uriah would have sex with Bathsheba, and so be duped into thinking that her future child was in fact his own flesh and blood.

Once David saw that his plan A failed, he resorted to plan B – he arranged to have Uriah killed, by placing him deliberately in the most dangerous part of a battle. Both of David's unrighteous plans included involving other people in his deception. If plan A had worked, Bathsheba would have been trapped into living a lifelong lie about the paternity of her child. Plan B could only work because David made one of his staff complicit in killing an innocent man. Even if we are in the middle of trying to hide it, sin is rarely an entirely individual matter. You can read the details of this sorry saga, and some of its consequences, in 2 Samuel 11 - 20.

The truth of the situation was revealed by God to the prophet Nathan. Nathan went to David and confronted him in a clever way by inviting David to express his moral judgment about a similar situation, which Nathan had invented for this purpose. David was condemned out of his own mouth. To his credit, David acknowledged his guilt.

Nathan declared the following consequences, in addition to the general observation that there were so many more good things that would have come David's way, but which would forever be blocked because of his sin. The sword will be a constant threat to David's family; his own household will rebel against him; his wives will be given to another man, who will have

---

146 1 Samuel 13:14

sex with them in public; and Bathsheba's unborn child will die.[147]

Nathan also declared that God had forgiven David, and that he would not die because of his sin. Perhaps one of the most shocking fulfillments of this prophetic judgment from Nathan was that Absalom, David's son who led a revolt against him, set up a tent on the roof of his father's palace in Jerusalem and had sex in public view with the ten concubines David had left behind when he had fled from the city.[148]

Whatever view you take about generational sin, it is abundantly clear that David's sin had consequences for other people, including the unborn baby in Bathsheba's womb.

You can go on from this section in 2 Samuel and read further to consider the life of another of David's sons, Solomon. Solomon started well as king and received tremendous wisdom as a gift from God, yet even so his reign did not end as well as it began. An argument can be made out that there is a significant connection between Solomon's failings and his father's sin. If Solomon's own moral failures were caused by generational sin – the sins of his father David being visited upon him – was there in fact any escape route for him? Is there any escape route for us today?

There is another concept that develops in the Old Testament that has a bearing on how we can deal with our own family tree. This concept is 'identificational repentance' - repenting to God for sins committed by other people as if you yourself have responsibility for them. Sometimes this is referred to a 'generational repentance'. This is identifying with the sins of your family, your city, tribe or nation – calling their sins your own sins, standing with them before God as you ask God for mercy on their behalf.

One example of this kind of prayer can be found in the book of Daniel. Daniel was a devoted lover of God who rose to a prominent position in the government of Babylon during the time of the Jewish exile there. Jeremiah the prophet was alive at the same time as Daniel. Daniel was reading part of what would become the book of Jeremiah in our Bibles. He understood from this prophecy that the time was approaching for the Jews to be able to

---

[147] 2 Samuel 12:7-14

[148] 2 Samuel 16:21&22

return to their own land. Here is part of his response:

*Then I set my face toward the Lord God to make request by prayer and supplications, with fasting, sackcloth, and ashes. And I prayed to the Lord my God, and made confession, and said, 'O Lord, great and awesome God, who keeps His covenant and mercy with those who love Him, and with those who keep His commandments, we have sinned and committed iniquity, we have done wickedly and rebelled, even by departing from Your precepts and Your judgments. Neither have we heeded Your servants the prophets, who spoke in Your name to our kings and our princes, to our fathers and all the people of the land.'*[149]

I doubt that there was a more righteous man than Daniel in the whole of his community, and yet Daniel prayed as if the sins of his nation, including the sins of his ancestors, were his own: '<u>we</u> have sinned' is what he said, not '<u>they</u> have sinned'.

You will find a similar prayer being said by Ezra.[150] Ezra was involved in the process of the return of the Jews from exile in Babylonia and Persia. He was descended from the High Priests and he was expert in the Jewish religious law. He was distressed to find that so many of his people had broken that law by intermarrying with heathen peoples around Jerusalem, something that God had forbidden because of the danger of idolatry. The language of his identification with the sin of his countrymen is striking:

*'O my God, I am utterly ashamed; I blush to lift up my face to you. For our sins are piled higher than our heads, and our guilt has reached to the heavens.'*[151]

As with Daniel, Ezra does not set himself on a higher and holier plane than his people. He claims their sins as his own.

At the risk of over-simplifying what identificational repentance is all about, great men of God such as Daniel and Ezra were choosing to position themselves with their people, as opposed to creating some kind of 'them and us' gap between the people who were praying and the people who were being prayed for. I see this as a healthy way to pray.

---

[149] Daniel 9:3-6 [nkjv]

[150] Ezra 9:5-7

[151] Ezra 9:6

If in your consideration of your family tree you find that some sins emerge that your ancestors have committed, then it is perfectly healthy and appropriate to pray a prayer of identificational repentance. But please do not pray this as an 'us' and 'them' type of prayer. Be like Daniel and Ezra and stand with your family, identify with your family.

The disciples around Jesus were, it seems, well acquainted with the idea that children can bear the ill effects of their parents' sins, as witness this episode:

*Now as Jesus passed by, He saw a man who was blind from birth. And His disciples asked Him, saying, 'Rabbi, who sinned, this man or his parents, that he was born blind?' Jesus answered, 'Neither this man nor his parents sinned, but that the works of God should be revealed in him.'*[152]

I am fascinated by Jesus' answer. He seems to swerve around the interesting question of whether such an affliction as blindness could ever be the result of the punishment for sin being passed down from one generation to another.

And yet, on more than one occasion in the Gospels, Jesus does make a clear connection between the decision we might make to carry on with our own sin and the possibility of something bad happening to us as a direct result. For example, here is part of the account of a man who had suffered with some kind of crippling illness for 38 years, and who was healed by Jesus at the Pool of Bethesda:

*Jesus said to him, 'Rise, take up your bed and walk.' And immediately the man was made well, took up his bed, and walked. And that day was the Sabbath. The Jews therefore said to him who was cured, 'It is the Sabbath; it is not lawful for you to carry your bed.' He answered them, 'He who made me well said to me, 'Take up your bed and walk.' Then they asked him, 'Who is the Man who said to you, 'Take up your bed and walk'?' But the one who was healed did not know who it was, for Jesus had withdrawn, a multitude being in that place. Afterward Jesus found him in the temple, and said to him, 'See, you have been made well. Sin no more, lest a worse thing come upon you.'*[153]

Job, which may well be one of the oldest books in the Old Testament, is

---

[152] John 9:1-3 [nkjv]

[153] John 5:8-14 [nkjv]

largely concerned with some related issues, to do with sin and suffering. Put bluntly, one can ask, 'why do bad things happen to good people?' Another question is, 'if God really is there and if he really is just, why does he allow undeserved suffering?' Job had no idea at the time what was going on, but his afflictions were to do with a debate between God and Satan about whether any human being would truly love and worship God simply for who God is, regardless of life's circumstances. Seeing Job's problems, his friends concluded that clearly Job must have brought all of this upon himself, he must have sinned. What Job ended up with was a bigger concept of God.

I am so glad that the Gospel records of Jesus' life and teachings include something of his own commentary upon complex moral problems such as this:

*There were present at that season some who told Him about the Galileans whose blood Pilate had mingled with their sacrifices. And Jesus answered and said to them, 'Do you suppose that these Galileans were worse sinners than all other Galileans, because they suffered such things? I tell you, no; but unless you repent you will all likewise perish. Or those eighteen on whom the tower in Siloam fell and killed them, do you think that they were worse sinners than all other men who dwelt in Jerusalem? I tell you, no; but unless you repent you will all likewise perish.* [154]

For Jesus, there seems to be a clear link between sin and calamity; but it is too simplistic to conclude that the worst things happen to the worst sinners.

In a very brief look at the issue of generational sin, we have seen how various passages from the Old Testament suggest that the consequences of sin passed down from one generation to another, for up to four generations.

There are, however, other passages from within the Old Testament itself that suggest perhaps some kind of change has taken place:

*'In those days they shall say no more: 'The fathers have eaten sour grapes, And the children's teeth are set on edge.' But every one shall die for his own iniquity; every man who eats the sour grapes, his teeth shall be set on edge.' Behold, the days are coming, says*

---

[154] Luke 13:1-5 [nkjv]

*the Lord, when I will make a new covenant with the house of Israel and with the house of Judah - not according to the covenant that I made with their fathers in the day that I took them by the hand to lead them out of the land of Egypt, My covenant which they broke, though I was a husband to them, says the Lord.*

*But this is the covenant that I will make with the house of Israel after those days, says the Lord: I will put My law in their minds, and write it on their hearts; and I will be their God, and they shall be My people. No more shall every man teach his neighbour, and every man his brother, saying, 'Know the Lord,' for they all shall know Me, from the least of them to the greatest of them, says the Lord. For I will forgive their iniquity, and their sin I will remember no more.* [155]

As if to emphasise the point, there is a very similar passage in Ezekiel,[156] and that passage does not even point to a future age when this change will come about. It is as if Ezekiel is announcing the dismantling of something with immediate effect.

I believe it is reasonable to conclude that are we are now living in the future era about which Jeremiah prophesied. Our teeth do not have to be 'set on edge' by our parents' sour grapes. Perhaps we could also conclude that this means generational sin is no longer an issue for us?

There is, however, a problem with such a conclusion. The problem is this: why does reality - the real-life situations around us - tend to indicate that problems are, in fact, passed down from one generation to another? Why, for example, do alcoholic parents sometimes seem to produce alcoholic children? Why do we seem to be, so often, 'chips off the old block'?

Whenever our theology is at odds with our experience, we have to ask ourselves what is wrong with the picture. Is our theology faulty, or do we need to adjust our understanding of what is happening in our world? It is at this point that I want to submit what I believe is a rounded, balanced approach to the issue of generational sin. I am taking as my model something that happened at the beginning of Gideon's exploits with God:

*Now it came to pass the same night that the Lord said to him, 'Take your father's*

---

[155] Jeremiah 31:29-34

[156] Ezekiel 18:1-4

*young bull, the second bull of seven years old, and tear down the altar of Baal that your father has, and cut down the wooden image that is beside it; and build an altar to the Lord your God on top of this rock in the proper arrangement, and take the second bull and offer a burnt sacrifice with the wood of the image which you shall cut down.* [157]

Gideon lived during the period of the Judges of Israel. Indeed, he became one of those Judges, one of the heroes who defended the emerging nation of Israel against attacks from their enemies. Gideon was living in a period of oppression. The Midianites, fierce camel riders from the East, were terrorising the people. Gideon was hiding his family's modest grain harvest by threshing it in the wine press, when he had an encounter with God, who later that same night tells him to dismantle his father's idolatrous shrine and replace it with proper worship.

Gideon's conversation with God on that fateful day began with God making an amazing declaration about Gideon. God greeted him by describing him as a mighty man of valour – quite a statement for someone hiding grain in a winepress. But Gideon had to do something very dramatic and decisive, early on in his dealings with God, to make sure he was able to accomplish what God had planned for him. He had to make a break with his father's compromise over demonic worship. Without doubt, if Gideon had failed to make this break, he would have failed to fulfil the destiny that God had spoken over his life. He would never have become the Judge he was destined to become.

When you consider the details of your own daily life, if you see health problems, bad habits or other negative issues that seem to be hard to break free from, perhaps there is something ungodly in your family line where you have not yet made a break in the same way that Gideon made a break. If you know something of your family's history and you can see unhealthy patterns emerging and even showing up in your own life, this may well be a clue that some prayer and/or ministry into the significance of what your ancestors did will help you to get free.

It is not necessarily the case that you have to repent for the sins of your parents. However, if you love them and want the best for them, standing

---

[157] Judges 6:25&26 [nkjv]

with them in a prayer of identification repentance would be a good thing to do, even if you are not sure about generational sin.

As you consider your family tree, you might discover that you have adopted the sins of your ancestors. If you have carried on with those sins, if you have failed to break with them, then they are most certainly our own sins. You are responsible for your own sins, even if in reality it was your ancestors who, in effect, taught you how to sin. It's not necessarily the case that they even understood what they were doing.

Near the beginning of this Chapter, I mentioned the commandment which requires that we honour our parents. As we close this Chapter, I want to reflect a little on what it means for you and me to honour our parents in the context of having a healthy approach to dealing with generational sin.

Readers of this book will have a very wide range of thoughts and feelings about their parents. For some of you, the very idea of talking about God as a loving heavenly Father may be almost impossible to process because your human father was absent or abusive. Others may feel that their parents were perfect, or that it would be some kind of betrayal or disloyalty to them to spend any amount of time investigating what, if anything, there might be in your family line that is standing in the way of you experiencing greater freedom.

Taking Gideon as an example, God told Gideon to do something which flew in the face of his father's practices and lifestyle. Was Gideon, as a result of obeying God, dishonouring his own father? No. Honouring our parents is not the same as carrying on with things our parents have taught us if those things are in fact ungodly.

God's plan for families was, from the start, that families would be a means by which we enjoy blessing. It is part of God's plan that as sons and daughters we show love and respect to our mothers and fathers, that we honour them.

It is good that, as we look at our family trees, we find in those trees whatever we can sincerely be thankful for. It is also important that we listen to anything the Holy Spirit might want to say to us about the need to make a break with any ungodly things in our family trees, especially if we can see bad fruit in that tree that is also evident in our own lives. We need to be willing to say sorry to God for any ways in which we have ourselves sinned by taking on and repeating any of our ancestors' sins. This is without in any way condemning or judging anyone.

The New Testament speaks of other trees that are not the family tree. There is Jesus referring to himself as the vine and us his followers as the branches in John 15. Also there is Paul talking about us being grafted into an olive tree, representing the whole of God's household, in Romans 11. These references do not, however, mean that as followers of Jesus we can simply ignore the reality of our actual human family trees.

Apart from issues to do with sin that we may need to address in our family trees, let's not lose sight of the good that is within those trees. Let's remember that Father God placed each one of us within a family tree with the intention of blessing us. In particular, even to the extent that we had difficult relationships with our parents, let's forgive them and rejoice in the fact that they brought us into the world. Let's honour our parents. Let's identify with our family tree and let's bless it in the name of Jesus.

# Enemy Territory

Jiè | Boundary

# CHAPTER 9

In 1974, the last confirmed surrenders by Japanese 'holdouts' took place. 'Holdouts' were Japanese soldiers who had fought in the 2nd World War but carried on as if the war had never ended - either because of a refusal to accept the truth, or because of poor communications. Hiroo Onoda was relieved of duty by his former commanding officer on Lubang Island in the Philippines in March 1974, followed by Terko Nakamura, who surrendered on Morotai Island in Indonesia in December 1974.

All of this was a long time after the war actually ended. Victory in Europe was officially declared on 8 June 1945, and in Japan the relevant date was 2 September 1945 - that being the date of Japan's unconditional surrender. So, in effect, for almost 30 years, Hiroo Onoda and Terko Nakamura lived in a false reality.

It is sad to think of people who carry on living as if they are at war, when in fact the war is over. What is also sad - and not only sad, but positively dangerous - is to live as if there is no war when, in fact, war is being waged around you. And yet, this is the mindset of many Christians in today's world. We have an enemy - the Devil, or Satan - and he is doing whatever he can within his kingdom to exercise influence over planet Earth, and to attack the Kingdom of God as it spreads around the globe.

Why would Christians, just like the Japanese 'holdouts', choose to try to live in a private version of reality that is so out of step with what is actually going on around them? This could be for a number of reasons. Maybe the idea of Christian life as being life in a war doesn't sit well with the idea of Jesus having won a decisive and final victory through the Cross. Maybe Jesus' ushering in of a new covenant is seen as meaning that Christians, as new creations, cannot possibly be under any kind of influence or control by demonic forces. Maybe any kind of talk of war with the enemy is seen as giving the Devil way too much attention and credit. Maybe, if we do everything 'right', life is meant to be a problem-free bed of roses. Maybe we have fear of the kingdom of darkness, so we prefer to brush the whole unpleasant subject under the carpet. Maybe any mention of the Devil sounds like old-fashioned nonsense.

There are, doubtless, other reasons that I haven't listed. Some of the reasons will have some element of Biblical truth within them, and some will not. None of them is a good reason to ignore the war, as I hope to make clear. What I want to do is to get to grips with what Jesus tells us about this subject, and how this is supplemented by other New Testament contributors. My aim is that we all have a healthy and balanced appreciation that there is, indeed, a war on. But there is no need to live in fear and we can have absolute confidence that Jesus is calling us to live a life of fruitful service in the Kingdom of Heaven, here and now.

One of the things that was distinctive about Jesus' public ministry was his announcement that the Kingdom of Heaven, or the Kingdom of God, was near, or was coming, or was at hand. By implication, Jesus was saying that a clash of kingdoms was under way. Another thing that was distinctive about him was the level of reaction there was to him from demons who were oppressing people, and his ability to command those evil spirits to end their oppression.

This display of true authority was a huge challenge to those religious leaders who couldn't accept Jesus' teachings, so part of their strategy was to try to tarnish his reputation by suggesting that really it was all just a demonic trick: that Jesus was an agent of Satan, and Satan was in effect stage-managing fake deliverances. This is what Jesus had to say in response:

*Then a demon-possessed man, who was blind and couldn't speak, was brought to Jesus. He healed the man so that he could both speak and see. The crowd was amazed and asked, 'Could it be that Jesus is the Son of David, the Messiah?' But when the Pharisees heard about the miracle, they said, 'No wonder he can cast out demons. He gets his power from Satan, the prince of demons.' Jesus knew their thoughts and replied, 'Any kingdom divided by civil war is doomed. A town or family splintered by feuding will fall apart.*

*And if Satan is casting out Satan, he is divided and fighting against himself. His own kingdom will not survive. And if I am empowered by Satan, what about your own exorcists? They cast out demons, too, so they will condemn you for what you have said. But if I am casting out demons by the Spirit of God, then the Kingdom of God has arrived among you. For who is powerful enough to enter the house of a strong man like Satan and plunder his goods? Only someone even stronger - someone who could tie him up and then plunder his house.'*[158]

---

[158] Matthew 12:22-29

Jesus here uses the imagery not only of kingdoms, but of houses, and the ideas of land, buildings and territory are things that we will keep encountering as we look at this question of life during wartime. Later in the same Chapter of Matthew's Gospel,[159] Jesus uses the picture of a house to speak about someone's life. He talks about a demon being cast out of someone - the demon's 'house' - and then eventually returning to re-occupy that house, bringing some of his unsavoury friends with him.

The purpose of Jesus' warning is that experiencing a deliverance is a one-off event, but what is even more important is whether we then re-align our lives within God's Kingdom so that our lives - our 'houses' - are no longer vulnerable.

In comparison, in the extract from Matthew that I have quoted just now, Jesus is again talking about a 'house', but it is a different house altogether. It is Satan's own house. Countering the accusations of the religious leaders, Jesus says that what is being demonstrated in his ministry is a genuine clash between two opposing kingdoms, and that his Kingdom, the Kingdom of Heaven, wins. Satan's house - the kingdom of darkness - has no security left. There is no lock that Satan can put on his front door that can keep Jesus out.

We find an echo of this in what Jesus says to his disciple Peter. The context is the significance of Peter understanding in the Spirit who Jesus truly is, and then receiving revelation from Jesus about who he - Peter - truly is. Jesus speaks about what the Church will be like when it moves in this kind of understanding and he says this:

*This is the rock on which I will put together my church, a church so expansive with energy that not even the gates of hell will be able to keep it out. And that's not all. You will have complete and free access to God's kingdom, keys to open any and every door: no more barriers between heaven and earth, earth and heaven. A yes on earth is yes in heaven. A no on earth is no in heaven.*[160]

What Jesus teaches here is a key to the mindset he wants us to have, as his followers, when we think about Satan's activities in the world. We might

---

[159] Matthew 12:43-45

[160] Matthew 16:18&19 [The Message]

feel a temptation to either pretend the enemy does not exist, or that he is utterly powerless. Alternatively, perhaps we fear him, and think in purely defensive terms - the enemy is advancing, and we must somehow defend ourselves against him.

Jesus clearly has a very different perspective. What he says to Peter is all about being on the attack, on the offensive, as opposed to being defensive. In Jesus' worldview, the issue is not how God's people can be saved from an advancing kingdom of darkness. Rather, the issue is this: will God's people live in the reality and fulness of the fact that their destiny is to raid hell itself?

This is completely consistent what Jesus said at other times about his Kingdom:

*'...from the time John the Baptist began preaching until now, the Kingdom of Heaven has been forcefully advancing...'*[161]

He announced that God's Kingdom was not something that was a long way away from people:

*...Jesus began to preach, 'Repent of your sins and turn to God, for the Kingdom of Heaven is near.'*[162]

The apostle John made this statement about Jesus as a comment on why it was that Jesus came into the world, and what it was that he achieved:

*...the Son of God came to destroy the works of the devil.*[163]

And the apostle Paul said this about what happened on the Cross:

*You were dead because of your sins and because your sinful nature was not yet cut away. Then God made you alive with Christ, for he forgave all our sins. He canceled the record of the charges against us and took it away by nailing it to the cross. In this way, he disarmed the spiritual rulers and authorities. He shamed them publicly by his victory over them on the cross.*[164]

Paul's statement here about God shaming the kingdom of darkness in

---

[161] Matthew 11:12

[162] Matthew 4:17

[163] 1 John 3:8

[164] Colossians 2:13-15

public would have been understood by the readers of his letter as a reference to the way vanquished enemies were paraded through the streets of Rome. The sense is clearly that a decisive victory has been won.

The Gospels are as full of accounts of Jesus driving out unclean spirits as they are full of accounts of Jesus healing people. The time came when he called his extended team of 72 followers to do the same work. Here is what was said when they reported back on what they had seen and heard during their ministry time:

*When the seventy-two disciples returned, they joyfully reported to him, 'Lord, even the demons obey us when we use your name! 'Yes,' he told them, 'I saw Satan fall from heaven like lightning! Look, I have given you authority over all the power of the enemy, and you can walk among snakes and scorpions and crush them. Nothing will injure you. But don't rejoice because evil spirits obey you; rejoice because your names are registered in heaven.* [165]

Let's take a little time to unpack what kind of authority Satan had, or has. When Jesus talks about having seen Satan fall from Heaven, does this mean that Satan was already powerless at the time when Jesus was sending out the 72?

When Jesus was tempted by Satan in the wilderness at the start of Jesus' ministry, Satan offered Jesus all the world's kingdoms in exchange for worship. Jesus refused to bow the knee to Satan, however we see nothing in the Bible account of their conversation to suggest that Jesus doubted Satan's ability to make the offer. Jesus' resistance to the enemy was all about worship being only for God and not for any created being being or created thing, no matter how powerful or attractive Satan might appear to be. What Jesus did not say, however, was that Satan could not offer to trade the kingdoms of this world for worship.

The claim of authority over the kingdoms of this world went through a fundamental shift by the time the resurrected Jesus was ready to take his place in Heaven at the Father's right hand. The following statement from Jesus is taken from the Great Commission, recorded in Matthew 28:

*Jesus came and told his disciples, 'I have been given all authority in heaven and on*

---

[165] Luke 10:17-20

*earth. Therefore, go and make disciples of all the nations, baptising them in the name of the Father and the Son and the Holy Spirit.* [166]

To summarise: Jesus calls us to have a positive, aggressive, offensive approach. It is not in his plan that we live in fear of the enemy, in fact he wants us to live in the reality of the victory that he has won. The fact is that we - as God's people - are winners, not losers.

Given that Jesus' work on the Cross was so pivotal, does this mean that, on and from that moment in history, we don't really have any active enemy any longer? Leaving aside for one moment what the Bible says about this, a glance around the world around us tells us that this surely cannot be true. There is so much evil, pain and grief. Surely there is still an enemy who is very much still at work.

If it is easy for us all to agree that there is still a kingdom of darkness in the world, it might be harder for all Christians to be clear about what relevance this kingdom of darkness has to them. There are two big issues. Firstly, doesn't the fact that each Christian is a new creation, with God's Holy Spirit deposited within, mean that we are immune from any kind of demonic control or influence? Secondly, aren't most, if not all, of our problems self-inflicted? In other words, if we live exactly the way that God wants us to live, won't God protect us from any trouble?

I am going to point to a number of Scriptures that tell us the truth about the war we are living through, but in advance I want to give you my summary response to those two big issues. Christians are not immune from being influenced or oppressed in some way by evil spirits. If we major on whether or not Christians can be possessed or controlled, we risk being sidetracked by what is, relatively speaking, a side issue. Suffice to say that even if we cannot be possessed, we certainly can be oppressed.

A key theme, and one that is hinted at in the title of this Chapter, is that if we think of our life as a house, or as a piece of ground, sometimes we allow the kingdom of darkness to occupy part of that space. Our Great Commission is to extend God's Kingdom, but our effectiveness in this task is tied to how thoroughly we are applying God's Kingdom to our own

---

[166] Matthew 28:18&19

territory, our own house, our own hearts and minds.

When it comes to what it is of our own stuff that needs to be sorted out so that we can be better able to attack hell, the answer in God's Word might surprise you. It is not primarily a matter of our stuff getting sorted out if only we can tune into whatever God is saying about a particular key or secret that we must know. Instead, the main area that is contested is whether we will walk the path of forgiveness, the path of not being judgmental, the path of non-bitterness.

This path runs alongside the path of repentance. Repentance - true repentance, not just saying sorry - demolishes so many of the opportunities that otherwise the enemy would have to claim the right to occupy part of your house. Repentance is about agreeing with God that if he says something is sin, then it really is sin. It is also about co-operating with the Lord as he adjusts the way we think, even the way we think that maybe led us into the sin we are repenting of. As Paul says in Romans, he wants us to allow him to change the way we think.[167]

It is likely that some, possibly even many, of the problems and sufferings that we experience from time to time are the result of our failures to live the way that God wants us to live. Also, another cause of problems for us is what other people do to us. Some of these problems we face may well be avoidable.

Be that as it may, it is bad theology to hold that, if only we could live perfectly in accordance with God's will for us, we will enjoy a trouble-free life. The truth is, we are living during a war. Despite the reality of the war, there is much life to be enjoyed, many exploits to engage in, much fruit to enjoy, and even much fun to be had. That said, the reality of the war is that sometimes, some of us will suffer loss. Added to that, any thorough reading of the New Testament will show you that Jesus' followers can expect suffering and persecution.

We live in a period that some have called 'the now and not yet' - the Kingdom of Heaven has indeed come, ushered in by Jesus, but we won't see it in all of its fulness until Christ's return. Another way of thinking of

---

[167] Romans 12:2

this is as an overlap between two kingdoms. The kingdom of darkness is being squeezed out by the Kingdom of Heaven. The final outcome is not in any doubt, but in the meantime we live in a period where we see evidence of two completely different kingdoms at work. They are at war.

This overlap can make parts of the Bible look like apparent contradictions, when in fact all they are doing is describing accurately various aspects of the now and not yet state of affairs. So, in Chapter 8 of Romans, Paul describes Jesus as being seated already in the place of highest authority - at God's right hand:

*Who then will condemn us? No one - for Christ Jesus died for us and was raised to life for us, and he is sitting in the place of honour at God's right hand, pleading for us.*[168]

Although Jesus is now sitting in this place of authority, Satan still has some ability to be active. As Paul closes his letter to the Church in Rome, he makes this comment:

*The God of peace will soon crush Satan under your feet. May the grace of our Lord Jesus be with you.*[169]

How soon is 'soon' in Paul's mind? We can see many victories along the way, but the completion of this crushing of Satan will happen when Jesus comes back. In his first letter to the Corinthian Church, Paul speaks about Jesus' return and says:

*After that the end will come, when he [Jesus] will turn the Kingdom over to God the Father, having destroyed every ruler and authority and power. For Christ must reign until he humbles all his enemies beneath his feet. And the last enemy to be destroyed is death.*[170]

We find a similar idea in Hebrews, describing Jesus as our High Priest:

*But our High Priest offered himself to God as a single sacrifice for sins, good for all time. Then he sat down in the place of honour at God's right hand. There he waits until his enemies are humbled and made a footstool under his feet. For by that one offering he*

---

[168] Romans 8:34

[169] Romans 16:20

[170] 1 Corinthians 15:24-26

*forever made perfect those who are being made holy.*[171]

It is our privilege, then, as followers of Jesus, to be actively involved in seeing God's Kingdom brought to bear more and more upon the Earth - even to the point, as Jesus said to Peter, that even hell's gates will not be able to keep us out. God's will for you is that you make a contribution to the process of enemy kingdom territory being taken for Heaven's Kingdom. When I use the word 'territory' here, I do not mean we are called to establish a new political state. Thinking in terms of political control was part of what tripped up some people who lived at the same time as Jesus. They were assuming that the arrival of the Messiah must mean the political overthrow of the Roman Empire.

I have tried to sketch a big picture. Now I am going to focus on some specific incidents in Jesus' ministry and see what these can teach us about the issue of spiritual warfare. Also I will look at what some of the letters in the Bible to the early Church have to say on the same subject.

Let's carry on with the idea of territory. Shortly before his arrest, Jesus said this:

*'I will no longer talk much with you, for the ruler of this world is coming, and he has nothing in Me.'* [172]

The language here is not explicitly about land, but it does carry the idea of a claim. We could paraphrase this as Jesus saying that Satan has nothing 'on' him. Since Jesus could say this about himself, our target should be that, as much as is possible, we can also say that Satan has no kind of claim or hold over us. You might think that we can say this automatically, and that this flows simply from the fact we are Christians. That kind of view doesn't agree with God, as is clear from what Paul says to the Ephesians:

*So stop telling lies. Let us tell our neighbours the truth, for we are all parts of the same body. And 'don't sin by letting anger control you.' Don't let the sun go down while you are still angry, for anger gives a foothold to the devil.*[173]

---

[171] Hebrews 10:12-14

[172] John 14:30 [nkjv]

[173] Ephesians 4:25-27

If we feel anger and don't deal with it well, we are giving the enemy a 'foothold'. There is a similar warning in Hebrews:

*Look after each other so that none of you fails to receive the grace of God. Watch out that no poisonous root of bitterness grows up to trouble you, corrupting many.*[174]

There is a warning here that bitterness can be a problem, and the picture is of a root of bitterness growing. If there is a root, clearly there must be some kind of ground for the root to grow in, so there is a sense here of our hearts being compared to territory.

Many of us struggle at some time or another with forgiveness. Forgiveness is, for Christians, optional in the sense that no-one else can make us do it and it is our choice when - and if - we forgive. However, it is not optional in the sense of what Jesus tells us as his followers. Satan has an interest in our refusing to forgive, or in postponing forgiveness, as Paul makes clear here:

*When you forgive this man, I forgive him, too. And when I forgive whatever needs to be forgiven, I do so with Christ's authority for your benefit, so that Satan will not outsmart us. For we are familiar with his evil schemes.*[175]

Paul is telling us that Satan tries to be smarter than us, and that he has evil schemes. At least one of those schemes is that we withhold forgiveness. If you find yourself withholding forgiveness, just ask yourself how comfortable you are about co-operating with the enemy!

It is possible - even for Christians - to be influenced in some way by the enemy: to experience, so to speak, some of our own personal territory being occupied in some way by our opponent. Jesus is of course our example to follow, and our model. He said, as we have already seen, that the enemy had no claim over him, no foothold, no landing place.

There is no reason in principle why we cannot get at least very close to being able to say the same thing as Jesus, with complete integrity and accuracy. However, it is not the case that all Christians are automatically in this position from the very first moment that they are born into the Kingdom of Heaven.

---

[174] Hebrews 12:15

[175] 2 Corinthians 2:10&11

While Jesus was with his twelve disciples, we know that it was possible for Satan to try to influence Jesus' decisions through advice from his own team. We know that the betrayal of Jesus by Judas Iscariot was the result of Judas responding to promptings from Satan.[176] Here is another example of precisely this sort of thing taking place. The context is of Jesus explaining to the disciples that it was going to be necessary for Jesus to die on the Cross, and that he would rise from the dead afterwards:

*But Peter took him aside and began to reprimand him for saying such things. 'Heaven forbid, Lord,' he said. 'This will never happen to you!' Jesus turned to Peter and said, 'Get away from me, Satan! You are a dangerous trap to me. You are seeing things merely from a human point of view, not from God's.'[177]*

This is very strong language from Jesus. There is no gentle correction here from the Lord, instead he very bluntly tells Peter that he is allowing himself to be the Devil's mouthpiece.

You might think that, while this was true of Peter before Jesus' death and resurrection, it couldn't possibly be true for us. If this is what you think, then please think again.

Jesus breathed the Holy Spirit into Peter and the other disciples after his resurrection and before his ascension into Heaven. After that, Peter was part of the team of apostles who were at the centre of the outpouring of the Holy Spirit on the Day of Pentecost. Peter was the one who could answer the crowd's question - namely, 'what do we have to do to get saved?' The Peter who lived after these events was, clearly, in the same position as regards being a son of the King as we Christians are today. And it is that Peter - the 'born again' Peter - who said this:

*So humble yourselves under the mighty power of God, and at the right time he will lift you up in honour. Give all your worries and cares to God, for he cares about you. Stay alert! Watch out for your great enemy, the devil. He prowls around like a roaring lion, looking for someone to devour. Stand firm against him, and be strong in your faith. Remember that your Christian brothers and sisters all over the world are going through*

---

[176] John 13:2

[177] Matthew 16:22&23

*the same kind of suffering you are.*[178]

The emphasis in Peter's warning might be more about external pressures such as persecution, but in any event he clearly identifies, for Christians, that the Devil is a real enemy.

We can find a very clear statement in James' letter to the effect that Christians can experience evil desires, and that Christians face a choice between aligning themselves with either God, or with God's enemy, the Devil:

*What is causing the quarrels and fights among you? Don't they come from the evil desires at war within you?....You adulterers! Don't you realise that friendship with the world makes you an enemy of God? I say it again: If you want to be a friend of the world, you make yourself an enemy of God....But he gives us even more grace to stand against such evil desires.....So humble yourselves before God. Resist the devil, and he will flee from you.*[179]

We are all in a war - a spiritual war. Jesus was acutely aware of the fact that his own apostles were going to face attack after his own ascension into Heaven. These next verses make this very clear, and they also shed some fascinating light on what we looked at earlier, namely that although Satan is now defeated, he still has some room to move and cause trouble:

*'Simon, Simon, Satan has asked to sift each of you like wheat. But I have pleaded in prayer for you, Simon, that your faith should not fail. So when you have repented and turned to me again, strengthen your brothers.'*[180]

Do you see what is going on here? The Devil asks for permission to persecute the Early Church, and it seems that what God does in response is not simply to deny permission, instead he focusses on how the Christians will respond to the trouble. How I behave - and how you behave - counts.

There is a very famous passage in Paul's letter to the Christians in Ephesus about the armour of God. The kit that Paul describes would have been understood by his readers as a description of standard Roman military

---

[178] 1 Peter 5:6-9

[179] James 4:1,4,6a&7

[180] Luke 22:31&32

gear. There are both defensive and offensive components to this. The armour includes weaponry and I do not believe it is described only for the purposes of defence. That said, Paul is clearly calling us to be wise about enemy attack - an attack upon ourselves as well as an attack upon other people around us:

*A final word: Be strong in the Lord and in his mighty power. Put on all of God's armour so that you will be able to stand firm against all strategies of the devil. For we are not fighting against flesh-and-blood enemies, but against evil rulers and authorities of the unseen world, against mighty powers in this dark world, and against evil spirits in the heavenly places. Therefore, put on every piece of God's armour so you will be able to resist the enemy in the time of evil. Then after the battle you will still be standing firm.*[181]

I don't know about you, but sometimes, if I find myself struggling with some kind of issue of sin in my life, it can feel as if God is being a little unfair in his various requirements. It can feel that to live my life in the way God wants me to live it is a little bit like I am giving up some of my own freedom, or perhaps my own fun. Perhaps you have felt the same way?

The attractiveness of the idea of being independent of God's ways, and of experiencing pleasure even if it is forbidden, or perhaps because it is forbidden in the first place, is what got all of us into trouble at the very beginning of humanity's story - in the Garden of Eden. If you or I find ourselves disagreeing with the Lord about something, perhaps it will help resolve the disagreement more quickly if we have a grasp of the fact that disagreeing with God means agreeing with Satan.

I am living in a time of war; there is a real, albeit defeated, enemy, who is still looking to do anything he can to destroy not only me, but all the people I love, and everyone else as well. In light of these facts, I will have a much more successful life if I set myself against any kind of co-operation with my sworn enemy's battle plans.

I mentioned it earlier, but I did not quote in full the passage in the Gospels where Jesus compares a person's life to a house, and paints a picture of the problems anyone will face if they fail to make their house hostile to unwelcome demonic guests. Here, as we close, is that passage:

---

[181] Ephesians 6:10-13

*'When an evil spirit leaves a person, it goes into the desert, seeking rest but finding none. Then it says, 'I will return to the person I came from.' So it returns and finds its former home empty, swept, and in order. Then the spirit finds seven other spirits more evil than itself, and they all enter the person and live there. And so that person is worse off than before. That will be the experience of this evil generation.* [182]

The context of what Jesus is saying here is that he is attacking the refusal of the religious leaders truly to receive Jesus' message. The personal application for each one of us is that we can experience a moment when God's Kingdom comes and delivers us from some kind of enemy oppression or bondage. The big question that arises is, will we make any change in the way that we live, or will we carry on just the same as before?

I urge you to pay serious attention to this. It may well be true most Christians will spend most of their lives living with some kind of area of their 'house' where there is a landing place for the enemy. However, there is a great deal we can do to make our houses as unpleasant for demons as possible.

If we live with compromise with the Devil, God will of course still be blessing us, but what sort of level of higher fruitfulness and success will we be missing as a result? We will still see some good things happen in terms of God's Kingdom being extended, but what things would we have seen if our spiritual weapons had been sharper still?

Within the house of your life, ask the Holy Spirit to guide you to any places where the kingdom of darkness has made itself at home. These places, or structures, could be a set of ungodly responses, such as something to do with unforgiveness, bitterness or judgment. They could be habits or addictions. They could be a set of beliefs - heart beliefs most likely, rather than intellectual, head beliefs - that are based on lies. Then pursue the process of tearing these things down. The dismantling process might well take some time, but much of the work can be done quite rapidly, if you really mean business with God.

May you be blessed as you allow the Lord to walk with you through the garden of your heart, and as you seek to remove any claims that the enemy

---

[182] Matthew 12:43-45

might have on you, and as you seek to demolish any structures that are designed (by the enemy) as landing points for enemy action.

May you, when you see Jesus face to face, know that you truly have fought the fight well, that you have run the race, and that you have proved to be a good and faithful servant to the Kingdom of God. May you have had a good war.

# Funny Money

Kù ∣ Storehouse

# CHAPTER 10

This Chapter is about money - or, more accurately, our attitudes towards money. You might ask, what is anything about money doing in a book exploring believers' freedom in Christ?

Around 500 years ago, Martin Luther observed that any believer needed to experience not one, but three, conversions. The first conversion is of the soul, the second is of the mind, and the third is of the purse (or wallet). The Bible is often misquoted as saying that money is the root of all evil. In fact, what the Bible says is that not money, but the <u>love</u> of money, is the root of many types of evil (or of every type of evil, depending on which translation you are reading).[183] The main point here is that money, in and of itself, is not the problem. The problem is our ability to love money.

The key thought for us in this Chapter is this:

*Each of you should give what you have decided in your heart to give, not reluctantly or under compulsion, for God loves a cheerful giver.*[184]

So, money can be a cheerful thing. Money can be funny. I suggest that, to the extent we think at all about being a cheerful giver, our concept of this has more to do with putting on a brave face and smiling as we give. Maybe we act as if it is a joy when really it is at best a chore, or is at worst positively painful. I have seen one or two video clips of people who look like they are having a good time taking part in a church offering. These happy folk are a good example to us all, but at the moment they seem to be in the minority. Why is this so?

God doesn't need our money. However, the way he has ordered our world seems to indicate that maybe he chooses to act as if he does need our money after all. Perhaps part of what he is doing is teaching us something about connectedness: about how it is never part of his plan for us to live as if we can be entirely independent of each other. Whatever the reasons are,

---

[183] 1 Timothy 6:10

[184] 2 Corinthians 9:7

we need to face up to our responsibility to deal with money in a way that is consistent with how Jesus dealt with it. Jesus gives us this stark challenge:

*You cannot serve both God and money.*[185]

To go along with the key thought about God loving cheerful giving, the value that I am going to invite you to consider is the value of generosity. I am not going to major on the issue of tithing – in other words, giving God a tenth of your wealth. I will certainly say something about tithing, but I want to see tithing in the context of the much bigger picture of the high value that God places on generosity.

Tithing is, at least for some Christians, a contentious subject. One side says that unless we are careful to give God at least 10%, we are disqualifying ourselves from at least some of God's blessings. The other side says that tithing as a requirement was superseded along with all the rest of the Jewish religious law when Jesus died for us, and to teach tithing is to promote law over grace and amounts to bringing legalism into the Church.

I believe that tithing remains an important principle for Christians, and that if we refuse to tithe, we put a blockage in the way of God's plans to bless us in various ways - and I am not necessarily talking about financial blessing. I respect the contrary view - being the view that because we are living in the good of the grace that God has revealed to us in Jesus, religious requirements such as tithing no longer apply. I respect that view, but I disagree with it.

Based on my own experience, very often the argument against tithing is used by people who are in fact giving less than a tenth of their income to God. Doubtless there are some Christians who are giving more than a tenth to God while at the same time holding firm to the belief that tithing is only an Old Testament concept. But I suspect that very often the anti-tithing argument conveniently gets us off the hook - that in many cases an argument against tithing is a justification for not giving to any significant degree.

In any event, the anti-tithing argument, however strong or weak it is, does not get us off the hook. God's call to us to come and be generous, just

---

[185] Matthew 6:24

like he is generous, is a much bigger challenge than the challenge of tithing. If we are challenged by tithing, then most likely we will be challenged by generosity. Generosity is a much bigger challenge than tithing.

I'm not trying to say that those in the 'anti-tithing' camp deliberately dream up arguments against tithing because they are mean and are coming up with schemes that are intended merely to justify a level of giving that is somewhere below 10%. As I have already said, I have respect for the arguments against tithing, and this is partly because I used to agree with them - and I certainly was not on any conscious level just trying to protect my bank balance.

By the time my thinking on this subject had changed, I had been involved in helping to lead my local church for quite a long time. At that time, the idea that my theology on any given subject could be wrong was very new to me. Now, I am much more used to the experience of my theology being open to change as part of the process of God's Spirit dealing with me.

During my spiritual journey I came under conviction, not only about the error of my previous and sincerely-held anti-tithing beliefs, but also about my views having had a negative effect on my local Church. I felt strongly that I had done a disservice to my Church in general and to my pastor in particular. I felt I had acted as a cork in the bottle, as a restraint on the pastor being able to teach clearly what the Bible has to say about finance. So, the time came when I felt it was appropriate to repent publicly, in front of the Church congregation, over this money issue.

For the record, here in a very brief form is what I feel you should know about tithing and its relevance to followers of Jesus in the 21st Century. To characterise tithing as nothing more than part of the Jewish religious law, as simply part of what was handed down along with the Ten Commandments, is to turn a blind eye to the truth that tithing was around long before Moses and the Ten Commandments.

When Abraham had his encounter with the mysterious figure of Melchizedek - the man who was both a king and a priest - Abram (as he was called at the time) gave him a tenth of everything he had.[186] Two

---

[186] Genesis 14:17-20

generations later, and over 400 years before Moses, Jacob had a divine encounter at a place he named Bethel and he made a promise that, if God would do certain things for him, he would give God a tenth.[187] All of this happened before the Ten Commandments were given. It had nothing to with the Jewish religious law.

Moving on to the golden age of Israel's history, King David wrote in one of his Psalms about the coming Messiah that,

*The Lord has taken an oath and will not break his vow: 'You are a priest forever in the order of Melchizedek.'*[188]

The Old Testament closes with the short and very beautiful book of Malachi. Just before Scripture in effect falls silent for a little over 400 years, there are some major final points made by God to his people. What are those points? There's a lack of respect for God in the way the people present their sacrifices at the Temple. There's a lack of integrity on the part of the priests in the Temple. There's a failure to honour marriage. There is a coming 'Day of the Lord' which will be preceded by a prophet coming like Elijah (this was fulfilled by John the Baptist) who would bring reconciliation between fathers and their children. And...there is a call to stop robbing God, a call to honour the tithe. This is backed up, uniquely, by God's call on his people to test him, and see whether he won't in fact flood them with blessings if they will just honour him.[189]

Tithing is not some kind of mere footnote in the Old Testament story. It is there very clearly long before the religious law was ever given, and it is given high prominence as the prophetic voice in the Old Testament falls silent, looking forward to the coming of Jesus.

When we move across to the New Testament, we find in Hebrews a fascinating study of the role of Jesus as the supreme and perfect High Priest. The writer of that book draws upon the prophecy contained within Psalm 110 that we have already seen and clearly sets before us the truth that

---

[187] Genesis 28:16-22

[188] Psalm 110:4

[189] Malachi 3:6-18

Jesus is indeed identified as a priest 'in the order of Melchizedek'.[190] If Jesus really is (and I emphasise the word is - not was) a priest in that order, what does that mean for us in terms of our relationship with him?

We don't know much about Melchizedek. We know that he brought bread and wine to share with Abram. Does that ring any bells for you? We know that Abram gave him a tenth of everything he owned.

Jesus is many things to me. He's my saviour, my brother, my friend, my lover and my Lord. He is also, according to Hebrews, my great High Priest, in the order of Melchizedek. For me, this means that he is due a tithe.

Let's now move back to the main point of this Chapter: generosity. The way that Jesus himself dealt with money, and the points he made about the world of finance and commerce in his teachings, are fascinating. Jesus constantly spoke about himself ushering in the Kingdom of God, or the Kingdom of Heaven. We need to understand that this Kingdom – the Kingdom where people can be healed, where people can be set free from demonic oppression, where broken hearts can be healed, and where relationships can be restored - has its own set of economic values. The economy of the Kingdom is very different from the economic system that operates in the world around us. We will take a little look at the Kingdom economy.

In Matthew[191] we are told about an incident when Jesus was challenged about whether or not he paid a particular tax - the Temple Tax. Jesus had an interesting discussion with Peter about whether they were liable for this tax, but in any event Jesus told Peter that he had a solution that would mean no-one would have to be offended. He told Peter to cast one of his fishing lines into the nearest lake, and to take the silver coin he would find in the mouth of the first fish that he caught.

What would life be like if we could find the cash to pay our taxes in such a supernatural way? Strangely enough, given Jesus' ability to source finances like this, he nonetheless made use of the generosity of others. His ministry team was, at least in part, funded by a group of women, including Chuza,

---

[190] Hebrews 7:1-15

[191] Matthew 17:24-27

the administrator of King Herod's household, and Susanna.[192]

Judas Iscariot was Jesus' treasurer. John 12:1-8 gives an interesting little insight into the state of this treasurer's heart. He took offence at the extravagant and sacrificial worship Jesus received from Mary, Lazarus' sister, who 'wasted' a vast amount of very expensive perfume to anoint Jesus' feet. Judas made a judgement about both Mary and Jesus here, dressed up in the self-righteous pretext that a better use of the sacrifice would have been to help feed the poor. How ironic that Judas soon afterwards took a bribe of silver coins, not in an act of worship towards to Jesus, but the opposite: an act of betrayal.

As part of his Sermon on the Mount teaching, Jesus makes some striking observations about how to deal with wealth:

*'Don't store up treasures here on earth, where moths eat them and rust destroys them, and where thieves break in and steal. Store your treasures in heaven, where moths and rust cannot destroy, and thieves do not break in and steal. Wherever your treasure is, there the desires of your heart will also be. Your eye is a lamp that provides light for your body. When your eye is good, your whole body is filled with light. But when your eye is bad, your whole body is filled with darkness. And if the light you think you have is actually darkness, how deep that darkness is! No one can serve two masters. For you will hate one and love the other; you will be devoted to one and despise the other. You cannot serve both God and money.'*[193]

We all have treasure, but we don't all have the same kind of treasure and we don't all keep our treasure in the same kind of place. There are connections between our treasure, our hearts, and our eyes. Money is a master who, if we let it, will demand our obedience. In truth, we have a choice to make. This choice will determine whether we live in the reality of the economy of God's Kingdom, or whether we subject ourselves to the demands of the world's economic system as part of the price we pay for obeying the money god.

Our choices about what we treasure are ultimately choices of the heart, not of the head, and in the long term the nature and location of our treasure

---

[192] Luke 8:1-3

[193] Matthew 6:19-24

will be a sure indicator of the condition of our heart. Whatever our treasure is, and wherever it is, we will find ourselves looking at it, or looking for it. It will take up many of our thoughts and our dreams, and many of our life decisions will be influenced, if not controlled, by questions such as: will this add to, or take away from, my treasure pile?

The fact is that Jesus wants us to have the same attitudes and thoughts about money that he himself displayed during his public ministry around 2,000 years ago. This fact will sometimes, for us, be an uncomfortable fact. This is because our attachment to money and some of the stuff that it can buy is so strong, and sadly sometimes in comparative terms our grasp of the realities of Heaven and the values of the Kingdom of God are relatively weak.

This is where 'the rubber hits the road'. This is the crux of the third conversion that Martin Luther spoke of, and which I mentioned at the start of this Chapter - the conversion of the 'purse'.

Jesus approved of sacrificial giving, even to a point that we might regard as unreasonable or irresponsible, as evidenced by this incident:

*Jesus sat down near the collection box in the Temple and watched as the crowds dropped in their money. Many rich people put in large amounts. Then a poor widow came and dropped in two small coins. Jesus called his disciples to him and said, 'I tell you the truth, this poor widow has given more than all the others who are making contributions. For they gave a tiny part of their surplus, but she, poor as she is, has given everything she had to live on.*[194]

We probably don't have any trouble at all in understanding Jesus' point about assessing what someone is giving by looking at it as a proportion of how much a person has. In absolute terms, what the widow gave was insignificant - just two small coins - but in relative terms it was a fortune, because those two small coins were all that she had. She wasn't feeling around in her pockets for some loose change as if she were giving God some kind of tip. She emptied herself.

What may well be much harder for us is to embrace the approval that Jesus implicitly seems to be giving to the act of sacrifice itself. He seems to

---

[194] Mark 12:41-44

be saying that the widow has done a very good thing. Applying the principles and values of the world around us, this doesn't really make any sense. The widow should have kept for herself the little that she had, and Jesus ought to have told her so.

In this next passage, we see a very clear challenge from Jesus about the way our love of money robs us of real treasure:

*Someone came to Jesus with this question: 'Teacher, what good deed must I do to have eternal life?' 'Why ask me about what is good?' Jesus replied. 'There is only One who is good. But to answer your question - if you want to receive eternal life, keep the commandments.' 'Which ones?' the man asked. And Jesus replied: 'You must not murder. You must not commit adultery. You must not steal. You must not testify falsely. Honour your father and mother. Love your neighbour as yourself.' 'I've obeyed all these commandments,' the young man replied. 'What else must I do?' Jesus told him, 'If you want to be perfect, go and sell all your possessions and give the money to the poor, and you will have treasure in heaven. Then come, follow me.'*

*But when the young man heard this, he went away sad, for he had many possessions. Then Jesus said to his disciples, 'I tell you the truth, it is very hard for a rich person to enter the Kingdom of Heaven. I'll say it again - it is easier for a camel to go through the eye of a needle than for a rich person to enter the Kingdom of God!'*

*The disciples were astounded. 'Then who in the world can be saved?' they asked. Jesus looked at them intently and said, 'Humanly speaking, it is impossible. But with God everything is possible.' Then Peter said to him, 'We've given up everything to follow you. What will we get?' Jesus replied, 'I assure you that when the world is made new and the Son of Man sits upon his glorious throne, you who have been my followers will also sit on twelve thrones, judging the twelve tribes of Israel. And everyone who has given up houses or brothers or sisters or father or mother or children or property, for my sake, will receive a hundred times as much in return and will inherit eternal life. But many who are the greatest now will be least important then, and those who seem least important now will be the greatest then.'*[195]

On more than one occasion, I have been part of a group that has discussed this passage. Almost without fail, once the passage has been read, someone in the group almost rushes to say something along the lines of,

---

[195] Matthew 19:16-28

well, the reason Jesus told this man that he ought to sell everything he had was because Jesus knew that this particular man had a particular hang-up about money and possessions.

It's as if what seems to be the obvious, and rather shocking, challenge of what Jesus is saying needs to be qualified and explained away before anyone makes the foolish move of perhaps wondering if Jesus is actually issuing a challenge to all of us. I believe it is a mistake to hurry to qualify this incident in such a way that it becomes largely irrelevant to most of us.

Reading the story, it's clear that the disciples didn't think they were off the hook. Jesus doesn't say in so many words that this rich young man was an extra special case. Instead, he makes a comment about how hard it is for rich people to get into the Kingdom. Probably not many of us see ourselves as rich, and probably most of us think that 'the rich' are a club to which we do not belong, and that 'the rich' are an elite minority. In contrast, the disciples were worried, as if they saw themselves as being part of the group that was in trouble, on the basis of what they had just heard Jesus say.

Peter's response - that they have given up everything for Jesus - might or might not be totally accurate. Possibly this is an example of enthusiastic exaggeration, possibly Peter is being accurate about his own position, but not everyone else's position. Otherwise, it's hard to see why the general reaction of the disciples is to identify most people, and maybe even themselves, in the category of camels trying to get through a narrow place.

It's possible that what is disturbing the disciples here isn't that they themselves are rich, and are therefore in difficulty; but that the rich are supposed to be enjoying God's special favour. If even the rich are going to have such a tough time accessing the Kingdom, even though they are blessed with wealth, what hope can there be for the rest of humanity?

As with many Bible passages, if you are inclined to do research, you can find that a great deal has been written about the eye of the needle and the camel, with various interpretations. The main thing to grasp, however, is the contrast in size between the camel and the eye of the needle and what Jesus says about the challenge we will face if we are rich.

Jesus gives them (or us?) hope when he says (my paraphrase) that it's almost impossible for a rich person to enter, but then again God can do the impossible. What is the impossible thing? Does it involve the rich person giving their money away, just as Jesus had just recommended to the rich man? Or is it to do with somehow staying rich but not being controlled by the money? And who is rich, and who is poor?

Let's move forward in time just a little to look at how the first Church - the one in Jerusalem - and then the Early Church in general engaged with the issues of finance and generosity.

When the Holy Spirit fell upon the first believers in an upper room in Jerusalem on Pentecost, thousands of people came to accept Jesus as Lord and Saviour in that one day and the first Church was catapulted into an amazing new adventure.

Often we Christians talk of wanting more of the Holy Spirit, or of wanting to see revival come to our Church, our city, or our country; but if the coming of the Holy Spirit would have the same effect upon us that it had upon those first believers, would we really and truly want it? I am not talking about the manifestations of the Holy Spirit on the Day of Pentecost itself - the apparent drunkenness and so on. I am talking about the manifestation of the Holy Spirit in the way these people lived their ordinary lives from day to day. The Bible tells us something about what that daily life of the first Church was like:

*They sold their property and possessions and shared the money with those in need. They worshiped together at the Temple each day, met in homes for the Lord's Supper, and shared their meals with great joy and generosity - all the while praising God and enjoying the goodwill of all the people. And each day the Lord added to their fellowship those who were being saved.*[196]

The Bible doesn't say in express terms that every Church in the future must be exactly like how the first Church was in the early days after the outpouring of the Holy Spirit on the day of Pentecost. Primarily what the Bible is doing in this passage is reporting facts, not telling us what God's opinions are. We can, of course, ask the Holy Spirit for guidance about what a Spirit-filled, sold-out-for-Jesus community of believers ought to look like in our time and in our culture.

Whatever conclusions you reach as a result of a discussion with the Holy Spirit on this question, one thing is clear: something was going on in the Jerusalem Church that was marking its members out as belonging to a

---

[196] Acts 2:45-47

radically new and different type of community. They were people who were so gripped by the life and vitality of what they had seen and experienced in God that it challenged fundamentally what they thought was important about the everyday practicalities of life. Apart from anything else, this had an impact on their domestic finances.

As if to show that the description of Church life in Acts 2 was not just some brief, uncharacteristic phase and that the first Church quickly progressed to some other, superior, more sensible, way of doing things, there is a very similar statement in Acts 4. This is in the context of continuing Church growth, persecution and evidence of the Holy Spirit's work in signs and wonders:

*All the believers were united in heart and mind. And they felt that what they owned was not their own, so they shared everything they had. The apostles testified powerfully to the resurrection of the Lord Jesus, and God's great blessing was upon them all. There were no needy people among them, because those who owned land or houses would sell them and bring the money to the apostles to give to those in need. For instance, there was Joseph, the one the apostles nicknamed Barnabas (which means 'Son of Encouragement'). He was from the tribe of Levi and came from the island of Cyprus. He sold a field he owned and brought the money to the apostles.*[197]

My belief is that what Acts tells us about what the life of the first Church was like gives us clues about what sort of things should be happening in any Church, regardless of its culture and location, where Christians are looking to live lives that are full of the Spirit. Our Churches might not follow exactly the same pattern as the first Church, perhaps they do not need to. However, I believe we should expect to find some kind of connection, some kind of similarity, some kind of resonance, between what we see going on in the everyday life of our own communities of faith, and the first Church in Jerusalem.

I do not claim to know to what extent any of the other major early congregations of Christians beyond Jerusalem followed more or less the example that was set inside Jerusalem itself. However, as you read the various letters to the various Churches that are recorded for our benefit in

---

[197] Acts 4:32-37

the New Testament, it is clear that there was a challenge to pay attention to the needs of others, and to be prepared to make generous financial donations to those needs.

We see these sorts of issues being worked through by Paul with the Church in Corinth. Paul was organising financial support for the first Church in Jerusalem from amongst various other Churches, including the Church at Corinth. We see in Paul's letters to that Church that he is working with them on a number of important issues to do with chaotic meetings, lack of discipline, sexual immorality and other things. It is, I suggest, no coincidence that he also needs to walk them though some issues to do with finance; there is a connection between how we deal with money and how we deal with the rest of life.

He encourages the Christians in Corinth to put aside an amount each week for this offering.[198] Possibly this is because he knows that, otherwise, they will be unable to deliver on whatever promises they have already made to Paul about the size of their contribution. They were the first Church to offer to help, but Paul tells them he wants them to finish what they started. He wants them to deliver on their promise.[199] Paul tells them he is not expecting to give what they don't have, but he wants them to be eager about giving out of the resources that they do in fact have.[200]

If all of this strikes you as mundane or unspiritual, the truth is that dealing with financial difficulties was part of the reality that faced Paul and other pioneers who spread the gospel and helped to extend God's Kingdom. The situation is no different today. Just as Jesus had people around him who gave him support with their money, the work of extending God's Kingdom today will require finance. And each of us has a part to play in making that finance available.

As an interesting contrast, and a challenge, Paul draws the attention of the Christians in Corinth to the way that the Churches in Macedonia have

---

[198] 1 Corinthians 16:1&2

[199] 2 Corinthians 8:10&11

[200] 2 Corinthians 8:12-15

responded. Those Churches are, says Paul, very poor and yet they have 'overflowed in rich generosity' and given even what they cannot afford.[201] It is worthwhile reflecting on the challenge that Paul lays down for them:

*I am not commanding you to do this. But I am testing how genuine your love is by comparing it with the eagerness of the other churches. You know the generous grace of our Lord Jesus Christ. Though he was rich, yet for your sakes he became poor, so that by his poverty he could make you rich.*[202]

One of the blockages to our operating in a generous way is a poverty mentality. We can say something like, you know I would love to be able to give, but I simply don't have any money to spare. Paul's challenge reminds us that God has been exceedingly generous towards us. He was rich, and he became poor so that he could make us rich.

Who is poor, and what is poverty? If we see ourselves as poor, what standards (or whose standards) are we using to measure poverty? For those of us who live in the West, the vast majority of us, including many of the very poorest, enjoy what looks like wealth to much of the rest of the world.

As a very famous Bible verse tells us:

*For God loved the world so much that he gave his one and only Son.*[203]

Why is it that God loves a cheerful giver? When we behave generously towards others, we are demonstrating that for us, personally, the penny has dropped, the scales have fallen from our eyes. We have woken up to the fact that God has been extremely generous towards us. Also, being generous is one of God's own character traits. When he sees us being generous, he sees us carrying the family likeness. To use again a word I used earlier when talking about the example that is given to us by the first Church in Jerusalem, there is a resonance in Heaven when we act generously here on Earth.

Fundamentally, the big question is this: are we confident that God is really going to look after our needs, even if in an act of generosity we give

---

[201] 2 Corinthians 8:1-3

[202] 2 Corinthians 8:8&9

[203] John 3:16

away to someone else the stuff that that we think is essential for our survival? In the Sermon on the Mount, after Jesus tells us that we cannot serve both God and money (we looked at this statement earlier in this Chapter), he has these words of comfort:

*'That is why I tell you not to worry about everyday life - whether you have enough food and drink, or enough clothes to wear. Isn't life more than food, and your body more than clothing? Look at the birds. They don't plant or harvest or store food in barns, for your heavenly Father feeds them. And aren't you far more valuable to him than they are? Can all your worries add a single moment to your life? And why worry about your clothing?*

*Look at the lilies of the field and how they grow. They don't work or make their clothing, yet Solomon in all his glory was not dressed as beautifully as they are. And if God cares so wonderfully for wildflowers that are here today and thrown into the fire tomorrow, he will certainly care for you. Why do you have so little faith? So don't worry about these things, saying, 'What will we eat? What will we drink? What will we wear?' These things dominate the thoughts of unbelievers, but your heavenly Father already knows all your needs. Seek the Kingdom of God above all else, and live righteously, and he will give you everything you need.* [204]

If, when it comes to my heart attitudes, I am living more like an orphan than a son, then I will need to do everything I possibly can to collect, and then to keep, what I need for life. If I don't look after my needs, then who will look after me? An orphan has no concept of there being anyone else who will care. In contrast, a son or daughter of the King who really knows who and what they are will not live under a compulsion to gather together as much as they can. He or she will not crave security in things as a protection against the day when their basic needs for shelter, food, clothing and warmth are not being met.

May each one of us approach our Father in Heaven with open hearts, open minds and open wallets and purses. May any insecurities we have about whether God really will look after us be healed, and may we experience the day by day reality of the joy of knowing that we have a generous Daddy. May we become evermore aware of our connections with

---

[204] Matthew 6:25-33

other people, and participate in the wonderful flow of giving and receiving, and of receiving and giving.

# The Sex Bomb

Chún | Pure

# CHAPTER 11

There is a very simple idea that lies at the heart of this Chapter. It is set out in a short and clear way in one of Paul's letters to the Church in Thessalonia:

*God's will is for you to be holy, so stay away from all sexual sin.*[205]

This statement, short and clear as it is, raises a number of questions and problems. What exactly is sexual sin? Is our interpretation of what the Bible says on this subject too clouded by the cultural conventions of our day? Is there any difference between sins relating to sex and any other sins? What if we cannot stop, or do not want to stop, whatever it is that we might be doing that God says is a sexual sin?

We run up against what look like some basic freedoms, some would say fundamental human rights, which seem to point in another direction. There is the freedom to love whoever we choose. There is the freedom to pursue pleasure, perhaps provided no-one else is hurt in the process.

At least in some cultures around the globe, we move in an environment which seems increasingly sexualised. The advertising and entertainment that surrounds us is heavy with messages - some of them subtle, some of them blatant - to do with the 'normality' of having sex. With whoever, whenever, however. The internet has proved to be an extremely effective vehicle for the spread of pornography.

When anyone connected with the Church tries to address some of the issues about our sexualised world, there can be additional pressure caused by the Church's own mistakes. It is all too easy to fall into the trap of being a hypocrite. The sexual misdemeanours of others might be highlighted while our own remain hidden, or our sins in other areas are somehow seen as unimportant in comparison with what we say are the more serious sexual sins of others. As an institution, the Church has tragically provided the cover for the sexual abuse of vulnerable people, including children.

---

[205] 1 Thessalonians 4:3

The task of setting out an accurate and balanced approach to the subject of sex, sexuality and sexual sin sometimes feels to me a little like negotiating a path through a minefield. There are so many mistakes that have been made, and that can be made again. The prospects of error and offence loom large.

This is partly why this Chapter has the title that it has. Calling someone a sex bomb means (the precise definition varies from one dictionary to another) that a woman is sexually attractive. It's interesting that in this common expression there is the idea of linking sexual attractiveness with destructive power.

Why is my title not <u>a</u> sex bomb, but <u>the</u> sex bomb? I am not writing exclusively about issues to do with sexually attractive women, nor am I writing exclusively about sexually attractive men. The bigger issue here is how our values - both our personal values and the values of society at large - can find themselves shaken by a sexual revolution.

It is as if a bomb has exploded in our midst; it is the sex bomb, and it raises all sorts of questions about both relationships and identity. In the reality of this explosion, the challenge for us is to make sure we are tuned in to what God is saying to us where we are right now. In the midst of the explosion of the sex bomb.

God pronounced what he did in making humanity in his image, male and female, as very good:

*Then God said, 'Let us make human beings in our image, to be like us. They will reign over the fish in the sea, the birds in the sky, the livestock, all the wild animals on the earth, and the small animals that scurry along the ground.' So God created human beings in his own image. In the image of God he created them; male and female he created them. Then God blessed them and said, 'Be fruitful and multiply. Fill the earth and govern it. Reign over the fish in the sea, the birds in the sky, and all the animals that scurry along the ground'…Then God looked over all he had made, and he saw that it was very good![206]*

In some circles it is a subject of controversy whether there are really any differences between men and women, at least if you scratch below the

---

[206] Genesis 1:26-28,31

surface of cultural conditioning and get to the deeper level of what is fundamentally true, as opposed to what society expects of the two genders. The Bible, however, is clear that it was in God's plan to reflect his character and nature not in just one, but two genders. Neither men nor women carry the family likeness, the 'image' of God, to the exclusion of the other. The Bible is also clear that part of God's plan in establishing humanity in this way was that there would be fruitful multiplication, that there would be babies.

The Genesis creation accounts include a statement about marriage. This is in the context of the first man, Adam, having something removed from him as part of the creation of the first woman, Eve, and his recognition of her as his life partner.

A verse from this passage in Genesis 2 is later quoted by Jesus when he is being asked questions about marriage and divorce:

*Then the Lord God made a woman from the rib, and he brought her to the man. 'At last!' the man exclaimed. 'This one is bone from my bone, and flesh from my flesh! She will be called 'woman,' because she was taken from 'man.''This explains why a man leaves his father and mother and is joined to his wife, and the two are united into one. Now the man and his wife were both naked, but they felt no shame.*[207]

Part of what we see here is that the act of sexual intercourse is not simply something that people can do, and then carry on separately as if they are both unaffected by it. We are told that the man and the woman, by 'joining', become one. This is an important truth and we come back to it later when we consider whether there is something special about sexual sin, as opposed to other types of sin.

Sex was God's idea in the first place, and it is part of what he declared, as we have already seen, to be very good. The Song of Solomon is, apart from anything else, a celebration of sexual love. Quite rightly, this book is referenced as having something to say about the relationship between the Church, as the Bride of Christ, and Jesus as the Bridegroom. That said, we should never forget that the book is also about sex between a man and a woman. Some people who have Bibles somewhere on their bookshelves

---

[207] Genesis 2:22-25

might be shocked to find that it contains such raunchy material as this:

*How beautiful are your sandalled feet, O queenly maiden. Your rounded thighs are like jewels, the work of a skilled craftsman. Your navel is perfectly formed like a goblet filled with mixed wine. Between your thighs lies a mound of wheat bordered with lilies. Your breasts are like two fawns, twin fawns of a gazelle. Your neck is as beautiful as an ivory tower. Your eyes are like the sparkling pools in Heshbon by the gate of Bathrabbim. Your nose is as fine as the tower of Lebanon overlooking Damascus. Your head is as majestic as Mount Carmel, and the sheen of your hair radiates royalty. The king is held captive by its tresses. Oh, how beautiful you are! How pleasing, my love, how full of delights!*[208]

There is no getting away from the fact that the writer of this book was most definitely talking about sexual love, whatever other perfectly valid spiritual principles can be bolted on to this when we are thinking about the relationship between Christ and his Church. As if to provide an interesting counterpoint to the celebration of the erotic that the Song Of Solomon clearly contains, this same book carries within it a refrain that hints at the potentially destructive power of this kind of love. The writer says this in two parts of the book:

*Promise me, O women of Jerusalem, by the gazelles and wild deer, not to awaken love until the time is right.*[209]

As we move along in our consideration of what God's Word has to say about this subject, how did Jesus deal with questions about sexual morality? His words are piercing:

*'You have heard the commandment that says, 'You must not commit adultery.' But I say, anyone who even looks at a woman with lust has already committed adultery with her in his heart. So if your eye - even your good eye - causes you to lust, gouge it out and throw it away. It is better for you to lose one part of your body than for your whole body to be thrown into hell. And if your hand - even your stronger hand - causes you to sin, cut it off and throw it away. It is better for you to lose one part of your body than for your whole body to be thrown into hell. You have heard the law that says, 'A man can divorce his wife by merely giving her a written notice of divorce.' But I say that a man who*

---

[208] Song Of Solomon 7:1-6

[209] Song of Solomon 2:7,3:5

*divorces his wife, unless she has been unfaithful, causes her to commit adultery. And anyone who marries a divorced woman also commits adultery.* [210]

This is radical stuff on a whole number of levels. Time and again in the Sermon on the Mount, Jesus takes a statement from the Law (the Jewish religious code handed down by God to his chosen people via Moses) and turns it on its head. Jesus opens up the world of heart attitudes, secret motivations, and shifts the focus away from external appearances to internal, hidden realities.

It is not the case that Jesus takes the Law - which is hard for someone to observe perfectly, even for one day - and says to his own followers, if you thought the old code was hard, wait until you see the new code that I am going to burden you with! A study of Romans is very useful in showing clearly that God's plan has always been that people will be saved not by observance of a set of rules, but by trusting in Jesus on the basis of what he did for us on the Cross.[211]

So - no, Jesus is not laying upon us the burden of a yet more unbearable set of rules to obey. What Jesus is doing is revealing to us more of the character of the person who wrote the Law in the first place: God himself. Jesus is inviting us to start a journey of having our own hearts changed so that we will, more and more, have a truly godly character. Jesus is announcing the new age spoken of by the Old Testament prophet Ezekiel:

*Then I will sprinkle clean water on you, and you will be clean. Your filth will be washed away, and you will no longer worship idols. And I will give you a new heart, and I will put a new spirit in you. I will take out your stony, stubborn heart and give you a tender, responsive heart. And I will put my Spirit in you so that you will follow my decrees and be careful to obey my regulations.* [212]

As with other moral issues, when in the Sermon on the Mount Jesus addresses sexual issues, it does not make for comfortable reading. Jesus takes the commandment about not committing adultery and teaches that

---

[210] Matthew 5:27-32

[211] Romans 3:21-26

[212] Ezekiel 36:25-27

lustful looking amounts to adultery of the heart. He recommends drastic measures; self-mutilation, no less.

The Gospels do not contain any record of Jesus' followers cutting off their own hands or gouging out their own eyes as an anti-lust measure. This means one of a number of things. Perhaps the writers of the Gospels, under the inspiration of course of the Holy Spirit, did not feel it necessary to record such details. Alternatively, Jesus' followers generally were not troubled by any lustful feelings. Another possibility is that they were a disobedient bunch who refused to take what Jesus said seriously. Finally - and most likely - Jesus' hearers understood perfectly well that Jesus was using a figure of speech. Actual self-mutilation is not what is needed. What is needed is an attitude of the heart that takes seriously the danger that is posed by lust.

Jesus does something truly extraordinary when he teaches that what the Law allowed as regards divorce in fact gave men room to commit adultery. We know from the Gospel accounts that the disciples asked Jesus privately about this, and I imagine they were struggling with a major shift in worldview that was being presented to them. How could it possibly be adultery for a man to marry again after a divorce?

The only 'escape clause' Jesus allowed was if the divorce was on the basis of the first wife having been unfaithful sexually. Remarriage generally was permitted in the Law of Moses, so it could not be adultery, could it? And yet, Jesus says that remarriage is, indeed, adultery - unless the previous divorce was triggered by the other party having a sexual relationship outside of the marriage.

If we read Jesus' teaching on sexual morals with an open mind and an open heart, we will know that most of us fall seriously short of his standards, at least some of the time. Like a laser light, Jesus zeroes in to the underlying point: are we faithful, or unfaithful? And do we care enough about the connection between our bodies and our hearts to take proper care of what we do with both?

Most of us are, at least some of the time, falling short of the kind of life that Jesus wants us to live. As we look around us, most other people are similarly in trouble, at least some of the time. To the extent that we spend any energy considering the sexual morality of other people, it would be healthy to be filled with compassion. Many of us, possibly most of us, are all pretty much in the same boat - or at least, we have been in a similar kind of boat at some point.

If I had to select one passage in the Bible that has the most to say to us today when it comes to striking a healthy balance when it comes to sexual issues, here it is:

*Jesus returned to the Mount of Olives, but early the next morning he was back again at the Temple. A crowd soon gathered, and he sat down and taught them. As he was speaking, the teachers of religious law and the Pharisees brought a woman who had been caught in the act of adultery. They put her in front of the crowd. 'Teacher,' they said to Jesus, 'this woman was caught in the act of adultery. The law of Moses says to stone her. What do you say?'*

*They were trying to trap him into saying something they could use against him, but Jesus stooped down and wrote in the dust with his finger. They kept demanding an answer, so he stood up again and said, 'All right, but let the one who has never sinned throw the first stone!' Then he stooped down again and wrote in the dust. When the accusers heard this, they slipped away one by one, beginning with the oldest, until only Jesus was left in the middle of the crowd with the woman. Then Jesus stood up again and said to the woman, 'Where are your accusers? Didn't even one of them condemn you?' 'No, Lord,' she said. And Jesus said, 'Neither do I. Go and sin no more.* [213]

One of the things that screams out from this incident is: where was the man who was committing adultery with the woman? Why was only the woman brought before Jesus? I suspect this reflects a culture where men saw women as the cause of their own lustful feelings. More generally, it illustrates a hypocrisy trap that many of us could easily fall into. The sins of other people can become our focus, when in reality we ought to be paying attention to dealing with our own sins.

Jesus refuses to condemn the woman. At the same time, he issues her with a challenge. He tells her to stop sinning. He does two things here at the same time that seem to contradict each other. This is when, in contrast, we probably find ourselves drawn to doing just one of these. Either we major on not condemning, or on pointing out the other people's errors and telling them to behave better. Jesus holds two apparently contradictory principles in balance, or tension, at the same time.

---

[213] John 7:53-8:11

We would all do very well to keep this story very much in mind if and when we find the behaviour of other people offensive, distasteful or just downright ungodly. This doesn't only apply to behaviour has something to do with the whole area of sex and sexuality.

One reason why Jesus' example might seem just too hard for us to follow is that we might have a false concept of what condemnation is. Jesus told the woman that he didn't condemn her. Did this mean he was saying that what she had done was OK, that it didn't matter? Clearly not. Otherwise, why did Jesus tell her to stop sinning?

Condemning someone is about writing them off as a hopeless case, making a final decision that they do not make the grade. We look at the underlying Greek word here for condemnation - *krino* - in Chapter 12 (Word Power). It has the sense of a final decision being made in a court of law.

Jesus didn't, so to speak, write the woman off simply because what she had done was wrong. He was prepared to keep open the possibility for her of a better future, while at the same time being clear with her about what was right, and what was wrong. We could very easily minimise the meaning of this 'niceness' of Jesus. We could say that her being able to walk away from this encounter with some kind of hope, some kind of relationship with God, was conditional upon her obeying Jesus' instruction to her - don't do that bad thing again.

It isn't within the Gospel account, but try to imagine what would have happened if this same woman had been brought again to Jesus - maybe days, weeks or months later - having committed adultery again? Would Jesus say, during that second interview, that this time the woman had blown it and that now he really was going to condemn her? Surely not.

I am sure that, if the woman were to fail again and again, and if she were to come back to Jesus again and again, she would find she was given more than just one further chance - she would get a second chance, and on and on. Just how many chances would Jesus be prepared to give the woman after the second chance? How many chances has he given you, if you apply this question to your own sins, whether or not they are sexual sins? What sort of number of chances do you think is a good number, a fair number?

I am risking labouring this point because it is too easy to move on. It is too easy to look at Jesus' kindness, his mercy, his refusal to condemn, and then quickly to take a position which is almost enthusiastic in its drive to be unkind, unmerciful, and condemning. And all of this can be done in the name of holding faithfully to God's standards and in the name of being zealous and faithful about a commitment to what the Bible says is right and wrong.

Let there be no misunderstanding. In the realm of sexual morality, I want to be holding completely to Biblical standards. Great care, however, should be taken to ensure that in working out how those standards apply in practice, we are never more harsh than Jesus would be, and that we aim to be as kind as Jesus would be, at least to the extent that we ever can come close to his level of kindness.

In all honesty, I would prefer it if God were less concerned than he seems to be about what I do with my body, and what you do with yours. If we disagree with God about this, we know who is in the right and who is in the wrong. I might neither like it nor understand it, but the body matters to God. Although there is nothing to be gained in trying to persuade God that some of our sins are less of a problem that some of our other sins, sexual sins do appear to have a special status:

*Don't you realise that your bodies are actually parts of Christ? Should a man take his body, which is part of Christ, and join it to a prostitute? Never! And don't you realise that if a man joins himself to a prostitute, he becomes one body with her? For the Scriptures say, 'The two are united into one.' But the person who is joined to the Lord is one spirit with him. Run from sexual sin! No other sin so clearly affects the body as this one does. For sexual immorality is a sin against your own body. Don't you realise that your body is the temple of the Holy Spirit, who lives in you and was given to you by God? You do not belong to yourself, for God bought you with a high price. So you must honour God with your body.*[214]

When we allow ourselves to look clearly at what God says about sexual conduct, it is so easy to get bogged down with pointing the finger at what other people are doing that is wrong, or with feeling that God is being some kind of prudish spoilsport. However, the heart of the matter is this: we are embodied spirits. Our bodies are intended to represent who and what we truly are. Even more than that, our bodies are also intended to be able to

---

[214] 1 Corinthians 6:15-20

hold in some way the Spirit of God himself. It is because of the very high calling and great destiny that God has for you that he wants your body to come into alignment with those things.

May each one of us, without fear, be able to embrace the love and higher calling that lies behind these words:

*God's will is for you to be holy, so stay away from all sexual sin.*[215]

I will close this Chapter with some thoughts about how we deal with people who, from our point of view, are living in a way that is not consistent with God's standards as to sexual purity.

First of all, there is always the danger of hypocrisy. Although it is true that the Bible says sexual sin is special in the way that it affects our own bodies, the Bible also tells us that all sin is sin.

I can, if I want to, draw up a list of specific sins, including some sexual sins. You could also draw up your own list. Quite possibly, there would be some big differences in those two lists. Who is right, and who is wrong? We could also try to give scores against specific sins on these lists as to how serious those sins are, and what priority should be given to stopping some of those sins as more of a priority than other sins. Again, most likely our lists would differ, if only slightly.

The big question is, what kind of list would God himself write? Does he, indeed, have any interest in such lists? Compared to God, our understanding is so limited, our assessments are so imperfect, our discernment is so flawed. I would not want to be dealt with according to any such list that anyone else had written, unless it was God's list.

When it comes to sin - including but not limited to sexual sin - there is so much that we don't see, we don't know and we don't understand. In contrast, God does see, he does know and he does understand.

The mandate we carry as part of Jesus' Great Commission is not to beat the world up with messages about how miserable it is - rather, our mandate is to do what we can to introduce the world to the real, authentic, Jesus.

It is healthy to keep remembering the attitude of Jesus and the woman who was caught in adultery. Jesus refused to condemn her. Yes, he was

---

[215] 1 Thessalonians 4:3

clear about standards - but he refused to condemn.

Some sins are obvious, some are hidden - and I am not just talking here about sexual sins. We could easily become agitated about some issue to do with sexual conduct and yet be totally unmoved by a heart issue such as greed. We can have an idea that a particular sin must definitely be addressed and dealt with before a person can be 'acceptable'.

In doing so, we have applied some kind of pecking order to sin. In doing so, we have failed to respect that other person's own journey of faith, and we have failed to respect God's entitlement to set his own agenda for when, and in what order of importance, certain sins should be addressed. We have, in effect, placed ourselves in the position of judge - dare I say, in the position of one who condemns. We would not seem to be doing very well in comparison with the way Jesus dealt with the woman who was caught in adultery.

I am not going to try to pretend that in these situations everything is always easy. I suggest that in such situations, there is a question that we would always be well advised to take on board - namely, 'who am I to judge'?

Rather than waste a lot of time and energy pointing the finger at other people, the key relevance of the subject of sexual purity to the general theme of this book - freedom - is that what I do with and to my body matters to God.

Any sexual relationships that I have had carry implications about my having been joined in a sense that is more than merely physical. For every sexual relationship that has been and gone, I have given part of myself away - there has been a tearing of 'one flesh'.

What Jesus says about what lust is, and how serious it is, raises big questions about the thoughts that I entertain. There might be issues about whether sex itself is some kind of escape from another issue I am avoiding. There might be issues about whether how I see my gender and my sexuality generally are good or bad, and whether there is something there that needs to be repaired.

I need to give Jesus permission to do whatever work he feels is needed in order to move me along the route to my personal best. If other people knew how much progress (or how little progress) I am making, they might have views about what my priorities ought to be. They might disagree with me about whether certain things I do are in fact sins or not.

If those other people are trusted friends to whom I have given the right to speak into my life, then of course I would be wise to pay attention to them. If those other people are just other people, then I would prefer them to stop pointing their fingers at me, and to concentrate on what Jesus is saying to them for themselves.

Just as much as I want people like you and me to be able to live alongside each other without condemning each other, I also want each of us to take very seriously that God may well, in his own time and his own way, have important things to say to each of us about our sexual identity and/or our sexual practice.

As we pursue our personal best, let's each bear in mind something that we know about God's will for us - I have already repeated it, but it is worth repeating yet again as a closing comment:

*God's will is for you to be holy, so stay away from all sexual sin.*[216]

---

[216] 1 Thessalonians 4:3

# Word Power

Zào | Make

# CHAPTER 12

This Chapter is all about the significance of the words we use. There are two themes that we will consider. The first is the power of the spoken word, both for good and for bad: the ability of words to bring blessing or to invoke a curse. The second is the way the things we say can reveal something about what is going on inside, in our hearts.

Very often our words are signs, showing us that we need to change. Amongst other things, we will look at how easy it is to judge other people. Our words can damage not only others, but also ourselves. There is very often a clear connection between the attitudes of our hearts and the words that come out of our mouths.

It might seem odd to you to think of words as having any great significance, or power. Some say that 'talk is cheap'. If someone's actions don't match what they say, we might think they are some kind of hypocrite. We might think that what counts is not what you say, but what you do. As the saying goes, 'actions speak louder than words'.

Most of the time we don't spend any great care or energy thinking about what we say before we say it. In any given day, possibly most of what we say is fairly mundane, everyday conversation. Some of the time we will be reacting to something funny, irritating, boring, or whatever. Although a process must be going on in our brains before we speak, mostly we are hardly even aware of it. Talking is as natural as breathing, and our words disappear into the air around us just like breath. Our words might seem just as insubstantial as just so much hot air.

On the other hand, if we think someone is a hypocrite because of an inconsistency between their words and their actions, doesn't this mean that we know, deep down, that there shouldn't be any such mismatch? And aren't we all hoping that someone, somewhere, will listen - not just hear, but pay proper, careful attention - to what we have to say?

It's very clear from the Bible that in God's economy, words are powerful. The account of creation in Genesis sets the scene for us:

*In the beginning God created the heavens and the earth. The earth was formless and empty, and darkness covered the deep waters. And the Spirit of God was hovering over the surface of the waters. Then God said, 'Let there be light,' and there was light.*[217]

God's words have creative power. Genesis also tells us that Mankind was made in God's image or likeness. Part of what this means is that we have received some kind of authority to shape the world around us, with our words as well as our actions:

*Then the Lord God said, 'It is not good for the man to be alone. I will make a helper who is just right for him.' So the Lord God formed from the ground all the wild animals and all the birds of the sky. He brought them to the man to see what he would call them, and the man chose a name for each one. He gave names to all the livestock, all the birds of the sky, and all the wild animals. But still there was no helper just right for him.*[218]

There is more to this passage than just the amazing idea that God, who I am sure could have come up with very good names for the animals himself, was content to pass this job to Adam. There is a link between the naming process and it becoming clear that none of the animals could deal with Adam's 'alone-ness'. It's as if part of what naming the animals was all about was this: Adam uncovering what the character, or nature, of each animal was - and how alone he was.

Just as with creation, so with our becoming followers of Jesus, words play a crucial part. Jesus is himself described as the 'Word' at the start of John's Gospel.[219] None of us gets the chance to receive Jesus unless someone else speaks, or communicates in some other way:

*But how can they call on him to save them unless they believe in him? And how can they believe in him if they have never heard about him? And how can they hear about him unless someone tells them?*[220]

Being born again, joining God's family as an adopted son or daughter, requires that we go beyond just an internal, unspoken 'yes' to him:

---

[217] Genesis 1:1-3

[218] Genesis 2:18-20

[219] John 1:1-5

[220] Romans 10:14

*If you confess with your mouth that Jesus is Lord and believe in your heart that God raised him from the dead, you will be saved. For it is by believing in your heart that you are made right with God, and it is by confessing with your mouth that you are saved.*[221]

Revelation describes at one point a war in heaven between the angels, led by archangel Michael, against the Devil and his demons. The 'brethren', in other words all believers, have suffered at the Devil's hands. A voice in Heaven declares that the brethren have overcome the Devil,

*...by the blood of the Lamb and by the word of their testimony, and they did not love their lives to the death.*[222]

So this tells us that our experience of victory over evil requires two things - the work of Jesus on the Cross and our agreeing with that work. We apply that work to our own lives by agreeing with it in terms of the words we actually speak.

Let us spend a little while looking at Jesus' use of words. Jesus was amazed at the faith of the Roman Centurion who had grasped that Jesus could work a healing miracle simply by saying that the healing had happened, without Jesus even being in the same place as the person who needed to be healed.[223] One of his disciples, Peter, declared at one point that, even though many people had deserted Jesus because his teaching offended them, Peter and the other close followers could not leave him because he had

'*...the words that give eternal life*'.[224]

Many, though not all, of Jesus' works of healing and deliverance involved him making some kind of declaration. In addition, he demonstrated authority over nature itself simply by speaking to it. Once, when his disciples woke him up because the boat they were travelling in was being tossed around in a storm, he 'rebuked' the storm and everything was calm. They asked themselves:

---

[221] Romans 10:9&10

[222] Revelation 12:11

[223] Matthew 8:7-9

[224] John 6:68

*Who can this be, that even the winds and the sea obey him?*[225]

Jesus blessed things: he spoke something out over them, thanking God for them. He blessed loaves;[226] he blessed fish;[227] and he blessed wine.[228] Jesus also blessed human beings: he blessed children[229] and he blessed his disciples.[230] Perhaps surprisingly, we also know that Jesus was capable of cursing, again showing his ability to shape his environment with his words. The Gospels include this account about Jesus being disappointed with a fig tree that had no fruit to satisfy his hunger:

*He came to it and found nothing on it but leaves, and said to it, 'Let no fruit grow on you ever again'. Immediately the fig tree withered away. And when the disciples saw it, they marvelled, saying, 'How did the fig tree wither away so soon?'*[231]

In case you are tempted to think that what Jesus is showing us is an aspect of his divinity and that our approach to words is supposed to be completely different, consider what Jesus said to his disciples as his commentary on the fig tree incident:

*'Assuredly, I say to you, if you have faith and do not doubt, you will do not only what was done to the fig tree, but also if you say to this mountain, 'Be removed and be cast into the sea', it will be done.*[232]

Before we move on from this brief look at Jesus' example to us, I want to mention one of my favourite stories from the Gospels, even though this story is more about actions than words:

*…a leper came and worshipped him, saying, 'Lord, if you are willing, you can make*

---

[225] Matthew 8:27 [nkjv]

[226] Mark 8:6

[227] Mark 8:7

[228] Matthew 26:27

[229] Mark 10:16

[230] Luke 24:50&51

[231] Matthew 21:19&20 [nkjv]

[232] Matthew 21:21 [nkjv]

*me clean.' Then Jesus put out his hand and touched him, saying, 'I am willing; be cleansed.' Immediately his leprosy was cleansed.*[233]

The leper did not ask Jesus to touch him, he simply asked to be cleansed, to be healed of his leprosy. Leprosy raised issues of uncleanness from a religious, ritualistic point of view as well as from a health point of view. No-one who was free of leprosy would want to touch a leper, for fear of what would be transferred from the leper - uncleanness and possibly sickness. Jesus reversed all of that. It was not a question of the leper contaminating Jesus, but rather of Jesus decontaminating the leper. Jesus was changing, shaping the world around him.

I mention this because it fits with what I have been describing about the way God's world works. God is the supreme communicator. He has been speaking from the very start, calling things into being and shaping the environment. His desire is that we follow his example and speak to creation, to other people, and even to ourselves, in a way that is consistent with God's character and purposes.

This brings us to an important question. In the real world, what is our actual experience of how we use this power of words? It is probably quite easy to bring to mind examples of the ways other people have spoken to us in an unkind or unhelpful way. It may be more difficult for us to face up to our own shortcomings in this department. Is it possible that we are harming others in the way we use words? Is it possible that we are even harming ourselves?

The book of James contains an amazing passage about the destructive, negative power of the 'tongue', the words that we use:

*...if we could control our tongues, we would be perfect and could also control ourselves in every other way. We can make a large horse go wherever we want by means of a small bit in its mouth. And a small rudder makes a huge ship turn wherever the pilot chooses to go, even though the winds are strong. In the same way, the tongue is a small thing that makes grand speeches. But a tiny spark can set a great forest on fire.*

*And the tongue is a flame of fire. It is a whole world of wickedness, corrupting your entire body. It can set your whole life on fire, for it is set on fire by hell itself. People can*

---

[233] Matthew 8:2&3 [nkjv]

*tame all kinds of animals, birds, reptiles, and fish, but no one can tame the tongue. It is restless and evil, full of deadly poison. Sometimes it praises our Lord and Father, and sometimes it curses those who have been made in the image of God.*[234]

It's quite a statement (in verse 2) that if we could just control our tongues, we could control everything else about us. You might think that words are of so little value (and that changing the way we speak would be such a simple thing) that this cannot possibly be true. We have of course already looked at the significance of words. Even if our own culture tells us that words do not matter, God's wisdom tells us something else.

If you realise that some, perhaps even much, of what you say is damaging, how easy would it actually be to change the way you speak, to change the sorts of things that you say?

There is some teaching given by Jesus which helps us understand why and how there is a strong link between control of our tongues and control of the rest of our lives. Jesus was being criticised by some religious leaders for allowing his disciples to not wash their hands before they ate bread. This was not a hygiene issue, it was a religious issue, to do with ritual cleansing. And it was not a problem about the disciples breaking part of the Ten Commandments and the other laws which were handed to Moses centuries before by God himself. This ritual cleansing was merely a custom. Jesus took issue with his critics, and said this:

*Then Jesus called to the crowd to come and hear. 'Listen,' he said, 'and try to understand. It's not what goes into your mouth that defiles you; you are defiled by the words that come out of your mouth.'... Then Peter said to Jesus, 'Explain to us the parable that says people aren't defiled by what they eat.' 'Don't you understand yet?' Jesus asked. 'Anything you eat passes through the stomach and then goes into the sewer. But the words you speak come from the heart - that's what defiles you. For from the heart come evil thoughts, murder, adultery, all sexual immorality, theft, lying, and slander. These are what defile you. Eating with unwashed hands will never defile you.*[235]

The crucial thought here is that our words come from the heart. It follows that if our heart changes, our words will change. This is what the

---

[234] James 3:2-9

[235] Matthew 15:10&11,15-20

passage in James is concerned with: the challenge of self-control. If we try to change our words without changing our hearts, we will struggle. By contrast, if our words change, it's a sure sign that something important has taken place in our hearts.

At another time, when other religious leaders were trying to suggest that Jesus' authority over demons was some kind of Devil-inspired trick, Jesus said something very similar about the relationship between our hearts and what we say. He coupled it with a warning that in his role as our future judge, he will take note of our words:

*'A tree is identified by its fruit. If a tree is good, its fruit will be good. If a tree is bad, its fruit will be bad. You brood of snakes! How could evil men like you speak what is good and right? For whatever is in your heart determines what you say. A good person produces good things from the treasury of a good heart, and an evil person produces evil things from the treasury of an evil heart. And I tell you this, you must give an account on judgment day for every idle word you speak. The words you say will either acquit you or condemn you.* [236]

It might be difficult to come up with a comprehensive list of all the bad ways that we talk about others and ourselves. The New Testament makes some attempts to list some of the ways, although you could probably think of some more:

*...quarrelling, jealousy, anger, selfishness, slander, gossip, arrogance, and disorderly behaviour...*[237]

and,

*...bitterness, rage, anger, harsh words, and slander...*[238]

not forgetting,

*...anger, rage, malicious behaviour, slander, and dirty language.*[239]

Bear in mind that these letters in the New Testament were written to Churches; Christians were thinking, behaving and talking in these unhealthy

---

[236] Matthew 12:33-37

[237] 2 Corinthians 12:20

[238] Ephesians 4:31

[239] Colossians 3:8

ways. If we feel we are struggling over our use, mis-use or abuse of words, we can know that this is not a new problem. Our brothers and sisters in the Early Church faced similar challenges.

I am not going to try to do a detailed analysis of all the various types of ungodly talk we might engage in. What I will do is explore two particular areas. These are: judging; and negative self-pronouncements.

Judging is worthy of special attention for a number of reasons. It is not entirely obvious what judging actually is. Jesus is very clear in his teaching that we shouldn't do it. I believe that judging is foundational to unhealthy language. If we can grasp what the problem with judging is, and if we can learn how to spot when we are falling into the trap of judging, this will provide a good basis for dealing with other challenges.

Something very good about the connection between our words and our hearts is that, as we learn how to tune into what is really coming out of our mouths, we will find that the words we use give us clues as to what there is in our hearts that God would like our permission to change, areas where we would benefit from some Holy Spirit expertise in sorting out the gardens of our hearts.

So, let's address the subject of judging, of being judgmental. This is not just a question of words, it is also a question of heart attitudes. As we have seen, there is a connection between what we say and what is in our hearts. If in our hearts we are harbouring judgmental attitudes, most likely these will spill out from time to time in what we say, whether or not we deliberately intend to make judgments.

Jesus dealt with judging very clearly and firmly in his Sermon on the Mount:

*'Do not judge others, and you will not be judged. For you will be treated as you treat others. The standard you use in judging is the standard by which you will be judged.* [240]

Jesus is not telling us that we must never have an opinion about people, that we must never try to exercise some measure of discernment about people or assess how much we think we can trust them.

In the original texts the Greek word used here for judging is *krino*. This

---

[240] Matthew 7:1&2

word has the sense of a decision in a law court, of someone being sentenced by a judge in court, or of being condemned. It is exactly the same word that is used in this very well known passage:

*God sent his Son into the world not to judge the world, but to save the world through him.*[241]

God did not send Jesus into the world to *krino* the world, but to save it. Clearly whatever Jesus is forbidding has nothing to do with making sensible assessments about how much you can trust someone, for example.

We can see this difference in Paul's letter to the church in Philippi. Part of his prayer for those believers was that:

*...your love may abound still more in knowledge and all discernment...*[242]

The Greek words here for 'knowledge' and 'discernment' are not *krino*, nor anything like it; they are *epignosis* and *aesthesis*. Exercising discernment is not the same thing as being judgmental.

Jesus makes it clear later in John[243] that although Jesus has not been sent to judge the world, there will be a later point in time, at the end when Jesus returns, when he will in fact act as judge. There is something very important here to grasp which is foundational to knowing why it is wrong for us to judge.

God is perfectly entitled to judge us. In his magnificent wisdom, mercy and grace, he is delaying judgment. Jesus has come into our world to give all of us the opportunity to be reconciled with God, to become adopted members of his family and escape the otherwise inevitable consequence of our predicament - permanent separation from God.

It is an understatement to say that we each should be very grateful that God has suspended judgment so that we have had the time to accept the gift of eternal life. We should also be very grateful that this judge has been prepared to come to our planet as a human being, he has experienced first hand what it is really like to live here, and he has paid an enormous price in

---

[241] John 3:17

[242] Philippians 1:9

[243] John 5:24-30

terms of pain and suffering to make a way for us to receive God's amazing free gift. We could not have a better judge.

Since God is prepared to suspend judgment, and since he has paid such a price to make this suspension worthwhile, how dare you or I act as if we can put ourselves in God's place and bring forward the date for judgment?

To judge someone is to condemn that person. It can vary in its intensity or severity. You might quite consciously treat that person as a piece of rubbish, as being of absolutely no value. Toward the other end of the judgment spectrum, you might attach a label to that person, limiting them, or if you like, putting them in a box of your own making.

It is all too easy for us in our judgment-ridden, fallen world culture to make identity statements about people based on something they have said or done. We are all capable of doing stupid things. But if as a result I say a person 'is stupid' or 'is an idiot', then I have stepped over a line. Would you want me to label your character as stupid just because you did something stupid? I doubt it, so don't turn the tables and call me, or anyone else, stupid.

At the risk of being dogmatic about it, I'll say that it can never be right to say someone is stupid, or an idiot, or lazy, or a liar, or whatever. I make a statement as bold as this because there is a need to challenge careless talk.

Just suppose I used to be a dentist. It would be very common in social gatherings for other people to be talking and, if I came into the conversation, someone might say, 'oh, did you know he's a dentist?' Proud as I'm sure I would be of being a dentist, this label - dentist - could never be a complete statement of who I am. What about being a son, a father, a brother, a husband, and so on. Of course, this doesn't just apply to dentists!

I can just about accept that in ordinary conversation we describe something about what someone does in this way, although personally I feel it reflects a fixation on status, possessions, performance and activity. If in that hypothetical situation, I was talking to someone who observed that I was 'a dentist', I would not take offence. I understand that they are not really trying to sum up everything I am in a simple label, and I certainly wouldn't take it as some kind of attack on my character.

It is, however, totally another thing to say someone is stupid, and so on. This most definitely is a character attack. Jesus said something else about this in the Sermon on the Mount:

*'You have heard that our ancestors were told, 'You must not murder. If you commit*

*murder, you are subject to judgment.' But I say, if you are even angry with someone, you are subject to judgment! If you call someone an idiot, you are in danger of being brought before the court. And if you curse someone, you are in danger of the fires of hell.* [244]

I am so grateful to God that in all the times he has seen me do stupid things, he has never judged me and labeled me as a stupid person. I just did some stupid things, and God saw through my failings and saw my potential. Isn't that what we all need, isn't that what we all want so desperately? We must learn to extend that selfsame courtesy and grace to the people we bump into, however hurtful or irritating their behaviour might be. Let's not box them in with our judgments; let's give room for the possibility of change.

What is it that prompts us to judge others? I'm sure there can be all sorts of reasons. It might be something specific a particular person has said or not said, done or not done. It might not be anything about that person's behaviour at all, instead our judgment might be triggered by some association. It could be that person's skin colour, ethnicity, accent, the clothes they wear, the friends they have. The list of possibilities is a long one. On the other hand, in reality our judgment might have nothing to do with that person at all. We might simply be lashing out with judgments at anyone and everyone, as a symptom of hurts or rejection we have suffered at the hands of someone else entirely - perhaps a parent, a teacher, a lover, or an employer.

Coming back to how we can identify clues in the particular words we choose, then, if you find yourself saying that someone 'is' something, I recommend that you pause to ask yourself whether you are in fact attacking that person's character, whether you are in some unhelpful way boxing them in. Another set of potential clues is if you catch yourself saying that someone 'always' does such-and-such, or 'never' does so-and-so. 'Always' and 'never' are very strong words. If we attach these words to someone, quite possibly we are condemning them, we are judging them.

Words such as these are so powerful that they can even create an expectation between you and that other person which reinforces that

---

[244] Matthew 5:21&22

person's unwelcome behaviour. And probably, no-one will even be aware that this is happening. I believe this is part of what Jesus meant when, in a passage we looked at earlier,[245] he spoke about our being judged by the same standard that we ourselves use to judge. It is better to use no standard at all: simply, do not judge. But if we do judge, there are consequences for us. As we read elsewhere in the New Testament,

*Do not be deceived, God is not mocked; for whatever a man sows, that he will also reap.*[246]

If you complain that someone in particular never says nice things to you, or always says nasty things to you, part of the consequence of your own judgment may well be that you will reap the very things you are complaining about.

We will close this Chapter with, as I have mentioned, a consideration of what I am calling negative self-pronouncements. I am sorry if this phrase seems a little clumsy. Moving on from the idea that our own judgments can rebound against us, negative self-pronouncements are statements we make about ourselves which hurt us. They are a form of self-harm, they are a self-inflicted curse.

Negative self-pronouncements are the things we say (and so they are evidence of the things we think and believe) about ourselves. In a discussion about how God wants me to control my tongue, it would be very easy to focus exclusively on the impact my words have on other people. And yet, it's important to know that other people are not the only victims of our bad words. We also hurt ourselves, we also limit ourselves.

It might seem odd in a Chapter about words to spend any time at all on what we say to ourselves. After all, when we are alone, how many of us actually talk to ourselves? I would say that I talk out loud to myself only a little, but then again, how much is a little? I have no idea whether you would say something similar, and for all I know your idea of talking to yourself a 'little' might sound quite different to me if I could hear you! And the same could be true the other way round, if you were able to eavesdrop

---

[245] Matthew 7:1&2

[246] Galatians 6:7 [nkjv]

on my times when I am on my own.

Whether we chatter away to ourselves a lot or a little is not the main point here. We might or might not be aware of it, but we have thoughts and beliefs about ourselves, little scripts if you will, little loops of dialogue that run around our heads and hearts a lot of the time. To the extent that these largely unspoken 'scripts' are not in agreement with God, it will be good for us if they can be changed.

To some degree, some of the time, these 'scripts' will leak out into actual spoken words. It could happen while you are on your own, doing some mundane task. On the other hand, it could come out while you are in conversation with someone else. You could suddenly find yourself saying something negative about - you!

I cannot come up with a comprehensive list of the clues to look for. However, be on alert if you find yourself saying you are: too fat; too thin; too short; too tall - in fact, anything that is 'too' is most likely a pronouncement about yourself that needs to be shifted.

Again, if you find yourself saying that you 'never' or 'always' do something, pay attention! It is even possible for some of our bad statements about ourselves to turn into something like judgments, but judgments which are directed at ourselves - something like a vow, which is a very powerful thing. For example, someone who has been disappointed in love might start saying, 'I will never get married', really just as an expression of pain and loss over what has happened so far. The 'never' in a statement such as this can turn into a belief about the future, so that this negativity is carried forward into every new encounter with new people. Just as we should not put other people into boxes, we should not box ourselves in. God's opinion of you is far higher and better than that.

When you describe yourself as 'a' something or other, check whether this is a fairly unobjectionable description of your current job - as in, 'I am a dentist/garbage collector/rocket scientist/banker' and so on - or whether you are slipping into an unhealthy statement about your very identity.

Please, never, ever allow yourself to stay in the trap of thinking that it's OK to be negative about yourself because you are simply agreeing with God. You are not in agreement with God if you are being negative about yourself. If you are doing some bad things, he will be hating those things, but he will not be hating you. He is far too loving, and far too wise, to box you in.

I'd like to close this Chapter with a very fine and appropriate prayer from the Psalms:

*Keep your servant from deliberate sins! Don't let them control me. Then I will be free of guilt and innocent of great sin. May the words of my mouth and the meditation of my heart be pleasing to you, O Lord, my rock and my redeemer.*[247]

May you find the Holy Spirit helping you as you pay attention to your own words, as you follow the clues in your speech as they lead to the attitudes in your heart that need to change. As you give God permission to work in your heart, may you experience the wonderful freedom of a tongue that is released to bless and to encourage. And when you look at yourself in the mirror, may you be very happy with what you see.

---

[247] Psalm 19:13&14

# Freedom To Be

Shì ¦ To Be

# CHAPTER 13

In an earlier Chapter ('Freedom From Sin') we looked at the some of the things that, as followers of Jesus, we are called to be freed from. However, there must be more to freedom than just getting rid of the things that hold us back. Fundamentally, what is freedom for, what is freedom really all about?

There is a Bible verse that seems to answer this question very quickly and easily:

*It is for freedom that Christ has set us free.*[248]

The answer is: freedom is for freedom! The reason why we are being set free from bad stuff is so that we can be free. Freedom is something much bigger than just not being bound by negative things. We get a clue to this in one of Paul's letters to the Church in Corinth:

*For the Lord is the Spirit, and wherever the Spirit of the Lord is, there is freedom….And the Lord - who is the Spirit - makes us more and more like him as we are changed into his glorious image.*[249]

Freedom is part and parcel of who God is, and what he is like. And because God wants us, his kids, to become more and more like him, it follows that he wants us to operate in freedom rather than its opposite, which is slavery.

Freedom is part of the expression of who God actually is, and what he is actually like. When Moses was first receiving his commission from God to lead the Hebrews out of captivity in Egypt, Moses asked God to reveal his name. God gave Moses this answer:

*God replied to Moses, 'I am who I am. Say this to the people of Israel: I am has sent me to you.' God also said to Moses, 'Say this to the people of Israel: Yahweh, the God of your ancestors - the God of Abraham, the God of Isaac, and the God of Jacob - has sent*

---

[248] Galatians 5:1 [niv]

[249] 2 Corinthians 3:17&18

*me to you. This is my eternal name, my name to remember for all generations.* [250]

By ancient tradition, this actual name of God was thought to be too holy to be written in full and too holy to be spoken, and it is written in the Old Testament in a kind of code of four letters - YHVH, or YHWH. No one knows for sure how the name actually sounds, but 'Yahweh' might possibly be very close to it. The main point I want to make about this special name is its connection with the Hebrew verb 'to be'. At least part of the sense of this name is that God simply is who and what he is, and he will be who and what he will be. He can't be defined or limited by anything else, nor by anyone else.

God takes this name very seriously. At a later point in Moses' life, when he is giving the Ten Commandments a second time to the Hebrews (because Moses destroyed the first set of stone tablets as a sign of God's anger at the Hebrews so quickly worshipping a false god) God comes down and appears in front of Moses:

*Then the Lord came down in a cloud and stood there with him; and he called out his own name, Yahweh. The Lord passed in front of Moses, calling out, 'Yahweh! The Lord! The God of compassion and mercy! I am slow to anger and filled with unfailing love and faithfulness.* [251]

There are strong suggestions in the Gospels[252] that, more than once, Jesus made statements about himself that moved from simple 'I am'-type statements, to something altogether higher - statements that were more like God himself saying, 'I am who I am, and I will be who I will be'. When Jesus was arrested in the Garden of Gethsemane, he asks the guards who they are looking for. When they say they are looking for Jesus the Nazarene, his reply is, 'I am he' - and the guards all fall down![253]

Freedom - true freedom - is about living the same kind of life that God lives. It is about living our day to day, sometimes dull, sometimes hard lives

---

[250] Exodus 3:14&15

[251] Exodus 34:5&6

[252] John 8:57-59, 13:9

[253] John 18:4-6

in the same way that Jesus would live if he were in our shoes. The kind of freedom that God offers us is the freedom to live in a way that is consistent with the way that God himself lives.

We can think of freedom as being about breaking away from things that bind us, like a prisoner coming out of a prison cell. This is a very good and very important aspect of true freedom, but it is not the whole story. We can think of freedom as being the ability to do just exactly as we please. Certainly there is something important in this, but it doesn't always represent true freedom. We can sometimes have an idea about freedom that is more about breaking rules, about not being bound by whatever restrictions other people place on us.

We might think that true freedom must involve us sometimes being able to do the things that even God doesn't want us to do. Another way of putting this kind of view is that anyone who is truly free must be at least a little bit naughty, they must be a bit of a rebel - maybe, even a rebel against God himself.

In reality, such a lifestyle is not true freedom. Going back to the Garden of Eden, this is in fact part of the package that the Devil was able to sell (miss-sell, really) to Adam and Eve. There was just one restriction that God placed on Adam and Eve, and they found it impossible to resist the temptation to step over the boundary that God had set.

The Devil dangled in front of them the idea that God was in fact depriving them of something wonderful. If only they would eat the forbidden fruit, they would acquire knowledge that would put them on the same level as God himself. Sadly, what the knowledge of good and evil did for them was that it introduced them to a false reality - a deluded world where you can live in a way that is contrary to God's plan and character.

Consider for one moment a question that might seem ridiculous or blasphemous, or possibly both. If God really is truly free, is he free to sin? And a related question is this: from God's perspective, what is it exactly about sin that makes it so objectionable? In fact what is sin, when all is said and done?

The Bible tells us very clearly that God is not free to sin:

*And remember, when you are being tempted, do not say, 'God is tempting me.' God is never tempted to do wrong, and he never tempts anyone else. Temptation comes from our own desires, which entice us and drag us away. These desires give birth to sinful actions. And when sin is allowed to grow, it gives birth to death.*[254]

God is never even tempted. So if we think that at least one aspect of freedom is the freedom to, so to speak, break the rules, then we have some kind of disagreement between us and God about what true freedom is.

Although we have just seen that God is never even tempted, elsewhere in the Bible we read something about Jesus that might seem to contradict this. One aspect of Jesus being our great High Priest is that he is in fact acquainted with the kinds of temptations, or 'tests', that we human beings face:

*Since, then, we have a great high priest who has passed through the heavens, Jesus, the Son of God, let us hold fast to our confession. For we do not have a high priest who is unable to sympathise with our weaknesses, but we have one who in every respect has been tested as we are, yet without sin. Let us therefore approach the throne of grace with boldness, so that we may receive mercy and find grace to help in time of need.*[255]

What is important to know is this - that Jesus never did sin, and that, now he is seated at his Father's right hand, just like the Father, the Son is not 'free' to sin now.

Freedom, from God's point of view, must be about something other than the ability to be 'naughty'. From God's point of view, sin is something that takes freedom away. To sin is the very opposite of being free. The freedom that is offered to us through Jesus' sacrifice is not the freedom to do whatever we like. Rather, it is the freedom to become who and what we were destined and designed to be: sons and daughters of the Most High King. Our freedom is to be just like his freedom. Our freedom is to live a life that is consistent with who and what we are, as a reflection of God's own life, which is totally and perfectly consistent with who and what he is.

This brings us to a key Bible verse for this Chapter:

*For I consider that the sufferings of this present time are not worthy to be compared with the glory that is to be revealed to us. For the anxious longing of the creation waits*

---

[254] James 1:13-15

[255] Hebrews 14:14-16

*eagerly for the revealing of the sons of God. For the creation was subjected to futility, not willingly, but because of Him who subjected it, in hope.*[256]

The New King James version of the Bible speaks here about the 'revealing of the sons of God'. J.B. Phillips' translation of the New Testament expresses this idea in an especially striking and beautiful way:

*The whole creation is on tiptoe to see the wonderful sight of the sons of God coming into their own.*[257]

This is our destiny, this is our destination. It is not the Father's plan to leave us trapped in old, futile and destructive patterns of behaviour that limit us, with our only comfort being that, one day in the distant future, everything will be better. His plan is that, more and more, we begin to live here and now in the reality of who and what we already are - royal children. God wants this to be reality for us now.

This Chapter and Chapter 7 of this book - 'Freedom From Sin' - are in many ways companions to each other and once again I want to go back to the story of Adam and Eve's fall, the fall of all of us. In that companion Chapter, when we looked at the Genesis story, the focus was on the attractiveness of sin - its appeal to the lust of the eyes, the lust of the flesh and the pride of life. We also looked at the importance of identity when it comes to dealing with temptation. The more we truly know who we truly are, the more successful we can be in resisting the enemy.

This time, when we look at the Genesis story of the Fall, the focus is different. I want to look at what we all lost when Adam and Eve fell. It is important to have a clear picture of what was lost, so that we can understand what God, through Christ, is giving back to us: our freedom to be. We are also taking a look beyond the sins that we commit to some unhealthy basic concepts that may well, at least to a degree, dictate the way that we make decisions, the way we act and react. These 'toxic' concepts can poison the way we deal with everything and everyone that we bump into as we go through our daily lives.

---

[256] Romans 8:18-20 [nasb]

[257] 'New Testament In Modern English', J.B. Phillips

In a nutshell, some toxic concepts became part of our everyday landscape at the time of the Fall. Three of these concepts are often described together, namely shame, fear and control. Another major toxic concept is rejection, and the final one we will touch on is a sense of being an orphan - feeling disconnected from the reality that God is the Father who loves us. We cannot truly live now as free sons and daughters of God unless and until any strongholds of shame, fear, control, rejection and orphan-ness in our lives have been dealt with.

Here is part of the Creation story:

*Then God said, Let us make human beings in our image, to be like us. They will reign over the fish in the sea, the birds in the sky, the livestock, all the wild animals on the earth, and the small animals that scurry along the ground.' So God created human beings in his own image. In the image of God he created them; male and female he created them. Then God blessed them and said, 'Be fruitful and multiply. Fill the earth and govern it. Reign over the fish in the sea, the birds in the sky, and all the animals that scurry along the ground.*[258]

And -

*Now the man and his wife were both naked, but they felt no shame.*[259]

Mankind was made by God to be like God. We were made in his image, and he gave us this amazing planet over which we were destined to reign. And there was no shame, no need to to cover anything up or to run away and hide.

Sin - choosing to move in the opposite direction to freedom - had some immediate consequences for our ancestors:

*At that moment their eyes were opened, and they suddenly felt shame at their nakedness. So they sewed fig leaves together to cover themselves. When the cool evening breezes were blowing, the man and his wife heard the Lord God walking about in the garden. So they hid from the Lord God among the trees. Then the Lord God called to the man, 'Where are you?' He replied, 'I heard you walking in the garden, so I hid. I was afraid because I was naked.' 'Who told you that you were naked?' the Lord God asked. 'Have you eaten from the tree whose fruit I commanded you not to eat?'...Then he said*

---

[258] Genesis 1:26-28

[259] Genesis 2:25

*to the woman, 'I will sharpen the pain of your pregnancy, and in pain you will give birth. And you will desire to control your husband, but he will rule over you.'* [260]

It is worthwhile trying to get to grips with what shame is, and what the absence of shame is. It is easy to think about the naked Adam and Eve feeling no shame as being about nothing more than being naive - as if, at the time, they didn't really know what sex was all about. This kind of view is very wide of the mark. The shame that they felt when they fell was to do with a fundamental sense of their not being 'right', not being acceptable. What shame does is it brings a conviction that there is something wrong with us, something wrong about us.

As we follow through the story, it was this sense of shame that drove Adam and Eve to try to make themselves more acceptable, more 'right', by clothing themselves. The alternative was that each of them would see the other as they really were, which was - in their eyes - no longer acceptable.

Next, they experienced fear. Adam cannot face the idea of talking to God face to face, which up until now has been normal for him, so out of fear he tries to hide.

Finally, when God outlines what some of the consequences will be for these two people in the way they relate to each other, we see that there will be a desire to control that competes with an exercise of power.

So, in this Genesis account we see the seeds of shame, fear and control. Within the next generation, we see a family drama played out that clearly shows rejection rearing its ugly head, in the life of Cain. [261] Cain reacted badly to the fact that his younger brother, Abel, was enjoying success in being approved of by God. God gave Cain this warning:

*'Why are you so angry?' the Lord asked Cain. 'Why do you look so dejected? You will be accepted if you do what is right. But if you refuse to do what is right, then watch out! Sin is crouching at the door, eager to control you. But you must subdue it and be its master.'* [262]

---

[260] Genesis 3:7-11, 16

[261] Genesis 4:1-18

[262] Genesis 4:6&7

The classic way that rejection plays out is like this. We experience some kind of rebuff from someone else. There could be all sorts of reasons for this, but we decide to be wounded by it, to take it as a personal attack. Then, we turn this pain inward and start to reject ourselves - we tie ourselves up in knots by finding fault with ourselves, because there must be something wrong with us. Finally, we engineer a kind of self-fulfilling prophecy when, out of a fear of being rejected again, we try too hard to ensure that no-one ever rejects us again.

It's weird, but what this fear of rejection actually does is this. We try to avoid people who we think might reject us - so we have less contact with people and as a result feel more rejected. Also, for those people we do actually have contact with, we try far too hard to make ourselves acceptable. We become oddly super-nice and very perfect in the way we behave and we become super-sensitive about how other people are reacting to us. This over-exertion in itself can set us up for coming across as being not that easy to know, so that our latest circle of contacts are all the more likely to - guess what? - reject us. And so the vicious circle starts all over again.

Going back to the example of Cain, he did not make a good choice about how to react to what he saw as rejection by God. Cain killed his brother, Abel. God tells Cain that his brother's blood is crying out to God from the ground, and as a result the ground will no longer yield good crops for Cain - who was a farmer. God also tells Cain he will be 'a homeless wanderer on the earth'. This is bad, but Cain elaborates on the judgment that God has pronounced. What Cain tells God is this:

*'My punishment is too great for me to bear! You have banished me from the land and from your presence; you have made me a homeless wanderer. Anyone who finds me will kill me!*[263]

Note this: God did not say that Cain was banished from his presence, nor that anyone who found him would kill him. The toxic rejection concept is already at work in Cain's mind - in Cain's world.

Moving to the final of these toxic concepts, which is orphan-ness, so far as I am aware, there is no single story early on the Bible narrative that neatly

---

[263] Genesis 4:13&14

and simply illustrates this, or that shows us how and when it first made itself felt. Instead, orphan-ness is part of a general disconnection from a healthy and normal relationship with God as Father. I use the words 'healthy and normal' in the sense of how things were always meant to be, as opposed to how things often are - sad to say.

We can find hints and traces of orphan-ness in many places in the Bible. As we allow the Holy Spirit to work in our hearts, we might also find hints and traces of orphan-ness in our own behaviours. It would be wonderful if orphan-ness could always be dealt with by a quick fix, such as the immediate casting out of an orphan spirit or the instant mending of a broken orphan heart. Provided fixes really are fixes, I am all in favour of fixes that are quick. However, if we have spent a significant part of a lifetime living like an orphan, it might take a little time, work and patience on our side to learn what it is truly like to live as a son or daughter.

For me, one of the best illustrations of what orphan-ness looks like is a comparison of the lives of the first two Kings of Israel, Saul and David. You can read the story of their lives, and of the way they dealt with each other, in 1 and 2 Samuel.

Orphan-ness as a toxic concept is not, fundamentally, about whether we actually grew up with a couple of parents, nor is it about whether those parents were loving towards us. These things can be factors, but they are only factors, not the whole story. Fundamentally, orphan-ness is about our not being connected to the reality of God's love for us as Father.

King Saul had a distorted image of himself. He found it difficult to follow carefully any instructions from God that were communicated to him by the prophet Samuel. He was insecure, impatient, over-sensitive to the opinions of other people, moody, bad-tempered, and impulsive. His many character flaws poisoned not only his relationship with David but also with his own son, Jonathan.

David was certainly not perfect, but he was described by the prophet Samuel as a man 'after God's own heart'.[264] His life demonstrated integrity and trust in God, even when he was tested very severely. Both Saul and

---

[264] 1 Samuel 13:14

David had human fathers, but of the two men, it was David who demonstrated a real, living relationship with his God as Father. In one of his poems, David says this:

*The Lord is like a father to his children, tender and compassionate to those who fear him.*[265]

Moving across to the Gospels, one of the unusual things about Jesus' teachings was his concept of God as Father. Jesus spoke with authority about God as Father because Jesus knew who, and what, he was talking about. It's easy for us to say that we know God is Father - we know that God is Father, Son and Holy Spirit - but do we really know that God is <u>our</u> Father? When the circumstances and pressures of life might tempt you to believe that there is no one you can trust, that there is no one who will really care for you and look after you, are you able to draw on deep reserves of love and trust that Father is on your side?

Orphans have to protect themselves. They may well have a place to live, but they do not have a home. They place too much reliance on stuff - things that will help to make them feel OK. They find that their relationships with other people so often disappoint, because none of those relationships can fill the emptiness that they feel inside. They tend to be over-sensitive to what other people say and what other people do. What every orphan needs is to experience adoption into Father God's family. Every orphan needs to come home.

Funnily enough, bearing in mind that this book is about freedom, there is an early link between the concept of freedom and the need to come home. It has been claimed that the first known trace of any written reference to the concept of freedom is the ancient Sumerian word *ama-gi*. This word was found written on a clay tablet around 2300 BC and its literal meaning is 'return to the mother'. Possibly the idea behind this is of oppressed workers being released - released to go home.

One of the criticisms that Jesus faced from religious leaders of his day was that he spent time with people those leaders thought of as scum, as the dregs of society. In response to this criticism, one of the stories that Jesus

---

[265] Psalm 103:13

told was the story of the lost son, or prodigal son.[266]

In that story, Jesus is very clearly saying that God is like the father who, although he has been treated disgracefully by the son who has deserted him, spends his time looking out to the horizon, waiting for the day when his lost son comes back home. That lost son has squandered all his money, and is coming back to his father's house hoping that he will at least be treated like a slave. But the father rushes out to meet him, showers him with kisses, honours him with fine clothes and jewels, and throws a massive party to celebrate. The lost son has been found, and he has come home.

It is a good spiritual exercise to reflect on this story from time to time and ask the Holy Spirit to show us where we fit into that story, and to consider whether we really are home. We all need as much of a download from Heaven as we can get of the reality of God's love for us as Father.

How does Jesus fix these toxic concepts of shame, fear, control, rejection and orphan-ness? This is part and parcel of what was achieved through Jesus' sacrificial death and we looked at this in the first Chapter of this book, which was about the Cross. Bearing in mind that the first of the toxic concepts we have looked at was shame, and that shame was at the very root of the Fall, this verse from Hebrews about the redemptive work of the Cross is very relevant:

*…Jesus, the author and finisher of our faith, who for the joy that was set before Him endured the cross, despising the shame, and has sat down at the right hand of the throne of God.*[267]

Jesus despised shame. The toxic concepts of shame, along with fear, control and orphan-ness all get swallowed up in the Cross. And yet, in truth, we can live with these concepts: even if we have said yes to Jesus, even if we have acknowledged what he did on the Cross for us. The Cross is not just about death, it is also about life. Not only the life of Jesus resurrected after his death, but also the life that he lived on planet Earth before his death.

John, the disciple who was closest to Jesus, puts it like this:

---

[266] Luke 15:11-32

[267] Hebrews 12:2 [nkjv]

*And as we live in God, our love grows more perfect. So we will not be afraid on the day of judgment, but we can face him with confidence because we live like Jesus here in this world. Such love has no fear, because perfect love expels all fear. If we are afraid, it is for fear of punishment, and this shows that we have not fully experienced his perfect love.*[268]

These words remind us that the kind of life Jesus calls us to live is a life without fear. The kind of emotions that Adam experienced at the Fall are not supposed to be the emotions we experience as we walk with God. These words tell us that our life is a process. The love that we experience 'grows more perfect'. These words contain a challenge: we are to 'live like Jesus here in this world'. How did Jesus live in this world?

Let's leave to one side all the healings - the blind people who could see, the deaf people who could hear, the lepers who no longer had leprosy, the dead people who - well, you get the idea. Let's also leave to one side all the direct confrontations with the Devil and his demons, which of course often also as a result led to some kind of physical infirmity coming off people. The Gospels contain many examples of Jesus commanding evil spirits to leave.

Let's spend a moment considering some of the other amazing things about what Jesus' life was like. He turned water into wine. He cursed a fig tree, and it withered. He walked on water. He changed the weather by speaking to it. He just walked through a crowd that was trying to kill him. Twice, he caused mass multiplications of food so that thousands of people were fed. He directed expert fishermen, against their professional judgement, to do something that led to a miraculous catch of fish. He financed his ministry team's tax bill by finding money in a fish's mouth.

Aside from the amazing things that Jesus did, what does the Bible tell us about Jesus' attitudes? He lived a life of humility. He described himself as 'humble and gentle at heart'.[269] One of the many ways that he offended members of the religious establishment was the amount of time he spent and attention he gave to people on the edge of society - the immoral and

---

[268] 1 John 4:17&18

[269] Matthew 11:29

the poor. He turned usual ideas of leadership upside down by living as a servant to others.

John says that 'we live like Jesus here in this world'[270]. But when we spend any time thinking about how Jesus did in fact live, we can perhaps feel that Jesus sets a standard that is not just high - isn't it impossibly high?

We might try to tell ourselves that ordinary people like us can never seriously expect to live at the Jesus-like level. After all, would it not be unfair for God to expect us to be able to match Jesus, when Jesus is, after all, God?

However, God's will for you really is that, as John wrote in his letter, you will 'live like Jesus here in this world'. In that same letter, John wrote this:

*Those who say they live in God should live their lives as Jesus did.*[271]

Paul's letter to the Philippians makes it clear that, when we look at the way Jesus lived, although he never stopped being God, he functioned as a human being:

*Though he was God, he did not think of equality with God as something to cling to. Instead, he gave up his divine privileges; he took the humble position of a slave and was born as a human being. When he appeared in human form, he humbled himself in obedience to God and died a criminal's death on a cross.*[272]

It is the fact that Jesus was functioning out of his humanity rather than out of his divinity which means he can set us an example to follow that is not impossible, not cruelly difficult. Otherwise, he would be telling us to do something that is not achievable. Jesus himself made it clear that he is expecting us to do the same stuff, to live the same life:

*I tell you the truth, anyone who believes in me will do the same works I have done, and even greater works, because I am going to be with the Father.*[273]

The reality of our daily lives at the moment may well be that we are not

---

[270] 1 John 4:17

[271] 1 John 2:6

[272] Philippians 2:6-8

[273] John 14:12

really living in this world in the same way that Jesus lived. But let's not let our current shortcomings make us explain away, qualify or dilute the force of what God's word tells us. Instead, let's determine to leave behind us the things that hold us back; let's determine to get free; let's determine to achieve our personal best. May our experience adjust to the reality of God's truth, as opposed to trying to adjust God's truth to fall into line with the reality of our current experience.

Jesus' arrival on planet Earth as a human being marked a radical turning point in history. Of course, what he achieved through the Cross and his resurrection are fundamental. We started this book by looking at the Cross, but also the way he lived as a human being <u>before</u> he suffered on the Cross is also hugely important.

Jesus showed us what it is like to live in the way God intended us all to live. Totally free from the toxic concepts of shame, fear, control, rejection and orphan-ness. He lived a life of open communication with his Father in Heaven. He knew who he was and what he was. He lived and breathed in the reality of an intimate relationship with Father. He was totally secure in a relationship of complete love.

Fear, whether it was the fear of not having enough stuff around him to keep him fed, sheltered or safe, or whether it was the fear of death, could not manipulate him in any way. Perhaps we cannot even imagine what it might be like for us to be entirely without fear. And yet, on the basis of the Cross and the resurrection, Jesus is now as it were standing on the other side, and is calling out to us, encouraging us, to live life in the same way that he lived life. Because we can. Because of Jesus, we can.

I am going to suggest that there is a tantalising picture at the end of the Bible that points very clearly to the importance of our aiming to live this kind of life. It is the story of the two witnesses in Revelation:

*Then I was given a measuring stick, and I was told, 'Go and measure the Temple of God and the altar, and count the number of worshipers. But do not measure the outer courtyard, for it has been turned over to the nations. They will trample the holy city for 42 months. And I will give power to my two witnesses, and they will be clothed in burlap and will prophesy during those 1,260 days.'*

*These two prophets are the two olive trees and the two lampstands that stand before the Lord of all the earth. If anyone tries to harm them, fire flashes from their mouths and consumes their enemies. This is how anyone who tries to harm them must die. They have power to shut the sky so that no rain will fall for as long as they prophesy. And they have the power to turn the rivers and oceans into blood, and to strike the earth with every kind of plague as often as they wish.*

*When they complete their testimony, the beast that comes up out of the bottomless pit will declare war against them, and he will conquer them and kill them. And their bodies will lie in the main street of Jerusalem, the city that is figuratively called 'Sodom' and 'Egypt,' the city where their Lord was crucified. And for three and a half days, all peoples, tribes, languages, and nations will stare at their bodies. No one will be allowed to bury them. All the people who belong to this world will gloat over them and give presents to each other to celebrate the death of the two prophets who had tormented them.*

*But after three and a half days, God breathed life into them, and they stood up! Terror struck all who were staring at them. Then a loud voice from heaven called to the two prophets, 'Come up here!' And they rose to heaven in a cloud as their enemies watched. At the same time there was a terrible earthquake that destroyed a tenth of the city. Seven thousand people died in that earthquake, and everyone else was terrified and gave glory to the God of heaven.*[274]

There are a number of opinions and interpretations about who these two witnesses are, and what they represent. In my opinion, many of these theories are not mutually exclusive. What I want to focus on is that they represent the Church - Jesus' followers who are called to be witnesses to him. These two people serve as a tremendous example to us of what it would look like for Jesus' followers to live in the same way that Jesus lived - and what better witness could there possibly be?

Until the time finally came for them to die (just as there was a time for Jesus to die) they were un-killable. Nothing, and no-one, could stop them. They could even exercise control over the weather. They could speak dramatic signs into being and they could visit plagues upon people. Even though at one point they are killed, they are resurrected and then they are called to move up into Heaven - they do not die a second time. Maybe, one day, we will actually meet people like this. Maybe, one day, we will actually be people like this. There is no doubt that this is our target, our aim, our destiny. This is what we were made for, this is what a life of freedom points towards.

---

[274] Revelation 11:1-13

Some members of the Early Church were described in this way by some of their critics:

*...people who have been turning the world upside down...*[275]

As we continue to explore the subject of freedom, may we find this criticism, this insult, being directed at us, to the extent that we are disrupting this world by the way we reflect Jesus. Could there be any greater compliment - than being the type of people who are turning the world upside down?

---

[275] Acts 17:6 [nrsv]

PART TWO

# THINGS TO DO

# Build Accountable Relationships

# CHAPTER 14

One of the greatest challenges we face as we pursue getting free - drawing closer to our personal best - is that we can't always see ourselves accurately. Inevitably, we lack objectivity when we try to look at ourselves.

A good technique we can use, therefore, is to break this subjectivity by involving other people in our stuff. There are various reasons why this can seem very hard. Can I really trust someone else? If I manage somehow to be brave enough to reveal some of my secrets to someone else, will that kill our friendship? What if my friend is even more messed up than I am? And so on.

Despite what might seem to be very good reasons not to open up, God has not designed us to live in isolation from other people. If we are struggling with something, there is probably someone else who can help us.

There is a proverb in the Bible that puts it very well:

*As iron sharpens iron, so a friend sharpens a friend.*[276]

The extent to which we really know ourselves will vary. Sometimes the issues in our lives that really need shifting as a priority are the hardest for us to see clearly for ourselves. Sometimes when we really need to get some blockage in our lives sorted out, we are feeling a lot of stress and this might mean we are not a good state to see clearly what is really going on in our own lives. It's at times like these that a good friend is especially valuable. Not just someone who will sympathise with us, but also someone who will, if necessary, challenge and/or provoke us to make a change. Someone who will help us to see something that is hard for us to see if we are just left to our own devices.

For this technique to succeed, two things are necessary. The first is that you need to be willing to submit yourself to accountability. This is where you give someone else permission to speak into your life, even if at a time of crisis you act like no-one has the right to talk to you like this. The second

---

[276] Proverbs 27:17

is that you need to find someone, or some group, that is worth trusting with this kind of accountability.

It is often not difficult to find people who are ready and willing to get involved with your life. This does not necessarily mean they will be good for you. Finding people who are not only ready and willing, but also able to do this well: people who, in other words, will do you good rather than harm - that is another matter. Jesus warns all of us against the hypocrisy of being keen to point out others' problems before we have got our own issues sorted out.[277]

So, do not be flippant or casual about who you invite to speak into your life. Make sure you tune into whatever God might be saying to you about who can be trusted with such treasure. Here is a good guide: if you are thinking about inviting someone to do this, ask yourself whether that person is himself or herself living an accountable life. Do they have someone who speaks into their own life? If not, then you should probably choose someone else.

There are some other useful questions you can ask yourself about the person you are about to trust in this way. Does this person like me? Is this person on my side, does he/she have my best interests at heart? Looking at their own life, is there evidence that they have themselves been willing to aim for their personal best?

If you are a follower of Jesus then you need to be aware that you have an enemy, and one of the enemy's main strategies against you will be to try to isolate you. Do not allow yourself to become isolated. As well as having one, or a few, close accountable relationships, it is healthy also to be an active part of a wider Church family.

The Bible warns us specifically against giving in to a trend of not bothering to meet together.[278] The Bible also describes the Church a number of times as a body - in fact, as the body of Christ.[279] Being part of a

---

[277] Matthew 7:3-5

[278] Hebrews 10:24&25

[279] Romans 12:4&5, 1 Corinthians 12:12&13, Ephesians1:22&23, 4:11-13

community like this has so many benefits for us. It creates the possibility of other people having insights into our lives that will help us make progress. It helps us to see the bigger picture, to grasp that life is not about just us, but other people as well. It creates the possibility of our finding ways to help other people, as well as being helped ourselves. Living in community rather than living in isolation is one of God's ideas, and it is a good idea. Don't be a loner.

There is no set way to start an accountable relationship, but it is helpful to have a clear understanding at the start about what it is you are entering into. If you are someone who is thinking of giving someone else the right to speak into your life, then it is up to you to take the initiative and to issue the invitation.

You could consider using the following wording as a starting point for working on what you would like to say to that person. It's best if you put your invitation into your own words, but hopefully my suggested wording can be a useful starting point for you.

This might seem a little contrived or artificial, but it is generally true that any relationship that is worthwhile requires effort and intention. Sometimes you have to make a conscious decision to say the important things that need to be said:

*I am very grateful to God that I have been able to get to know you. I want you to know that I respect you as a man/woman of God. I believe your knowledge of God's Word and his ways are a great resource, and I would like to be able to draw on these to help me develop in my own walk as a disciple of Jesus Christ.*

*I have also noticed that you lead a humble life - you do not have a puffed-up opinion of your own importance, and you are secure enough in your own relationship with the Lord that you have given other people the right to speak into your life and to hold you accountable.*

*I would love you to help me in my walk with the Lord. If you are willing, please accept this invitation to become an accountability partner for me. If you accept this invitation, I am giving you the right to speak into all areas of my life. If you see me doing anything, or hear me saying anything, that is in any way out of line with what you feel is appropriate or healthy, please draw this to my attention.*

*If I try to avoid you, or if I fight against what you try to tell me, then you have my permission to persist and to challenge me. It would be such an honour for me to have you take up this place in my life - thank you for taking the time to consider my invitation.*

# Keep Confessing

# CHAPTER 15

The Oxford Dictionary defines 'confession' as an acknowledgement - whether of sins, fault, blame, whatever. To acknowledge something is defined as including agreeing to the truth of something, or owning it. This concept of ownership is very helpful for grasping what part confession can play in our set of tools for freedom.

Sin is a nasty business, and it is understandable why, as and when we are confronted by the reality of our own sin, we want it dealt with as quickly as possible, preferably in private and with the least possible fuss and bother.

Such is our haste that we may find we have a bad theology about what is, from God's viewpoint, the appropriate way to respond when sin is revealed. If you ask yourself the question, what must I do if I become aware of sin in my life?, quite possibly the word which will come to mind is - repent! This seems consistent with what Peter said to the crowd on the Day of Pentecost. They were convinced by the message about Jesus that Peter had just preached, and they asked him what they needed to do. This was his reply:

*'Repent, and let every one of you be baptised in the name of Jesus for the remission of sins; and you shall receive the gift of the Holy Spirit.* [280]

Repentance is certainly vital. However, I suggest that such is our rush to deal with sin that we perhaps might miss another important part of the process, namely confession. In fact, confession is really an essential part of what true repentance is all about.

Unless you come from the Catholic tradition, the very idea of confession may seem alien to you. It can seem weird to think about spilling the beans, as it were, to another human being here on planet Earth, as opposed to just being honest in private with God, who of course already knows all of your secret stuff anyway.

I was saved into the Protestant/Evangelical tradition. For people within that tradition, perhaps the baby has been thrown out with the bath water if

---

[280] Acts 2:38 [nkjv]

we think that confessing sins to one another cannot be of God because it feels 'too Catholic' - like going into the confessional and treating someone else as a priest.

If that is what you think, then possibly it is inconvenient for you that the Bible endorses confessing sins to one another:

*Confess your sins to each other and pray for each other so that you may be healed.*[281]

It is important to note the 'each others' in this reference. There is no need to assume that the only person who can ever hear a confession of sins is a Catholic priest. We are all called to be priests and confession is meant to be a mutual, a two-way process. I believe Peter was at least in part thinking of this when he wrote:

*Most important of all, continue to show deep love for each other, for love covers a multitude of sins.*[282]

One of the enemy's tactics is to make us feel trapped with a sense of shame about whatever sins we have committed. It seems very easy - almost natural - to carry around with us a belief that if our Christian brothers and sisters knew what we were really like, they would be shocked, and they would reject us. And so, sadly, our experience of Church life can be that we put on some kind of mask, covering up who we are, in the hope that we will be accepted, by pretending we are better than our true selves.

This shame-based reaction, the cover up, goes right back to when sin first poisoned Mankind's relationship with Father God, in the Garden of Eden. Although the enemy promised Adam and Eve that they would become just like God when they ate the fruit from the tree in the centre of the Garden, in fact their very first experience was of shame. They felt shame at their nakedness and they strung fig leaves together to cover themselves.[283]

I am not saying that every believer must therefore stand up in front of the whole Church and go into great detail about all of his or her sins. There

---

[281] James 5:16

[282] 1 Peter 4:8

[283] Genesis 3:4-7

is a place for public confession and repentance. I have seen this done, and it is very powerful. However, the norm is not public confession, but finding perhaps just one or two people with whom you can be real enough to lower your mask, let them see the real you and be honest about any sin which is sticking to you.

It is a very healing and releasing thing to hear another living, breathing human being agree with what God says and tell you to your face that you really are forgiven and accepted. Let's break the shame!

As part of the Methodist revival that John Wesley spearheaded in the 18th Century, small groups of Christians who were accountable to each other were established. These groups went by a number of different names - 'Accountability Discipleship Groups', 'Methodist Societies', 'Classmeetings', and 'Band Societies'. That revival had a tremendous impact upon the United Kingdom. In these little groups, followers of Jesus were committed on a regular basis to asking questions such as: 'What known sins have you committed since our last meeting?'; 'What temptations have you met with?'; and 'How were you delivered?'. These seem to be very strong and direct questions!

As the modern Church uncovers, or discovers, or rediscovers, the value of confession, may we be revived and may our nations be changed as a result. Only God can forgive sins. Only the sacrifice of Jesus on the Cross is effective in dealing with our sins. We must, in our dealings with the God who loves us, be honest with him about our sins. We must confess them to him.

Going on from that, we need to understand that sin is not an entirely private affair. Especially if we sense shame about a particular part of our lives, or if there is a sin which constantly seems to be recurring, part of God's solution will very likely be that some brothers or sisters in Christ should come alongside and help us.

If you want to develop in your walk with the Lord, and you know you do not really have any relationships within the Church where you can be brutally honest about yourself, I encourage you to ask the Holy Spirit to lead you to at least one or two people who can be trusted to do you good.

So, as we pursue freedom, let's be prepared to own, to own up to, our sins. Let's not hide away in shame, and let's not deflect blame by saying it is all somebody else's fault. Let's be real about what is really going on in our lives.

There is a passage in the Bible that is very useful to know when we are confessing our sins to each other. It is talking about confessing our sins to God, but since what it says is true about God's response, we can with confidence fall in line with God's response and say something similar to each other:

*If we claim we have no sin, we are only fooling ourselves and not living in the truth. But if we confess our sins to him, he is faithful and just to forgive us our sins and to cleanse us from all wickedness.*[284]

So - if you find yourself hearing someone else's confession, and if you know that they have not just confessed sins to you but also to God, you can make a confident statement based on this passage. I encourage you to pronounce over the person who has confessed to you that God is faithful and just, that God has forgiven the sins and he has cleansed that person from all wickedness.

---

[284] 1 John 1:8&9

# Forgive Often And From The Heart

# CHAPTER 16

When Jesus blew out of the water Peter's suggestion that perhaps seven was the maximum number of times you should have to forgive someone,[285] the main idea was that in fact Jesus does not accept any limit. Compared to Peter's seven times, Jesus went for 490 times - a number so big that, really, there is no limit.

Even if we agree that forgiveness is essential for our own wellbeing, we might not forgive very often. Perhaps we have been confronted with a small number of very big things to forgive. Possibly those things will have had a lot of pain attached to them. We might feel, whether or not we are conscious of this feeling, that the business of forgiving was necessary but not pleasant, and now it is done with and we can move on - no need for any more forgiveness.

There are two main areas where I want to encourage you to not give up on forgiving and to make it a natural and easy response to some of the stuff that life throws at you.

The first of these areas is being prepared to forgive the same person when he or she continues to hurt you. So, this area of challenge involves you deciding that forgiveness is not an occasional, once in a blue moon type of exercise. It is a common, everyday part of your life.

The second of these areas is being prepared to forgive someone for something when you think you have already forgiven them. Don't be surprised if, having gone through the process of forgiving someone, you find that months or years later you get the sense that you still need to forgive them, for the same thing.

Does that mean that you didn't really mean the forgiveness thing when you did it the first time? Does it mean that the forgiveness thing didn't work? Does it mean that, somehow or other, you messed up?

I believe this experience of being confronted by the challenge of

---

[285] Matthew 18:21-35

forgiving the same thing all over again is very common, and that it does not mean the forgiveness first time around was either fake or incompetent.

The challenge here is this: will we prepared to forgive to the depth that the Holy Spirit is calling us to? If we say yes to that challenge, we will enjoy the ongoing benefits of being free of everything that unforgiveness would otherwise dump on us. We will also become more and more comfortable with the process of forgiveness and it will be easier to forgive quickly and more often.

In the Matthew 18 passage mentioned just now where Jesus gives a major teaching about forgiveness, one of the many interesting things he says is that he calls us to forgive 'from the heart'. At least one reason why we can feel called to forgive the same person for the same offence all over again is that God wants us to go through the forgiveness process again, but this time at a deeper level than before. This is rather like the layers of an onion being peeled away; or like going deeper into the heart, so that we move from a perhaps relatively intellectual approach to forgiveness and go into something much more to do with our feelings.

I am going to outline an approach to forgiving someone that fits very well with the process of following what Jesus says - that we forgive from the heart.

It is very useful to be as specific and detailed as possible about what it is that needs to be forgiven. Sometimes when someone comes to me and asks me to forgive them for something they have either done or not done, I ask them to tell me what it is exactly that they think needs to be forgiven. For example, sometimes if a person comes to you and tells you they are sorry, they might mainly be sorry that you are upset. They might not actually be sorry for their actions.

The call to forgive does not mean that we lose any sense of our dignity as individuals. If someone asks for my forgiveness, there is no reason why I should forgive as if it is nothing. It is perfectly fair and reasonable, if someone asks you to forgive them, to invite them to be clear about what it is they have done that needs to be forgiven.

Applying that idea of the value of being specific, what should I do if I know that the Holy Spirit is prompting me to forgive someone, perhaps as a repeat of something I have already tried to address?

I recommend writing a list, being as detailed as you can about what that person owes you, and how that person has harmed you. Sins that call to be forgiven can be sins of omission as well as sins of commission. There may be two sides to the offence you have suffered. Possibly it is not just a question of what that person did to you, but also what that person failed to do. For example, someone who has suffered physical abuse from a parent during childhood has paid the price of not only what was done - the abuse- but also what was missing - security and affection.

When you have a list that looks to be complete, also consider how you have reacted to these offences. For example, have they made you bitter, or angry? Have they caused you to be somewhat shut down or closed off emotionally? However understandable some or all of those reactions might be, they might point to decisions you have made that are, in fact, sinful. It is healthy therefore, as part of the forgiveness process, to repent of your own sinful reactions and invite God's forgiveness of your sins.

As you reflect on your list, you might see some connection between whatever the offence is that you are forgiving and the reaction that you have to the offence. For example, if someone has betrayed me in the past, I might feel hurt, suspicious and angry. What we leave unforgiven can grow into something very unpleasant in our own lives over time - the offences done to us that remain unforgiven can yield bad fruit in our own lives.

God's call to us to forgive as often as is necessary does not mean we have to pretend to be great friends with people who have hurt us. However, it is wise to resolve as part of your forgiveness that as far as you can, you will not allow any remaining resentment against that person to linger anywhere in the depths of your heart.

As much as you can, as part of the forgiveness process, resolve to make this something you are doing from the heart, as sincerely as you can. Without pretending that you are now trying to be friends with the offender (if they are still alive), resolve to be reconciled with them at a heart level - so there is no longer anything in your heart that is seeking vengeance against them.

You can of course use your own words, and there is no 'magic' formula: but here is some wording that might help you shape the words that you want to use to express your forgiveness. May the act of forgiveness become increasingly natural and normal for you, and may you live in the benefits of a life that is lived on the level of forgiveness - rather than its opposite.

If you have made any kind of list as mentioned earlier, there is a helpful physical act you can perform once you have been through some statements/prayers of forgiveness along the lines of what I set out below. You can take hold of your list, and then tear it up and throw it away.

*Thank you Jesus for dying in my place that I might be forgiven. By an act of my will I now choose to forgive those who have hurt me or sinned against me.*

*I forgive _______________ , for _________________ (be specific as to what you are forgiving the person for).*

*I give to him/her the gift of unconditional forgiveness. He/she owes me nothing. I entrust him/her to you God. I bless him/her in your name.*

*Lord, I ask you to forgive me for my ungodly response to the offence and the pain. I have judged with wrong attitudes and words and in bitterness and anger (be specific). I ask you now to forgive me for my ungodly and sinful responses_________________.*

*(Speak out the ungodly ways that you have responded to the pain the people have caused you.)*

*Forgive me for these and any other sinful, hidden things in my heart that have given the enemy legal rights to torment me. I choose to repent of these ungodly and sinful responses and practices.*

*Thank you Jesus that I am forgiven, and you are setting me free. I ask you to come and move powerfully in my life to change me.*

*Please forgive me, Lord if I have in my foolishness blamed you and judged you for what others have done to me. I need to speak out the words "I release you Father" for those things my heart has held against you. Thank you for loving me and promising to set me free. Amen.*

# Follow The Signs

# CHAPTER 17

If you are serious about co-operating with God in dealing with your baggage, your 'stuff', then you will want to address the causes, as opposed to the merely superficial symptoms of those things. If you pay attention you can find clues to those causes in the words that come out of your mouth and the way you behave. These clues, or signs, might be more obvious to the people around you than they are to yourself. Sometimes we are unable to see our own baggage, our own stuff. This is why earlier in this Part Two I encouraged you to find other people to help you deal with your stuff (see Chapter 14).

So - if you know you want to make progress but you are not sure where to start, you can start by paying attention to the clues, or signs, in what you say and what you do. You can follow these signs and see where they take you. You can ask other trusted friends to help point out these signs to you.

A couple of very clear signs in what we say are the words 'never' and 'always'. Often these words are used in a negative way when talking about what someone else does, or what someone else fails to do. These words often carry with them a sense of judging, or bitterness, or both.

We can also very easily use words like these about ourselves. When we direct such words at ourselves, often they amount to either a vow (for example, 'I will <u>never</u> let someone get too close to me again') or as a negative self-pronouncement (for example, 'I <u>always</u> mess up' or 'I will <u>never</u> amount to anything').

Another sign that indicates we are judging someone, or that in general we might be living in a judgmental way, is labelling other people (or even ourselves) with inappropriate identity statements. For example, we might call ourselves 'stupid', or an 'idiot'. We put ourselves and other people in a box of judgment when we say things like this. I am not stupid, but sometimes I can do stupid things.

Similarly, we can put ourselves and other people in boxes when we use the word 'too'. Too fat, too thin, too poor, too busy, too whatever. This is all about comparing ourselves or others to some kind of sense of what is normal or acceptable.

If I am overweight, it is a wise thing to look at why this is so, what changes in lifestyle and diet I could make, and perhaps what drives me to eat unhealthy foods. But if I just label myself as 'too fat' - what am I too fat for? Am I too fat to be loved? Am I too fat to learn? Am I too fat to begin to make some changes? And when does 'too fat' become 'not too fat', or 'acceptably fat'? Whose measuring standard am I allowing to be applied to who and what I am?

When it comes to the things that we do, a major sign is the way we react to things, if those reactions seem inappropriate or out of proportion. We can all act, or perform, to some degree - we can make an effort to behave in a certain way when we are with other people. How we react, rather than how we act, can be different. Reacting is what we do in response to the sometimes unpredictable things that other people say or do. Reacting is what happens when we don't have time to plan in advance precisely how we are going to behave. Something instinctive kicks in. This can reveal what is going on in our lives at a non-superficial level.

A classic example is anger. In and of itself, anger is not a problem. It can be a perfectly legitimate emotion. Sometimes, God is angry. Unresolved anger, though, is not OK. And outbursts of anger at seemingly trivial things are a sign that something within us is out of balance.

Other behaviour that is less obviously negative can also be a sign. We might try very hard to be nice, or to be happy. We might try very hard to be not noticed, or to stand out as the most exciting and interesting person around. Don't get me wrong - being relatively shy and introverted is not in and of itself a sign that we are carrying some kind of wound. Nor is being the life and soul of the party a problem in and of itself. However, if we pay close attention, we can probably distinguish between behaviour that is just part and parcel of who we are, and other stuff that doesn't really suit us, that doesn't really fit.

Moving on to other possible signs, if we know the we are in the grip of some kind of compulsion or addiction, again this tells us that something is out of kilter in our lives. Any kind of addiction - whether it is to narcotics, chocolate, alcohol, pornography, gambling, whatever - gives us a clue. When we are under pressure we are trying to find comfort in something that truly is not the answer for us.

Aside from what we say and what we do, physical sickness can also be a sign. I am not trying to say that all illness is certainly your fault and that all you need to get healed is to fix some underlying issue in your life. However, sometimes there is a connection. Particularly if you are dealing with something that seems not to have any clear medical, scientific explanation, or if it is something that seems to be part of a pattern in your family tree, my advice is to consider whether there might be some other cause. In pursuing physical healing, it is good to look at every wholesome way of attacking the sickness. The worst thing that can happen is that we receive some healing in our hearts, but we remain physically sick.

To be clear - I do not want anyone who is suffering a physical problem to feel that I am blaming them in any way. But if I am sick - or if someone I really care about is sick - I would want to pay attention to this question: is there anything that might be getting the way of receiving a physical healing?

The physical problem might be a sign that is pointing to something. If we then find that we do indeed address some issue in our lives and still we do not immediately see our physical problem resolved, what have we lost? The only thing we have lost is some baggage that we are better off not carrying anyway. It is worth the risk!

James says something about how important it is that we pay attention to what we notice about ourselves - and I think we can include here paying attention to what our friends have pointed out for us:

*So get rid of all the filth and evil in your lives, and humbly accept the word God has planted in your hearts, for it has the power to save your souls…For if you listen to the word and don't obey, it is like glancing at your face in a mirror. You see yourself, walk away, and forget what you look like.*[286]

May you experience the Holy Spirit highlighting for you anything in your life that is a sign to follow, that you might experience a greater level of freedom. And if you notice any such signs in the lives of people close to you, may the Holy Spirit give you wisdom about when to say something, and when to remain silent, and how to pray for them.

---

[286] James 1:21, 23&24

# Know God's Word, Recognise God's Voice

# CHAPTER 18

A fundamental part of being a Christian is that we have a real relationship with God. And as in any relationship that is real, there must be communication, that we hear what each of us is saying to the other. Jesus at one point calls us his 'sheep', and explains that we will hear and know his voice.[287]

What could be more amazing than having an actual conversation with the maker of the Universe?! If we can accurately hear whatever he wants to say to us, what else could we possibly need? And yet, there is something else. There is huge value in our being familiar with what God has already said in his word - in other words, in the Bible.

The Bible says this about itself:

*All Scripture is inspired by God and is useful to teach us what is true and to make us realise what is wrong in our lives. It corrects us when we are wrong and teaches us to do what is right. God uses it to prepare and equip his people to do every good work.*[288]

This is Paul writing to his spiritual son, Timothy. When Paul talks about 'Scripture', he is not just talking about what we would recognise today as that part of the Bible called the New Testament. He is certainly including what to us is the Old Testament, to Paul these were the Scriptures that he had grown up with.

The writer of Hebrews says this about the word of God - meaning, both what God says to us that is brand new, and what he says to us through what has already been written:

*For the word of God is alive and powerful. It is sharper than the sharpest two-edged sword, cutting between soul and spirit, between joint and marrow. It exposes our innermost thoughts and desires. Nothing in all creation is hidden from God. Everything is naked and exposed before his eyes, and he is the one to whom we are accountable.*[289]

---

[287] John 10:27

[288] 2 Timothy 3:16&17

[289] Hebrews 4:12&13

Following Jesus is not a matter of having to obey a set of rules. Following him is not legalistic: we don't enjoy a relationship with God on the basis of our performance. We do not, therefore, have to read a certain amount of the Bible to qualify as 'proper' Christians. However, we are deluded if we try to convince ourselves that we don't need to read the Bible at all.

It is nice to receive messages from other people that perhaps include a verse from the Bible as part of a motivational or inspiring message. It is nice to see a photograph of something amazing from the natural world with a Bible verse superimposed on it. It is nice to hear good sermons that are clearly based on what the Bible says, and that help to explain parts of the Bible to us.

I am by no means against any of these things, but they are no substitute for each disciple of Jesus actually taking personal responsibility for knowing what the Bible - the whole Bible - says. Do not rely totally on anyone else spoon-feeding you with the truth as if you are always going to be a baby. Learn to feed yourself.

If you are not already familiar with the Bible, there a number of challenges about it. The Bible is a big book. It is a collection of a number of separate books, spanning an enormous amount of time. These separate books are not arranged in a strict time order, so if you just start reading from page one and carry on, you could well end up rather confused.

These books are written in a number of different styles. Some are historical records, others are poetic. Some say a lot about what will happen in the future - that is, of course, the future judged from the points in time when the books were written. Some of that future has now happened and is part of our past, but some of it is still the future, even for us today.

There are many good resources available, some of which are online and free, that can help you to find your way around the Bible. Using whatever good resources you can find, my advice is that you make it a good habit to read part of the Old Testament and part of the New Testament regularly - ideally every day, without trying to make this a legalistic rule.

All of the Bible is good, but especially if you are starting out, and you want a way of beginning to piece together for the first time an understanding of how the various books in the Bible flow together, I suggest you could make a start with these particular books:

<u>Old Testament</u>

Genesis: this is the book of beginnings, and it is good to start at the beginning! Genesis includes the story of how God began shaping a nation who were in a special covenant relationship with him, starting with Abraham.

Exodus: this is the story of Abraham's descendants, under the leadership of Moses, coming out of slavery in Egypt and starting the journey to the Promised Land. It includes the giving of the Ten Commandments and the rest of the Law.

Numbers: this continues the story of the journey to the Promised Land.

Joshua: this man takes over from Moses as leader of the Jewish people. He leads them into the Promised Land and begins a series of conquests.

1&2 Samuel, 1&2 Kings: this is a lot of history. Very importantly, it includes the life of David. It takes you from just before the Jews appointed their first king (Saul) and through the golden age of David's reign as the second king. David captures Jerusalem and makes it the capital of his new extended kingdom. After David's death, Solomon builds the Temple in Jerusalem. After Solomon's death, the kingdom quickly divides into two separate kingdoms - Israel in the north and Judah in the south. Most of the kings are ungodly. Hundreds of years go by and eventually Israel (the northern kingdom) crumbles under pressure from the superpower Assyria and its people are taken into exile. Later, Judah (the southern kingdom) also falls, this time to the next superpower, Babylon. Jerusalem is laid waste and the Temple is completely destroyed. People and plunder are taken into exile into the Babylonian Empire.

Daniel: this man is a young nobleman who is taken out of Judah into exile in Babylon some years before Jerusalem itself falls. He lives a long life and sees the passing of one superpower - Babylon - and the arrival of the next one - Persia. Daniel perceives towards the end of his life that he is close to seeing the fulfilment of Jeremiah's prophecy that Judah's exile would end after 70 years. The Persian Emperor issues a decree and the process of the Jews' return to Judah and the building of a new, second Temple can begin.

Ezra & Nehemiah: these two books carry on with the history of the return to Jerusalem, rebuilding the walls of the city and building the second Temple.

Psalms: this is a collection of poems. They are of varying lengths, but reading one or part of one can be a very useful daily exercise in focussing our attention on God as an act of worship.

<u>New Testament</u>

Matthew, Mark, Luke & John: each of the four Gospels is a portrait of the life of Jesus. They contain many of Jesus' own words and they need to be read again and again. There is a strong overlap between Matthew, Mark and Luke. John is rather different from the others.

Acts: this is the story of the first few years of the Church, starting with Jesus' ascension into Heaven.

Revelation: more words from Jesus, this time delivered to an elderly Apostle John who is living in exile on the island of Patmos. This book has a lot to say about how the Church should deal with persecution, and what will happen in the end times.

If each day you read at least one Chapter in sequence from those parts of the Old Testament that are mentioned above, and also something from the New Testament and a Psalm, or part of a Psalm, that would be a good basis for progress.

The objective is not that we become familiar with the Bible as a piece of literature for its own sake. The objective is, instead, that we get to know the person who inspired the Bible - God himself - as he speaks to us through the words of the Bible.

It is just as Jesus said to some religious leaders at one point:

*You search the Scriptures because you think they give you eternal life. But the Scriptures point to me! Yet you refuse to come to me to receive this life.* [290]

There is nothing virtuous or smart about deliberately remaining ignorant about what the Bible contains. Jesus himself knew the Scriptures very well. Matthew 4 tells us about the temptation Jesus went through at the start of his public ministry. When Satan came to him, each time Jesus responded with a quotation from the first few Chapters of Deuteronomy. Perhaps he was meditating on these passages at the time. This would make sense: Deuteronomy is Moses' farewell address to the people before he dies and hands over to Joshua the job of taking the people across the Jordan into the

---

[290] John 5:39&40

Promised Land. Jesus was about to usher in a momentous new era in human history.

In the Matthew 4 passage, we see that Satan also knows what the Bible says. At one point, Satan quotes from the Psalms to back up one of his temptations. So, the struggle that we see played out in this temptation is not about who knows the Bible the best. The struggle is about who knows the author of the Bible the best: it is about who is in relationship with the author of the Bible.

Our engagement with the Bible is important if it helps us in our relationship with the Lord. Whether we read whole chunks in one sitting or ponder about one verse or even just a couple of words, what really matters is our relationship. And if we value the relationship, we will value the part that the Bible can play in deepening that relationship.

We have already seen in Part One of this book that we do not all 'hear' God's voice in exactly the same way. His voice might come, for example, as some kind of picture or image, or as a gut feeling, or as a sense of some actual words. Whichever way we 'hear', the Bible can help us to hear. It is an amazing thing to sense the voice of the living author as we spend some time reading some of the words that he has previously breathed into - this is what 'inspired' means. The Bible is inspired. God has breathed into these words.

As we come to know the Bible better, we can at the same time get to know the author of the Bible better - so long as we treasure and value the relationship, and don't make the mistake of thinking that the Bible is just another book.

It is a useful spiritual discipline to write down anything that you sense God is saying to you as you read his word - to keep a record, a journal. The process of doing this will, over time, help you to fine-tune how you can pick out God's voice from the white noise of other voices: the noises of your own thoughts, of the enemy's lies and temptations, and the opinions of others.

It will help to sharpen your focus on what God is saying to you through the pages of the Bible. As you read over and review the notes that you make, you will begin to be able to see patterns and themes that develop, answers to prayer and promises that come to be fulfilled. Your journal will be a written evidence of a living and loving relationship.

Getting to know the Bible better helps us get to know God better. We do not have to choose between being a student of the Bible and being someone who can tune into the spontaneous flow of what God is saying at a particular moment in time. There is no contradiction between these two things, in fact they flow and fit together perfectly well. Here is an example of a type of prayer you could say any time that you settle in to spend some time reading God's word, and as you prepare to write in your journal whatever you feel God is saying to you:

*Father God, what is that you want to say to me today?*

# Meet The Healer

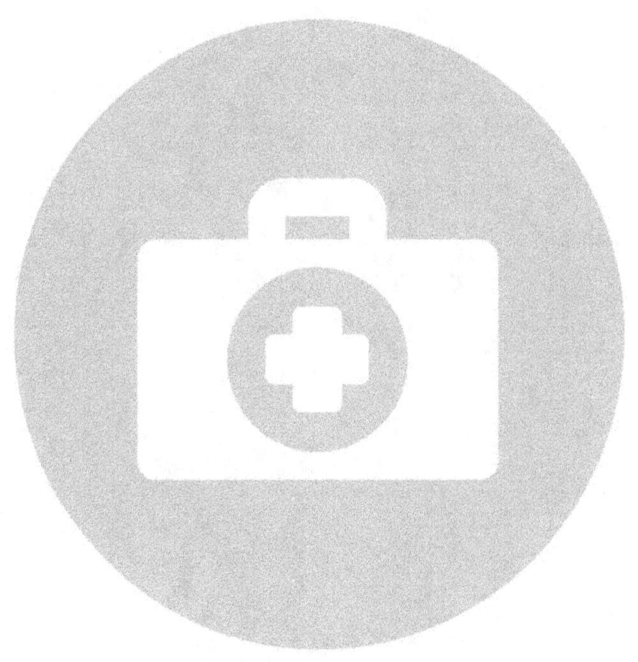

# CHAPTER 19

This Chapter is primarily about what to do when we are conscious of pain in our lives. Not physical pain, but emotional pain.

We all know that life can hurt us. Sometimes people do bad things to other people. Sometimes we ourselves have done bad things, at other times we have suffered bad things that have been done to us. Even when you think you are living right, sometimes bad stuff happens.

Most or all of us can probably think back to a period before we knew Jesus and we can be aware of painful things from those times. Most likely we can also think of painful things that have happened since we began walking with Jesus.

Of course, loving God and trying to obey him is no guarantee of a problem-free life! But how are we supposed to deal with people and events that might hurt us? And what, if anything, can we do about hurts we are carrying from the past?

It is one thing to have a bad experience. It is another thing entirely for that bad experience to cause a wound within us that is never healed and in effect haunts us for the rest of our lives. This is not God's will for you. This is what God is like:

*He heals the brokenhearted and bandages their wounds.*[291]

And we have seen before what Jesus said about the connection between freedom and truth:

*'…you will know the truth, and the truth will set you free.*[292]

The connection between freedom and healing is that Jesus can bring truth to bear into situations where we are carrying emotional pain from the past. What we need is to be able to receive Jesus' truth about those experiences.

Often what happens when we endure a negative experience is that, quite

---

[291] Psalm 147:3

[292] John 8:32

apart from the experience itself, the enemy takes the opportunity to sow into the soil of our hearts a lie. It is, then, the lie that continues to cause us pain, like an unhealed wound. The lies that are sold to us are many and varied, but they could include something like: 'no one cares about you'; 'you need to protect yourself'; 'never allow yourself to look weak or vulnerable'; 'you are disgusting'; 'you are worthless'; 'you must never trust anyone again' - and so on.

It is the most amazing thing to be able to have an authentic conversation with Jesus so that he can address the problem at the centre of our pain - namely the lies that we have, perhaps unconsciously, chosen to believe (in a moment of weakness and pain) and that fester in our hearts.

We know that the past is the past and it cannot be undone or re-written. Our understanding of what the past means to us today can, however, be changed. Jesus is part of the Trinity. He is God, and God knows everything and, mind-blowing as it is, can be everywhere. He not only knows about your past; he was present in your past (please forgive the pun), as it happened, even if that was during a period before you even knew him.

No-one is better qualified than Jesus to tell you what the truth is about your past. His memory is much better than yours. He is not a liar. So your recollection and the enemy's twisted opinions don't match up in any way to Jesus' assessment.

What each of us really needs, as an absolute priority, is to hear from Jesus. He can speak in a unique way into the detail of what you have experienced. Other people - trusted friends, family members who love you, even Church leaders or trained counsellors - can give you statements that are in line with what is true. However, only Jesus can speak the words of life that have the actual power to set you free, and to heal you. I think this is part of what Peter was meaning when he said this:

*Then Jesus turned to the Twelve and asked, 'Are you also going to leave?' Simon Peter replied, 'Lord, to whom would we go? You have the words that give eternal life'.*[293]

Based on my own experience, if I had to point to one thing that has been crucial for me in my own development as a Christian, it has been this:

---

[293] John 6:67&68

being able to have real encounters with Jesus when he can unpick and unpack for me some of the stuff in my history that gets in the way of my personal best. Of course, lots of other things are very important, but actually to hear from Jesus is spiritual dynamite!

In one sense, this is very easy to do. And yet, it seems, very few of Jesus' followers actually do it. One layer of complication is that, if we have taken on board a lie that we think is the truth, there might be some barriers in our hearts to letting Jesus speak clearly to us. This is because Jesus may well contradict the lie that we actually think is the truth.

It is good if you can find a trusted Christian friend to help you with this. Make sure that they are full of the Holy Spirit and know the Bible very well. Here is a suggested list of things you could work through together. The friend who is helping you needs to do the work of praying, asking questions and keeping notes of what happens so that you can review these later.

1. Identify what the most serious pain is that you are aware of. There might be a number of issues. Try to limit yourselves to addressing say no more than the three most serious issues - you don't have to try to solve everything in one session together.

2. Pray! Commit your time together to God, invite the Holy Spirit to come and in Jesus' name take authority over any attempts the enemy might make to disrupt and confuse.

3. Ask the Holy Spirit to lead you to where the pain is rooted. You might be reminded of an actual place or scene, or you might feel you are led somewhere else altogether. There is not necessarily any obvious connection between what the pain is, and where you think it took root. Remember that the Holy Spirit is much smarter than you are. You might sense a place almost immediately, only to dismiss it. Do not dismiss it too quickly - this could well be the work of the Holy Sprit.

4. If this doesn't work straightaway, do not despair. Do some more praying and try again. You are not making anything worse by making an attempt at healing.

5. As and when you identify a scene, take some time to describe it, and how you feel about it. Then, if he isn't already immediately obvious, ask Jesus to make himself known in the scene. If he doesn't appear, see 4. above - do some more praying and try again.

6. When you think you have identified Jesus as being there, ask him to confirm that he really is Jesus. This is vitally important - sometimes we

think we are talking to Jesus when actually we are talking to someone else. If you are not 100% that this is Jesus you are talking with, then in Jesus' name tell that person to go away. Then try again.

7. As soon as you are totally sure you are talking to Jesus, talk to him! Ask him anything you like - what is he doing, what is he feeling, what is he thinking, what is the truth about what was going on in your past, is there a lie that you have believed, what is the truth that you need to know, and so on.

8. If you get to a point where you feel that Jesus has done some significant work on an area of pain in your life, then if it feels appropriate, revisit a scene where you feel that this pain first began - and check if it now feels less raw, less painful.

9. Close your session in prayer, ask the Holy Spirit to seal any freedom that has been won and to continue to heal up the past hurts.

Here are some prompts that you might find helpful, either as part of a session along the lines of the above suggested format, or that you can work through on your own with the Lord:

*Take a few moments to let the Holy Spirit reveal to you the hurt that he wants to deal with right now. Then allow him to bring healing to it.*

*You might have received a memory, a thought or a picture. It could be an event or a situation that happened many years ago. It could be the name of a person or a picture of a person who said something that hurt you. Write down a summary.*

*Once you can picture the event, take note of your feelings. What emotions do you remember?*

*Ask God to show you where Jesus was at this event. When you see or sense him, flow with what God is showing you. It may mean letting go of some pain, anger or hatred. Picture yourself giving it to God.*

*Ask Jesus if there any lies that you have believed, and write them down if he tells you what they are. Ask Jesus for his opinion; what is the truth? Write it down. Say sorry for believing the lies.*

*If you haven't taken the time to forgive those involved in your memory who hurt you, do so now. Speak a blessing over them.*

*Allow the Holy Spirit to speak into your life. When you are finished, revisit the memory. What has changed?*

The following format is designed to help you work through dealing with ungodly beliefs. A few common beliefs are mentioned, merely to give you some idea of the general areas that might be relevant. The main thing is to tune into whatever the Holy Spirit prompts you about. Trusted friends might be able to help you:

*Look down this list of common ungodly beliefs and allow the Holy Spirit to alert you to areas where your beliefs are ungodly. Ask the Holy Spirit to show you what your ungodly belief is (listen for the "clang" in your heart as you identify the lie). There might be something that occurs to you which is not on this list:*

*I don't belong.*

*I will always be on the outside.*

*My feelings don't count.*

*No one cares what I feel; I will isolate myself so that I won't be vulnerable to hurt, rejection, and so on, any more.*

*I am not worthy to receive anything from God; I am the problem.*

*When something is wrong, it is my fault; I am a bad person.*

*If you knew the real me, you would reject me; I must wear a mask so that people won't find out how horrible I am and reject me.*

*I have messed up so badly that I have missed God's best for me; my value is in what I do.*

*I am valuable because I do good to others, because I am 'successful'.*

*I have to plan everyday of my life.*

*I have to continually plan/strategise.*

*I can't relax.*

*I only have value because of what I do.*

*I am unattractive.*

*God shortchanged me.*

*It is impossible to lose (or gain weight).*

*I am just stuck.*

*I am not complete as a man or woman.*

*I will always be _____________________ (angry, shy, jealous, insecure, fearful, etc.).*

*I will always have financial problems.*

*I must be very guarded about what I say, since anything I say may be used against me.*

*Authority figures will humiliate and violate me.*

*I will not be known, understood, loved or appreciated for who I am by those close to me; and God loves other people more than he loves me.*

*As and when you have identified one or more misbeliefs, you could pray along these lines:.*

*I confess my sin of believing the lie that _________________. I forgive those that have contributed to my forming this misbelief. I ask you Lord to forgive me for receiving this misbelief, for living my life based on it and for any way I have judged others because of it. I receive your forgiveness On the basis of your forgiveness, Lord, I choose to forgive myself for believing this lie. I renounce and break my agreement with this. I choose to accept, believe and receive the replacement truth that _________________.*

As you seek encounters with Jesus, who is your healer, may you find him quickly and easily. May you be blessed with an ever greater revelation of God's truth that leads to freedom indeed.

# Practise Generosity

# CHAPTER 20

We saw in Chapter 10 (Funny Money) that generosity is a vital value in God's Kingdom. Whether or not we feel comfortable with this, finding some way to fit in with the way that God does economics is an integral part of becoming more like Jesus. When we consider how Jesus dealt with money and possessions, Jesus gives us a clear example of what freedom looks like when it comes to stuff that so many people are preoccupied about.

If the gap between Jesus' values in this area and your own values is an uncomfortable gap for you, you can of course if you wish simply choose to ignore it. This is not, sadly, consistent with genuinely wanting to be a good follower of Jesus, a good disciple.

Another option is to tell yourself that you are open to being more generous, and indeed you will be more generous, once God has changed you on the inside so that generosity is no longer a problem for you. Superficially this looks like a more 'spiritual' option - it seems to have some integrity attached to it. Really, though, it is a cop-out.

We need to accept the spiritual discipline of doing acts of generosity, even if this does not feel entirely easy or natural for us. Quite possibly, the more that we act generously, the more our feelings will catch up and we will find ourselves enjoying not holding on quite so tightly to our money and our possessions. The main thing, however, is that we make a start, as an act of obedience to Jesus the Teacher.

In Matthew 25 there is an interesting teaching from Jesus about the judgement that will take place at the end of this age.[294] The picture here is of a final separation between sheep and goats. The sheep inherit God's Kingdom and eternal life, whereas the fate of the goats is eternal punishment. And what is the difference between the sheep and the goats? Is it the fact that the sheep at some stage in the past accepted Jesus as

---

[294] Matthew 25:31-46

saviour? No. Is it the fact that the sheep had a good attendance record at Church services? No. Is it the fact that the sheep read their Bibles faithfully? No. I could go on, but hopefully I have made my point. The key difference between the sheep and goats is their actions - what they did:

*Then the King will say to those on his right, 'Come, you who are blessed by my Father, inherit the Kingdom prepared for you from the creation of the world. For I was hungry, and you fed me. I was thirsty, and you gave me a drink. I was a stranger, and you invited me into your home. I was naked, and you gave me clothing. I was sick, and you cared for me. I was in prison, and you visited me.'*

*Then these righteous ones will reply, 'Lord, when did we ever see you hungry and feed you? Or thirsty and give you something to drink? Or a stranger and show you hospitality? Or naked and give you clothing? When did we ever see you sick or in prison and visit you?' And the King will say, 'I tell you the truth, when you did it to one of the least of these my brothers and sisters, you were doing it to me!'*[295]

Am I trying to say that we somehow earn our salvation? Or that we are saved not by grace through faith, but somehow by works? No, I am not - I am merely trying to draw due attention to what Jesus has clearly said. Our acts of generosity in and of themselves will not save us. If, however, our faith in God is for real, the challenge Jesus gives us is that this faith must surely show itself in some way.

This is why I say that none of us can afford to play the game of delaying our generosity until our hearts have caught up with what we know in our minds that we ought to be doing. Identifying ourselves as Christians without demonstrating, in some tangible way, the practical love that flows from our Heavenly Father is not really an option.

Quite often you will hear people say that they are moved, or that they feel compassion about some cause or other, perhaps about some crisis that they see going on somewhere in the world. Personally, I try to avoid using the word 'compassion' unless I am actually going to do something.

Mark's Gospel gives us an example of Jesus being moved with compassion. This was when a leper begged Jesus to heal him.[296] Jesus was

---

[295] Matthew 25:34-40

[296] Mark 1:40-42

moved with compassion and touched the leper (awesome in and of itself, when you think about what leprosy is) and Jesus healed him. The Greek word in Mark that is translated in English as compassion has the sense of a strong feeling in the inward parts. I am no Greek scholar, but my rough paraphrase for compassion is that is a gut-wrenching conviction. This demands that something is actually done.

Oh, that all of us would connect more with the same kind of compassion that moved Jesus! But of course, there would be implications. If we are moved with compassion, we must ourselves move, we must act.

What might be stopping us from practising generosity? Perhaps we feel we simply do not have enough to spare. God surely understands that if we only had a little bit more, then we could be generous. However genuinely we might feel something like this, it is based on a lie that we have received. Everyone, no matter how poor, can be generous. And if we don't have enough now to be generous, the likelihood is that we will never have enough - because we are focussed too much on what we do not have, rather than on what we do have.

Generosity is not merely a question of money. It is about our time and our things. Ask the Holy Spirit to guide you about what you can give and what you can do that would be generous. Consider whether there are any causes or issues that cause a stirring in your inward parts, and ask the Holy Spirit if this could be the beginnings of some God-inspired compassion that is welling up within you. Be prepared to be creative, spontaneous, and open.

A prayer along these lines might help you:

*Heavenly Father, thank you for everything that you provide. Help me, Lord, with my insecurities. Teach me to trust you with the details of what I need to live day by day. I want to learn each day about relying on you and being confident about being your child. Thank you that I am not an orphan, but I am a member of your royal family. I want to carry myself with the confidence and generosity that is consistent with my royal status - so please, Jesus, help me to see in the circumstances of my life how you would like me to behave. Amen*

# Rubbish In?
# Rubbish Out!

# CHAPTER 21

This Chapter is about taking steps to make sure that our lives are free of unhealthy and unhelpful distractions. It is about both our lives and also our homes - the physical places where we live - since our homes can be something of a reflection of what is happening in our lives. The title is something of a play on a common expression: 'rubbish in, rubbish out' - or alternatively, 'garbage in, garbage out'.

The idea behind that expression comes from the world of computing and software. If you feed poor quality information in, then you get poor quality results or reports. It is the same with our lives. There is a connection between what we allow to come into our lives, and what our lives are like.

The big question is, what are we allowing as inputs into our lives, and into our homes? In his letter to the Church at Philippi, Paul says this:

*Fix your thoughts on what is true, and honourable, and right, and pure, and lovely, and admirable. Think about things that are excellent and worthy of praise.*[297]

Just as we are encouraged to focus on good things, we should also address the question whether there are some bad things that take up our time and, possibly, even our affection.

Really, the spiritual discipline we are looking at here is an aspect of worship. At least in part, worship is about what and/or who we value. It is about what we spend time looking at, what we spend our time doing. It is about what we read, what we watch, what we listen to, what we admire, what we ponder.

It is straightforward that if we are spending time on things that are clearly sinful, we should stop; and that if we feel cannot stop, we should face up to our addictive behaviour. Equally, there could be a range of quite innocent things that maybe need some adjustment because we are simply spending too much time on them and they are getting in the way.

I am going to zoom in on something less straightforward. I am going to

---

[297] Philippians 4:8

look at the need to pay attention to not letting the occult have any room in our lives.

It is a characteristic of the occult that people often have no idea, or very little idea, of the real significance of what they are getting into but that occult practices and associations can have real power in the spiritual realm. This may seem unfair or bizarre - how and why does God allow this?

The book of Acts gives a number of examples of how the expansion of the Early Church led to a confrontation with the occult. Here is one example, of an event in the city of Ephesus:

*Many who became believers confessed their sinful practices. A number of them who had been practicing sorcery brought their incantation books and burned them at a public bonfire. The value of the books was several million dollars.*[298]

All credit to these new believers for destroying their occult stuff and not finding buyers for it. Although it was valuable, they rightly treated this stuff as the rubbish it truly was.

Such is the nature of the occult that it is not in any way fair. It will grab influence and power even when its victims do not properly understand what they are doing. This is consistent with the character of Satan, who is behind the occult. Jesus identifies him as a liar and a murderer.[299]

I am not going to try to produce a list of absolutely anything and everything that could possibly count as occult. Most importantly, you should give careful consideration to what there is within your home and what you are spending your time on, and ask the Holy Spirit to guide you. I will mention some things to watch out for, especially as some of these may seem less than obvious.

For example, most Christians know that horoscopes should be avoided, and yet there are some 'fun' activities available on social media that, in reality, are forms of horoscope. I recommend you avoid anything that claims to be able to say something interesting or significant about you based purely on your birth date.

Freemasonry is a movement that is probably full of in the main genuine

---

[298] Acts 19:18&19

[299] John 8:44

people who have no real idea about what they have entered into. Presumably they think that the vows they make as part of their initiation are merely part some kind of quaint and meaningless ceremony. Freemasonry is, however, without doubt an occult movement. If you or anyone in your family lines has been involved, you should be aware of this. Aside from dealing with any direct membership, watch out for any masonic regalia that might be sharing space with you. This could include artefacts that hark back to ancient Egypt; obelisks and similar items can often point to a masonic link.

It is quite easy to acquire jewellery from areas around the Mediterranean that feature an eye in the middle of the objects. Often this will be a connection to the all-seeing eye, the evil eye or something similar.

Sometimes when friends or relatives come back from a holiday in some lovely exotic part of the world, they might bring you back an ornament from that region as a gift. It may well seem rude or ungrateful to even think about throwing away or destroying something that has been given to you as gift by someone close to you. However, how much do you know about who produced that object, and what their motives were? At least consider whether it might be a representation of a demon or a false god, or whether the person who made it and/or sold it has attached a curse to it.

This leads me to mention something related to the occult, which is false religion. Many people who follow religions other than Christianity may well be genuine seekers after truth, but why would you want to have anything around you in your own personal space that represents worship of some kind of other god? Something that I personally notice a great deal is the placing of many Buddha figures around people's homes and gardens - as if this is just a great piece of design, or perhaps it is seen as being symbolic of inner calm.

I do not want to be prescriptive about what is definitely OK, and what is definitely not OK. Some of these things are, in my view, very clear but there are bound to be some items that are subject to interpretation and perhaps are matters of opinion and judgement. However, I would strongly urge you to at least consider this subject seriously. Take a good look around at the stuff that is in your home, and the stuff that you are letting in to your life through what you see and what you hear. May the Holy Spirit be your guide.

# Break With The Past

# CHAPTER 22

We cannot, of course, change the past. We can, however, change the way that our past continues to affect our present and shape our future. Through the Cross, we are given a new life by our heavenly Father. We are new creations. We can continue to live in the benefit of whatever blessings come down us through our family history and our personal history, but we need to make sure we have put an end to anything that might pollute our lives as we move forward.

This process is not just about issues that there might be in the lives of our parents and other family members; it is also about making sure we have cut off anything unhealthy to do with our own previous relationships and other associations.

In Chapter 8 (The Family Tree) we looked at the story of Gideon. His story is a very good example for us. In order for Gideon to move on up into the high destiny that God was giving him, the first thing that Gideon had to do was to make a break with the idol worship that his father had tolerated.

It is a good idea to do some kind of inventory of your own family tree. To the extent that you know these things already, or can find them out, then taking both your father's line and your mother's line, try to list the things that are not consistent with God's Kingdom. I am not going to try to set out an exhaustive list, but those things could include some of these things: ungodly beliefs; ungodly practices; violence; abuse; rejection; shame; mental illness; addictions; sexual sins; untimely death; occult involvement; hereditary illnesses; religious restrictions; and anything else that strikes you as relevant or noteworthy.

When you pray through your own personal family inventory, I do not believe there is much to be gained in trying to work out how much of your prayers are identificational repentance (confessing the sins of someone else as if they are your own personal sins) and how much they are your own personal responsibility.

Taking Gideon as an example, what really mattered was whether he was going to make a break with his family's idol worship, in a sense regardless of whether he personally had endorsed it in the past. When we bring our families to God in prayer, we want to be thankful for all the love and good things we have received from them. We want to honour them. We want to keep on receiving all the blessings that God sends down through our family lines, so why not stand with our family lines and repent on their behalf for anything that might be sinful?

When we do the inventory for our family lines, are there issues that jump out at us, that seem to have some kind of personal, live relevance for us? This may well be a clue that there is something there that is a personal sin issue for us that can be addressed.

Breaking with the past involves our being to take a new approach to both our family history, and also our personal history. It is not just about what has happened previously in the development of our family tree; it is also about what we ourselves have done, how we have lived.

As we consider our personal history, all sorts of issues could emerge. However, it is likely that we will find ourselves coming up against at least one of three key areas in particular. The first of these is any occult involvement that we may have had. The second is membership of any organisations or associations where we might have made ungodly promises as part of the price of membership. The third is the lingering effect upon us of any ungodly past sexual relationships.

On that third area, Jesus was speaking about marriage when he spoke about a man and a woman becoming 'one flesh'[300] - but any sexual union raises the possibility of a significant tie between the two people, even if the sex itself feels casual rather than committed. Whenever we have sex with someone, we give part of ourselves away. It is good to break any ties to past sexual partners, and as it were to call back the parts of ourselves that we have given away. We can also release those partners from any claim we might otherwise make to try to influence or control them in any way. Let's bless them in Jesus' name and move on with life.

The suggested prayers that follow are a template for prayers that you can use to deal with your family history and your personal history. May God bless you as you seek to seal off in the past anything that might hinder your flourishing into the son or daughter of God that you are destined to be.

---

[300] Mark 10:7&8

## Family History

*As a child of God, purchased by the blood of the Lord Jesus Christ, I choose to confess and acknowledge the sins of my ancestors. While I don't like the results of their sins on my life, I choose to forgive and release them, and not to hold them accountable for each and every way that their sins have affected me.*

*I confess _______________________ in my father's/mother's line.*

*I now renounce all of the sins of my ancestors, and release myself from their effects, based on the finished work of Christ on the Cross.*

*Lord, I am sorry for all the ways that I have entered into these same sins, and allowed the curses to affect me. I ask you to forgive me for this, and to wash me clean. I choose to receive your forgiveness.*

*Thank you, Lord, that I can cast my burdens on you. I receive my freedom. I now release my ancestors from my father's/mother's line into the freedom of my forgiveness. No longer will I blame them for who I am. I place the Cross of Jesus between me and my father's/mother's line so that the sins of the ancestors are stopped there.*

## Personal History

*I confess my own sins of _______________________________.*

*I now renounce all promises and vows I have made as a result of membership of the following groups, cults, clubs or associations _______________.*

*I now renounce my involvement in the following occult practices _______________.*

*I now break any ungodly soul tie that I have made as a result of my sexual relationship with _______________ . I call back in Jesus' name any part of my own self that I gave away through becoming one flesh with him/her and I release him/her from any tie to my life. I renounce any power to influence him/her through any ungodly soul tie and I bless them to experience your love and blessing for themselves.*

## General Repentance And Confession

*I affirm that I have been crucified with Jesus Christ and raised to walk in newness of life. On this basis, I announce to Satan and all his forces that Christ took upon himself the curses and judgements due to me. Thus I break every curse that has come upon me because of me or my ancestors. I also break all curses that have been released onto me by others. I also break all curses that I have spoken or thought about myself. I receive my freedom from every one of these curses.*

*Because of the above, and because I have been delivered from the power of darkness and translated into the Kingdom of God's dear Son, I cancel the legal rights of every demon sent to oppress me.*

*Because I have been raised up with Christ, and now sit with him in heavenly places, where I have a place as a member of God's family, I renounce and cancel each and every way that Satan and his demons may claim ownership of me. I cancel all dedications made by either myself or my ancestors, in the name of Jesus. I declare myself to be completely and eternally signed over to, owned by, and committed to, the Lord Jesus Christ.*

*All this I do on the basis of the truth revealed in the word of God, and in the name and with the authority of my Lord and Saviour, Jesus Christ. Amen.*

# Get Over Yourself

# CHAPTER 23

One of the paradoxes of the gospel is that each one of us is both significant and, in a sense, insignificant at the same time. Our significance is a truth, but our insignificance (for want of a better word just now) is also true.

You matter. You are highly valued. You are significant. This is not based on anything that you have done or earned. Instead, it is based on the fact that God places a high value upon you. When we say yes to what Jesus has done for us, we say yes to a wonderful new identity, a membership of a royal family. At the same time, the world does not revolve around you. You are not God. There is a lot that you do not know, possibly even about yourself. Some of the stuff that you even think you know may, in fact, be wrong, at least in part.

Part of your journey to becoming more and more like Jesus is getting more of a grip on how the world is from the only point of view that is really true - namely, God's point of view. To see things more and more from God's point of view, we need some kind of concept of the difference between him and us. We need to soak up more and more of the reality that he is God and we are - well, we are not God.

Of course, we all know that we are not God. And yet - don't we sometimes run our lives as if we are in charge? Don't we sometimes get frustrated or even angry with other people who somehow manage not to believe the things we believe, or who don't do things the way that we do things? Don't we sometimes get upset even with God himself when we don't get healed when we think we should, or don't get rewarded when we think we should? Don't we sometimes get tangled up with resentment or bitterness when we have been hurt or offended in some way and justice has not been done?

We need to get over ourselves. We need to embrace the fact that our agenda will not always match God's agenda. His idea of when it is the right time to do something can be very different to our ideas about timing. He knows things that we don't know. We need somehow to be able to move beyond how life's circumstances and hurts affect us personally and glimpse the bigger picture - God's world, God's Kingdom, God's agenda.

Paul touches on this subject when he writes this to the Christians in Rome:

*I give each of you this warning: Don't think you are better than you really are. Be honest in your evaluation of yourselves, measuring yourselves by the faith God has given us.*[301]

And to the Christians in Galatia he wrote this:

*If you think you are too important to help someone, you are only fooling yourself. You are not that important.*[302]

There is a great deal that we can know. We can study the Bible, we can be good students of life in general, we can receive revelations from the Holy Spirit. But even when we are functioning very well, we only get to see a small part of the big, very big, picture that God sees with total clarity.

In one of Paul's letters to the Christians living in Corinth, he talks a little about an experience he had of Heaven 14 years previously, and how he heard things that he does not feel he is even allowed to tell anyone else.[303] And yet, around 14 years after that amazing experience, Paul says this:

*Now we see things imperfectly, like puzzling reflections in a mirror, but then we will see everything with perfect clarity. All that I know now is partial and incomplete, but then I will know everything completely, just as God now knows me completely.*[304]

The stuff that we think we know to be true, our grievances, our sense of having been treated poorly, our impatience at things just not getting sorted out better and faster, and much else besides, is clutter that gets in the way between us and God. We need to get over ourselves, we need to find a way through that clutter.

Possibly you might find the title of the Chapter and its tone offensive because you feel it somehow minimises or overlooks the pain you have endured at the hands of other people. I do not intend any such thing, but it is vital that we do not stay trapped in the mentality of being a victim of other people.

Strange as it may sound, a strong sense of being a victim - perhaps

---

[301] Romans 12:3

[302] Galatians 6:3

[303] 2 Corinthians 12:1-6

[304] 1 Corinthians 13:12

almost having a victim mentality, or a victim mindset - can be part of the baggage that we need to work through in order to enjoy true freedom.

I can do no better that to quote Eva Kor on this subject. Eva was a Romanian Jew who as a young girl, with her twin sister, endured the horrors of Josef Mengele's experiments at Auschwitz during the Second World War. She has written extensively on the subject of forgiveness, even forgiveness of Mengele himself. Here are some of her own words:

*I believe with every fibre of my being that every human being has the right to live without the pain of the past…The victim has the right to be free.*[305]

If you feel like a victim, please do not stay stuck in that place. You deserve more, but as part of the process of moving on, you must be willing to let go of victimhood.

So, how exactly can we get over ourselves? One practical thing we can do that will help us in this task is to meditate about the Cross. You can ask the Holy Spirit to show you something about what the world looks like when you put yourself in the centre of your world. You can ask God if there is any pride in you that he would like to deal with.

Other helpful spiritual disciplines in this area could include all or any of these:

Have some kind of focus on the needs of other people rather than your own needs. For example, find a charity or other good cause that you can support.

Give one or two close friends permission to tell you when they disagree with something you say. And commit to staying friends with them even when you cannot persuade them that they are wrong, and you are right.

Try to find something about yourself that you can laugh at every day.

Find something that is fun (and not a sin) and do it, just to have some fun.

You might find that occasionally praying a prayer something along the following lines will help deal with issues of pride and self-centredness in your life:

---

[305] 'Surviving The Angel Of Death', by Kor & Buccieri

*Heavenly Father, thank you so much that you are God, and that I am not. Thank you for this amazing life that you have given to me. I am so sorry for any times when I have resented other people, or even you, for hurts that I have suffered. I choose to walk in the path of forgiveness. If I am sick, I will trust you with the details of when I will be healed. If I am in need, I will trust you with the details of when my needs will be met, and how they will be met.*

*Lord, if there is any part of my life where I am trying to be in control rather than letting you be Lord of my life, I am sorry - and please show me so that I can make a change. Holy Spirit, if there is any part of my life where you and I disagree, please guide me further into your truth. I give you permission to continue the process of renewing my mind and of changing me from one degree of glory to another. May I never forget that I am on a journey, I am a traveller, I am a disciple. Thank you so much for the Cross and for your amazing love.*

# Find A Retreat

# CHAPTER 24

I am not talking here about 'retreat' in the sense of 'defeat'. This is not about withdrawal from the heat of battle in the face of overwhelming opposition. This is about developing some kind of lifestyle, some kind of rhythm, so that you can recharge your spiritual batteries.

For these purposes a retreat can be a special place, or a special kind of place, or an activity. It can be a walk around countryside somewhere, or going for a run, or having a coffee in a favourite chair. It can be sitting on a bench looking across the ocean, a river or a field. It can be listening to some favourite worship music through some earphones even while other people are rushing around you and getting on with their busy lives. A retreat can look like a wide range of different things, and a great deal depends upon what works best for you.

A key element of a true retreat is this. It is a deliberate separating of yourself from all the usual things in life that will so easily distract you from two vital things: first, hearing what God wants to say to you; and second, being truly aware of what is going on in the depths of your own soul.

Probably most of us, if not all of us, will on any given day have a number of things that simply have to be done, sometimes at particular times of day. If you think of each day of your life as a calendar or a diary, these things are bookings in your daily list. If these firm bookings take up so much of your time each day that you simply don't have any time to make a booking with God for, say, even 15 minutes - well, you need to take a very serious look at what you are allowing to be booked into the calendar of your life.

Aside from these firm bookings, the rest of our days are filled with a mixture of mundane things, fun things, random things and so on. For a lot of the time, we allow ourselves to be surrounded by, and immersed in, mere noise. To borrow some words form an old song, often we are 'busy doing nothing'. Whatever it may be that we are sometimes barely paying any attention to at all, that thing seems to be alluring enough to stop us drawing away to another kind of place or space - where we could tune into a higher level of reality. The background noise of everyday life seems so easily to get in the way of something more.

The reason I am encouraging you to take the idea of a retreat seriously is because it is a key part of living the life of freedom, living the same kind of life that Jesus lived. We know that Jesus himself made a habit of finding a retreat. Luke, one of the writers of the Gospels, was a doctor by profession and his Gospel represents a very careful study of what Jesus did. Luke makes this telling observation:

*Jesus often withdrew to the wilderness for prayer.*[306]

If Jesus - God's Son - felt it necessary to go on retreat, how can we possibly think that we can get by without doing the same thing? We know that when Jesus arrived on Earth as a human being - when, as The Message puts it, he 'moved into the neighbourhood',[307] he put aside his rights and powers as God.[308] The model, or example, that Jesus sets for us is that it is possible for humanity to live and walk in a way that is pleasing to God - we can hear God's voice, we can be secure in a loving relationship with God, and we can experience the power of God's Holy Spirit moving in us and through us.

However, part of the example that Jesus gives us is making a habit of withdrawal into the wilderness for prayer. I doubt that Jesus did this merely to set us an example. I believe he did it because it was necessary for himself personally. And if he needed it, surely we need it!

One of the challenges some of us face when trying to establish some kind of retreat as part of our lifestyle, is not that we cannot find the time, but that we don't know how to fill the time that we set aside for retreat. Apart from the minutes that we might spend actually reading a passage from the Bible, or telling God what we want, or what we are feeling and what we think about him, what else is there?

To the extent that we might sense God speaking to us, then it's easy to feel that the time we have set aside is time well spent, and that something is happening. But what about when nothing seems to be happening?

We need to take the pressure off ourselves and God to be performing

---

[306] Luke 5:16

[307] John 1:14

[308] Philippians 2:5-8

constantly. A fundamental part of the idea of retreat is to allow space and time to relax, to recharge your batteries and to reflect. You don't have to spend all your time on retreat reading or talking - and you won't necessarily constantly be aware of what God is saying to you.

In my opinion, there is great value as part of a retreat to allow yourself simply to soak in God's presence. Personally, I find it very useful to have worship music playing in the background. Sometimes there might be a phrase in a song that helps me to focus on some aspect of God's love or his character. Other times, the music in a more general and gentle way helps me to relax into God's presence.

If you are not already regularly finding yourself in some kind of place of retreat, you could try asking yourself a few questions along the following lines. Whatever answers you get to questions like these will help you understand both what is stopping you, and what will help you to enjoy times of retreat.

1. Is there anything in my life that is taking up an unhealthy amount of time/money/attention?

2. At what time of day am I at my best to enjoy a period of retreat? For example, if you are a morning person and switch off very quickly in the evening, a period of retreat in an evening probably won't work well for you - most likely you will fall asleep.

3. What sort of things do I like doing that help me feel relaxed? It may be that the best kind of retreat for you will match the sorts of things that help to refresh you. For example, if you love to walk, then a retreat as you walk may well serve you better than an attempt to retreat in a comfy chair.

4. Is there something in my life that I ought to give up, or cut down on, so that I have some time available to retreat?

There are no rules about how often you must retreat, or how long a retreat must last in order to be valid. Our guide is the example of Jesus, who 'often withdrew to the wilderness for prayer'. If you can set aside in your diary even say 15 minutes once a week for a retreat, that will be a useful start. The key thing is to make a start - and as you find that going on retreat works for you, you will find the desire to make more space for it.

# Thanks

# CHAPTER 25

Many children are taught by their parents to say, 'please', and 'thank you'. This is good manners. But as adults, how regularly do we say, 'thank you', other than as a mere reflex? Is it almost an automatic, piece of everyday conversation that we do not really mean? How common is it for us to express genuine gratitude?

If you are not doing it already, it would be very good to develop a pattern of saying thank you to God for something every day. Some people say 'grace' before they share a meal. This is saying thanks to God for food, and provided it is done with sincerity rather than purely as a mindless habit, surely this is a good basis for building thankfulness into our everyday lives.

We know from the Gospels that Jesus often gave thanks for food, so perhaps we would be wise to follow his very good example. Being thankful is part of how we prepare ourselves to worship, as this Psalm tells us:

*Acknowledge that the Lord is God! He made us, and we are his. We are his people, the sheep of his pasture. Enter his gates with thanksgiving; go into his courts with praise. Give thanks to him and praise his name.*[309]

Being thankful is part of what gets us into a good frame of mind to start relating with the Lord in an appropriate way. Another Psalm tells us that being thankful is actually part of how we worship God:

*Make thankfulness your sacrifice to God, and keep the vows you made to the Most High.*[310]

In one of his letters to the Thessalonians, Paul gives us a command about thankfulness:

*Be thankful in all circumstances, for this is God's will for you who belong to Christ Jesus.*[311]

---

[309] Psalm 100:3&4

[310] Psalm 50:14

[311] 1 Thessalonians 5:18

Notice here that Paul is not saying we must say thanks <u>for</u> everything, but that <u>in</u> all circumstances, it is indeed God's will that we should give thanks. There may well be circumstances in our lives that are awful, and it might be too hard to see how anyone could give thanks for those. Nevertheless, no matter how bad some circumstance might be, God is still good and there will still be something that we can thank him for.

My practical suggestion here is easy to state, but perhaps less easy to live out. Try to find, each and every day, at least one thing that you can thank God for. It would be a very useful exercise to do this every day for a year, and to find something different every day - so that you finish with over 360 things for which you are thankful to God.

You might find yourself attempting to express thankfulness through, as it were, gritted teeth - as if you are saying thank you, but it hardly feels like you are meaning it. Do not let this kind of feeling put you off. That feeling is not hypocrisy, or pretending - it is in fact a very true act of worship. It is deciding to reach out for some kind of level of gratitude, even when it feels like everything around you is putting you under pressure to curse God rather than thank him.

Making a decision, as an act of your will, to be thankful is a powerful spiritual weapon. It is a doorway to living truly as a child of God rather than as an orphan. Rather than complaining and obsessing about what we do not have, we learn true appreciation of what we do have. We are weakening the barriers that might otherwise get in way between us and God. Barriers of resentment and bitterness, of striving and fear.

As an example, what follows is a short prayer saying thanks for something that we all share: our breath. I wonder how many breaths you have taken while you have been reading this Chapter? Breathing is an amazing thing, and something that many of us probably spend very little time ever thinking about. If you feel you can't think of anything to be thankful for, you can be thankful - if you want to be thankful - for breathing, at least.

*Heavenly Father, thank you for the breaths that I am taking right now. Thank you for the wonder of oxygen being taken into my lungs, and then into my bloodstream, so that I can remain alive. Thank you for the gift of breath that came to me once I was in the world outside my mother's womb. Thank you for the rhythm of breathing in and out that is part of my life - a constant reminder of your gift of life to me. I accept every breath as a gift from you. Thank you so very much for this precious gift of life. May I never forget your goodness and kindness to me. I love you.*

As you pursue a lifestyle of gratitude to God, may you grow in your awareness of his lovingkindness day by day.

I hope that some or all of this practical suggestion about thankfulness and the other steps I have outlined in this book will help you in some way in your walk with Jesus. May there be a lasting and joyous change for you. May you experience the truth of being changed from one degree of glory to another; of moving ever closer to your own personal best; of becoming more and more like Jesus himself.

# BIBLIOGRAPHY


The Bondage Breaker, Dr Neil T. Anderson (Monarch Books, 2007)

Celebration Of Discipline: The Path To Spiritual Growth, Richard Foster (Hodder & Stoughton 2008)

The Cross Of Christ, John Stott (IVP 2006)

The Divine Conspiracy, Dallas Willard (William Collins 2014)

Eros Defiled: The Problem Of Sexual Guilt, John White (IVP 1977)

Eros Redeemed: Breaking The Stranglehold Of Sexual Sin, John White (Eagle 1993)

The Father Heart Of God, Floyd McClung (Kingsway Publications 1985)

Grace & Forgiveness, John & Carol Arnott (New Wine Press 2009)

Healing The Wounded Spirit, John & Paula Sandford (Victory House 1985)

Ordering Your Private World, Gordon MacDonald (Thomas Nelson Publishing 2012)

Renovation Of The Heart: Putting On The Character Of Christ, Dallas Willard (IVP 2002)

Victory Over The Darkness, Dr Neil T. Anderson (Monarch Books 2007)

# ABOUT THE AUTHOR

Brian Spencer lives in Harlow, Essex, UK. He and his wife, Mary, lead Gateway Freedom Church. They are also part of the Core Team in the UK that supports the Partners In Harvest network of Churches.

You can contact Brian at: brianspencerauthorchat@aol.co.uk or you can follow his blog, 'Brian's Freedom Files', at: https://brianspencersite.wordpress.com

May the road rise up to meet you,
May the wind always be at your back,
May the sun shine warm upon your face,
And rains fall soft upon your fields,
And until we meet again,
May God hold you in the hollow of his hand.

(Ancient Irish Blessing)

www.ingramcontent.com/pod-product-compliance
Lightning Source LLC
Chambersburg PA
CBHW071554030726
47593CB00001BA/158